And the Glory

THE HUDDERSFIELD CHORAL SOCIETY
1836–1986

And the Glory

A History
in commemoration of the 150th anniversary of
THE HUDDERSFIELD CHORAL SOCIETY

R. A. EDWARDS

Printed and published by
W. S. MANEY & SON LIMITED
LEEDS

*This publication has been greatly assisted
by the generous support of the*
YORKSHIRE BUILDING SOCIETY

Printed and published by
W. S. MANEY & SON LIMITED
Hudson Road, Leeds LS9 7DL, England

in association with
THE HUDDERSFIELD CHORAL SOCIETY

ISBN 0 901286 17 6

Contents

	List of Illustrations	vi
	Foreword	vii
	Author's preface	ix
1	Beginnings	1
2	The Lost Years	11
3	Firm Foundations	22
4	The Continued Tradition	35
5	Fresh Fields	46
6	In from the Cold	62
7	Maturity and Excellence	80
8	Honour and Glory	99
9	The Aftermath	126
10	A Renewal	139
	Appendix I: Past Performances of the Society	147
	Appendix II: Society Officials since 1836	156
	Appendix III: Society Members 1985–86	160
	Bibliography	167
	Index	170

List of Illustrations

	PAGE
Thomas Parratt	24
James Battye	24
The old Cherry Tree Inn	24
Cover of the programme for the Society's concert in the new Philosophical Hall, October 1837	25
Title-page of the Revised Rules and Regulations booklet, 1842	25
Mrs Sunderland	52
Robert Senior Burton	52
The Armoury and adjoining Zetland Hotel, *circa* 1900	52
Huddersfield Town Hall in the 1880s	64
Ben Stocks	64
J. Edgar Ibeson	64
Joshua Marshall, Charles Hallé and others, sketched at the 1881 Music Festival marking the opening of the Huddersfield Town Hall	65
John Bowling	68
John North	68
Henry Coward	82
The Choir in Holland, 1928	94
Sir Malcolm Sargent and Sir William Walton with Herbert Bardgett and G. D. A. Haywood at the *Gloria* performance in 1961	109
Testimonial from the County Borough of Huddersfield, presented in 1961	121
Wyn Morris	132
Sir John Pritchard	132
Owain Arwel Hughes	132
The Choir in the Town Hall with O. A. Hughes for the *Messiah* concert, 1981	140
Brian Kay	145

Foreword

To mark its forthcoming 150th birthday celebrations, it is fitting that a new chronicle of the distinguished Huddersfield Choral Society should be published, and I am honoured to have been invited to write this foreword.

My own association with the Society began in 1949 and was to last almost twenty-five years, during which time several gramophone recordings and broadcasts, both radio and television, were made. I recall visits abroad to Belgium and America where the Choir received tremendous ovations; many 'special event' performances in Leeds, Liverpool, and London, and many more in the Society's established home — the Huddersfield Town Hall.

Every concert had that sense of important occasion, and one was conscious of becoming a welcomed visitor to a most prestigious musical body, based upon long and successful traditions. This, both for me and for my dear husband and daughter, was to deepen into a sense of belonging to the very family bond of 'The Choral', and I cherish fondest memories of so many great occasions.

I extend to all of you my warmest congratulations upon attaining this great landmark in your history, and may the next 150 years bring continuing musical joys and well-deserved acclaim.

Marjorie Thomas.

March 1985

Author's Preface

APART FROM occasional magazine and newspaper articles, no attempt to record the history of the Huddersfield Choral Society was made before 1936, the occasion of the Society's centenary. This was followed twenty-five years later by an up-dated publication which not only failed to correct some notable omissions from the former publication but, due largely to some uncorrected typographical errors, resulted in a less, rather than a more, accurate record.

In 1982, with the approaching 150th anniversary in mind, I decided to take action regarding the writing of a new history of the Society. This was a task which I had contemplated for a considerable time but it was with some diffidence that I submitted my proposals to the Society's officers and committee. Clearly, without their blessing and co-operation, the task would have been virtually impossible. It was only after beginning to work on the history that I became fully aware of the overdue, and indeed daunting, nature of the task I had undertaken. However, the discoveries that I began to make only served to heighten my interest and intensify my resolve to try to meet the challenge. Huddersfield lacked, so I soon learned, any serious publication devoted to the recording of its musical heritage, the jewel in the crown of which is undoubtedly its Choral Society. I hope that this account of that Society's past may prove to be a useful contribution to the record of Huddersfield's participation in, and contribution to, English musical life during the past century and a half.

The opportunity to write the book, made possible by the interest of the Society and that of the publishers, W. S. Maney and Son of Leeds, I regard as a privilege, and one which has afforded me great pleasure. As originally conceived, the book would have been a much larger one. It would have included more, both about the membership of the Society and about its music. However, a large book may have been tedious and it would certainly have been too costly — and too late.

For any errors, and for what some may regard as almost unforgivable omissions, I offer my apologies. I have done what I can to minimize both but cannot hope to have been entirely successful. Much of the account of the Society's affairs is here published for the first time, and regarding certain matters, I hope to have put the record straight. For example, the Society gave concerts for subscribers and the general public continuously from 1837, or even earlier, and not only from 1842 as previously recorded. Its early members were not, for the greater part, untutored, nonconformist mill-workers. Many were amateur, if not semi-professional musicians. Some were teachers as well as performers of music. It seems, moreover, that they were musicians first and members of particular congregations second — and many were Anglican at that! They were as likely to be found singing or playing in Anglican, or even Catholic, churches, as they were in nonconformist chapels.

I wish to record my thanks to the following:

Mr Peter Watkins, formerly of Greenhead Books Ltd, Huddersfield, for invaluable help and encouragement initially.

The officers and committee members of the Choral Society for their support and assistance, especially to Mr Richard Barraclough, Vice-president and ex-General Secretary; Mr Graham Fearnley, ex-Choir Secretary; Mrs Sue Green, ex-Publicity Officer; Mr Donald Haywood, Sponsorship Secretary and ex-President; Mr George Slater, Past President; Mr Paul Michelson, President; Dr John Hughes, General Secretary; and Mr Bill Drake, Sub-scribers' Secretary and ex-President, for their particular efforts on my behalf.

All those members of the Society who have kindly given or loaned material and all those others who have given or loaned material and allowed me to interview them. These latter include Miss Judith Sherratt, Miss Hilda Wilmhurst, Mr A. Guy Crowther, Mrs F. R. Armitage, Mrs Nancy England, Mr and Mrs Charles Marshall, Mr Philip Wood, and Mr Brian Kay.

The staff of the Public Library in Huddersfield, particularly Miss J. Helliwell and her colleagues of the Local History Department, and also the staff of the Reference Department for all their attention and assistance. The staff of the Public Libraries of Bradford, Brighouse, and Heckmondwike. Miss Fletcher of the *Huddersfield Examiner* and Mrs Welch of the *Spenborough Guardian* and *Heckmondwike Herald*. Mr Selwyn Green for his great help with the photography for the illustrations.

The Revd Andrew Hindley of the Huddersfield Parish Church. Mr Simon Lindley, Organist of Leeds Parish Church. Also Mrs Margaret Whittaker and members of her family for much help and encouragement, and Mrs L. Loizou for her excellent work in typing the manuscript.

Finally, to members of my family for their assistance and particularly to my wife, not only for her assistance, but also for her forbearance with my obsession. She never once begged me to change the subject!

CHAPTER ONE

Beginnings

THE MORE ONE DISCOVERS about the musical life of Yorkshire in general, and of Huddersfield in particular, during the early part of the nineteenth century, the less surprising it seems that a choral society was established in the town as long ago as 1836. What is surprising is that the formation of a choral society had to wait until 1836. The Huddersfield Glee Club (or Glee Society) was certainly in being in 1827 — 'the most celebrated in the county in its day' says Cudworth in his *Musical Reminiscences of Bradford*. The Huddersfield Friendly Musical Society held its first quarterly meeting in 1832, and the first Huddersfield Philharmonic Society came into being, it is believed, in about 1820. The district was not short of musical talent and enterprise: there were organists, instrumentalists, singers, and even composers of some merit, if not fame, living in and around the town.

In the neighbouring town of Halifax — also by no means lacking in musical life and talent — there had been a choral society since 1818, and in Bradford since 1821. There were undoubtedly choirs, other than church or chapel choirs, of some sort or another in many other neighbouring towns and villages. In the *Magazine of Music* of June 1889 an article by J. G. Schofield entitled 'The Huddersfield Choral Society' provides some interesting information concerning the musical scene in and about Huddersfield during the early part of the century. 'The early history of amateur musical culture in the neighbourhood is in great measure lost in obscurity' wrote Schofield (and no doubt this remains very largely true to this day) but he was indebted, he said, to an 'esteemed local octogenarian vocalist', a Mr William Blackburn, for many items of information. He is probably correct, therefore, when he relates that in the early nineteenth century 'a number of glee clubs, vocal societies and small bands of instrumentalists existed in most of the neighbouring villages and hamlets'. The most important of those, he tells us, were at Almondbury, Mirfield, Deighton, Kirkheaton, and Dewsbury. It seems that it was common for members of these groups to visit each other's villages on foot, covering distances from two to eight miles, in order to perform in concerts, or simply to practise, after working hours 'long before the existing restrictions of hours of labour in factories was instituted', and they did this in all weathers, winter and summer alike, walking home late at night.

The Huddersfield Philharmonic Society was formed 'in or about the year 1820' reports Schofield, who describes it as the precursor of the present Choral Society. 'Into its ranks were drafted the pick of the local amateurs, both vocal and instrumental' he writes. Later he tells us that not only the Philharmonic but many other smaller societies became merged eventually into the Choral Society and although its formal constitution dated from 1836, a 'less definitely organised form existed for some years previous to that date, the earlier meetings having been held at Paddock'. W. L. Wilmshurst, President of the Society from 1915 to 1917, and writer of its Centenary Memorial History in 1936, also tells of these meetings in Paddock but with him, 'some years before 1836' becomes 'six years before 1836'. At the time of writing I have discovered no means of checking the authenticity of this reference to six years.

In a series of articles entitled 'Incidents in the Life of a Veteran Organist', *The Huddersfield Examiner* of 1874 tells of the life and times of Richard Mellor who, after two years as organist at St Patrick's Roman Catholic Church went to Ramsden Street Chapel in 1840 where he remained as organist until 1874. Evidently, prior to the formation of the Choral Society, musical gatherings used to take place in the houses of local musicians at such places as Linthwaite, Golcar, Clough Head, Longwood, and Paddock School. 'At these meetings' we read, 'Mr James Battye, an eminent musician — witness his anthems, prize glees, etc. — led with the violin, his twin brother Mr Edward Battye played the violoncello, old Joe Gledhill, the bassoon and old Jos. Sykes, the trombone'. Then, a little later, comes 'these men laid the foundation of the present Choral Society by the monthly meetings at Paddock School'. With the exception of 'old Joe Gledhill', the names of these men are all to be found on the 1837 membership list of the Choral Society, still extant, the Battye brothers being founder members.

It appears that the Philharmonic Society's concerts were subscription concerts and were held in the Court House in Queen Street. The sum of five shillings (25p of our present currency, of course, but worth a great deal more in 1820) entitled a subscriber to an admission ticket for one gentleman and two ladies to the annual concert. If the reference to the Court House is to that building which still stands in Queen Street, with its year of erection, 1823, clearly marked above its portals, it would suggest that if this Philharmonic Society were in fact founded as early as 1820, then it could not have held its concerts there from the start.

In the *Musical Times* of 1 April 1902 appeared an article in which the view was expressed that the musical history of Huddersfield might be said to have begun in 1812, when Thomas Parratt, then barely twenty, became the first organist at the Parish Church. It is true that he began something of lasting value, for he was followed in this post approximately fifty years later by his son Henry who was still at the Parish Church at the beginning of the present century. Henry's younger brother, Walter, was the Sir Walter Parratt of later years, organist of St George's Chapel, Windsor, and master of the royal music. Thomas Parratt, who was one of the earliest members of the Choral Society, is said to have been the first professional musician to practise in Huddersfield, but the traditional musical character of the common people in the area seems to be legendary. In his 1936 centenary history, W. L. Wilmshurst writes 'Part-singing by small or large groups was of course practised in the West Riding for long before the advent (in the seventeenth century) of oratorio and opera. Numbers of local compositions, glees, ballads, and folk-pieces existed of which the traces have now disappeared but which were heard at church feasts and those annual village "sings" some of which still survive'. Again we read in the *Social History of English Music* by E. D. Mackerness that glee clubs and other musical societies — 'sometimes merely convivial assemblies' — were to be found in towns all over England from the second half of the eighteenth century onwards and that in quite small places subscription concerts were organized. It would have been remarkable if these activities had not found their way to the West Riding of Yorkshire.

Regarding the Huddersfield Friendly Musical Society, mentioned previously, the earliest document in the Choral Society's archives is a printed handbill giving notice of a concert by this Friendly Society, to be held in the Infants' School Room, Spring Street, on Wednesday evening, 9 May 1832. This concert was announced as constituting the first Quarterly Meeting of the Society and was to consist of a selection of the works of Handel, Haydn, and Gardiner, the first half being a selection from Handel's *Jephtha* (spelt 'Jeptha' on the programme, and undoubtedly very commonly pronounced that way). The second half was to begin with a Rossini overture followed by a selection from Gardiner's *Judah* (an adaptation from works by Haydn, Mozart, and Beethoven). The programme also included a 'Concerto Piano-Forte' given by Mrs Horn, the wife of Henry Horn, the Choral Society's first conductor or 'leader', as he was called in those days. The Choral Society's first concert, incidentally, took place at this same Infants' School Room in Spring Street.

The founder of the Huddersfield Friendly Musical Society was Thomas Hartley, so one reads in a report in the *Huddersfield Chronicle* of 1 April

1854, which gives an account of his recent funeral along with some remarks by way of eulogy. He was born in 1788 and was a local vocalist of repute and the landlord of the Woolpack Inn, Buxton Road. Known locally as 'a father of music' he was evidently, by the time of his death at least, much loved and respected. He sang in various church and chapel choirs and, we are told, gave free community singing lessons to hundreds of local children. He too was a founder-member of the Choral Society and was its first treasurer.

The occasion of the twenty-third annual dinner, held at the George Hotel, of the Huddersfield Glee Club is reported in the *Huddersfield Chronicle* of 11 May 1850. The President, John Freeman, reminded the assembly that 'there was a time when a man's education was not considered as complete unless he could join in a madrigal or glee'. This statement received applause, as did his further remark to the effect that there were few towns in which there was so much musical talent as in Huddersfield. The strict truth of this may be uncertain, but all evidence suggests that, musically, Huddersfield was no mean town. This Glee Club (or Glee Society, as it seems sometimes to be called) is not to be confused with the present Glee and Madrigal Society of Huddersfield formed only in 1875. It is interesting to note, however, that the late Sidney Crowther, in his centenary history (1875–1975) of the Glee and Madrigal Society states that there had been, in the 1880s, a similar society called the Orpheus Society and that there was 'still another, for the cover of the original minute book of the G. and M. bore the title Huddersfield Glee Society'. When Cudworth wrote of the original Glee Society as the most celebrated in the county in its day, he may not have been far from the truth, for certainly it awarded coveted prizes for best glees annually. In March 1839 the prize went to James Battye for his glee, *Hail, Memory Hail* — a favourite for years after at concerts in and around the town. In the following year the Glee Society awarded a prize to William Jackson, organist at Masham, for his Glee *The Sisters of the Sea*. Jackson subsequently became the conductor of the Bradford Choral Society and after that, of the Bradford Festival Choral Society. He was a composer of much renown in Yorkshire. Cudworth writes that in 1841 he composed his '103rd Psalm' for the Huddersfield Choral Society although G. F. Sewell in his *History of the Bradford Festival Choral Society* says this dates from 1856. His *magnum opus* was the oratorio *The Deliverance of Israel from Babylon*.

Evidently there existed, in the 1830s, a society called the *Ramsden's Arms Glee Club*. I have not been able to ascertain whether this was the same society as the Huddersfield Glee Club — being perhaps the original name; but even if they were separate organizations, they would probably have had many members in common. The meeting place, the Ramsden's Arms, still stands in Cross Church Street. The existence of this club is referred to in an article appearing in the *Huddersfield Chronicle* of 4 June 1864 concerning the retirement as a public singer of that celebrated local vocalist, Mrs Sunderland, whose memory is perpetuated in Huddersfield by the musical competition bearing her name, which is held annually in the town. The fame of this lady has resulted in there being more information available about musical affairs in the Huddersfield area than might otherwise have been the case.

Susan Sunderland was born on 30 April 1819 into the family of Mr and Mrs James Sykes of Spring Gardens, Brighouse, both of whom are said to have been musical. James was Head Gardener to a Mr Radcliffe of Lightcliffe. Apparently Susan's voice attracted attention from a very young age. The population of Brighouse in 1821 was less than four thousand but it seems not to have been lacking in musical ability. The Choirmaster at Brighouse Parish Church when Susan was a young girl was one Luke Settle, a blacksmith by trade and also a flautist of some repute! The story is told that the credit for discovering the talents of young Susan belongs to Luke. She was playing in her father's garden, when about 12 years old, singing merrily, when the blacksmith stopped to listen at the garden wall. 'I say, lass' he exclaimed after a while, 'tha's gotten a rare voice. If tha'll come down to my place, I'll teach thi how to use it.' Following upon this encounter she used to visit his forge and sang — mostly sacred songs — whilst he kept time on the anvil. He impressed upon her, it is said, the necessity of breathing deeply, opening the mouth wide, and making the words clear. Luke Settle had clearly not boasted idly when he said he would teach her how to use her voice!

An early wish of Susan's had been to sing in Bridge End Chapel in Brighouse. At that time, before most chapels and churches had organs, a Mr John Denham played the 'cello at the chapel. John Denham also sang, and it was he who was responsible for teaching Susan the rudiments of music. She did get to sing in Bridge End Chapel, and also at St Anne's Church in Southowram, *and* in the Parish Church at Brighouse. The man to whom she acknowledged her greatest indebtedness for musical tuition and subsequent success in her profession was, however, Mr Dan Sugden of Halifax, a double bass player and, according to Cudworth, justly esteemed as 'one of the ablest musicians in the West Riding'. He was so impressed with Susan's voice that he took no remuneration for singing lessons. She came to Dan Sugden's notice as a result of her membership of the Halifax Quarterly Choral Society. Although a Mr Frobisher was the leader of this society, Sugden was generally acknowledged as its chief member, says Cudworth, who adds that he was a man of commanding presence, could 'play every instrument in the orchestra' and was ever ready to give tuition to others. It was he who was responsible, it seems, for obtaining engagements for Mrs Sunderland at the Sacred Harmonic Society performances in London later in her career.

Susan's first public engagement was at the age of 14, in early 1834, at Deighton, near Huddersfield, where she sang 'Wise men flattering' from Handel's *Judas Maccabaeus*. She reports that her first earnings amounted to sixpence for singing at a wedding at Brighouse Parish Church, but her first real fee was five shillings from Dan Sugden for singing 'Ye men of Gaza' from *Samson* at a concert given by the Halifax Quarterly Choral Society.

On the occasion of the opening of the organ at St Paul's, Huddersfield in December 1835 Susan sang 'Rejoice Greatly'. The organist was Henry Horn who was to become leader of the Huddersfield Choral Society in the following year. Susan was appointed principal treble at St Paul's from 1 April 1836, the appointment lasting eight years. Later she also sang on Sunday evenings at the Parish Church where Thomas Parratt played the organ.

Henry Horn was one of the members of the Ramsden's Arms Glee Club. So also were Mr Brook, who later went to Lincoln Cathedral as a bass chorister, Timothy Knowles, who became a tenor of some note at the Chapel Royal, Windsor, Mr Dyson and Mr Bradley. Mr Dyson shares the name, if not the identity, of one of the early members of the Choral Society in Huddersfield. Both Mr Horn and his wife were pianists as well as organists and it was as a pianist no doubt that he served with the Glee Club. The members of this club persuaded young Susan Sykes to receive tuition from Mr Kaye, a Huddersfield schoolmaster, in order to improve her elocutionary powers. Being born of humble though respectable parents, she was reported as being only of meagre education with a pronunciation and delivery of a rude and uncultivated character, which all sounds a trifle patronizing. One wonders if her diction was quite so dreadful as described by this report. Be that as it may, she joined the Huddersfield Choral Society from the date of its formation in 1836 and was its favourite soloist for many years thereafter. She married Mr Henry Sunderland in 1838, a butcher by trade, of whom we seem to hear very little except that upon his death in 1893, aged 77 years, the *Brighouse Echo* reported that he retired from the butchery trade 'about 40 years ago'. He never took a prominent part in local public matters it seems, but was locally well known and highly esteemed. It was with his name of Sunderland that Susan's career blossomed, leading her to the forefront of English vocal musical life. They came to call her 'the Yorkshire Queen of Song' and she seems to have been universally loved and her talents applauded. She was said to have remarkable flexibility of voice, combined with great power as well as intensity of feeling. Her name will often be mentioned in this history but this account of her early development is sufficient to indicate the musical fertility of the soil into which this seed of talent had been sown.

Although it is true that for a century or more before the time under discussion, England could hardly have been regarded as the centre of the musical universe, it was by no means a musical desert. Native composers of immense genius had been few, if any, within these islands for too long, no doubt, but musical composition of the highest order is not the whole of music, and musical activity thrived not only in London but throughout the provinces during the eighteenth century. Musical activity developed particularly in the towns where wealth was increasing due to the Industrial Revolution, which gathered momentum towards the end of that century. The links between industry and the world of music at that time are variously manifested. The Handel Commemoration held in Westminster Abbey and the Pantheon in 1784 was, according to Mackerness in his *Social History of English Music*, in some ways the most important single event in the history of English music during the eighteenth century. Its director was Joah Bates from Halifax who had considerable financial interest in the Albion Mills, destroyed by fire in 1791. He and his wife, who was the singer, Sarah Harrop and once a Halifax factory worker, lost a fortune. Halifax was certainly a town of great musical repute in the North in those days, no doubt due in part to the influence of Joah Bates and his wife, whom Cudworth refers to as 'two of the foremost musicians of the age'. Charles Dibdin is quoted as saying that the town was reputedly the most musical place for its size in the Kingdom, and attributes the great veneration there for the works of Handel to Joah Bates. Evidently even the children lisped 'For unto us a Child is born' and the clothworkers 'sweating under their loads to the Piece Hall' used to be heard roaring 'For His Yoke is easy, and His Burden is Light'. Dibdin tells us that he had been assured that more than one man in Halifax could take any part in the choruses of *The Messiah* and regularly went through the whole oratorio by heart. The popularity of the German composers, particularly of the oratorios of Handel, was universal, and as the new century advanced the works of Handel, Haydn and, eventually, Mendelssohn, were always high on the list of popularity.

The spread of nonconformity which accompanied the Industrial Revolution, was as strong in Huddersfield as anywhere else. Its passion for the communal singing of hymns, anthems, and oratorio choruses exerted a great influence on the development of choral music. Despite the relative decline of the Anglican Church during the eighteenth century, and the growing strength of the nonconformist chapel communities, the founder-members of the Huddersfield Choral Society would seem to have been of Anglican association for the most part. Nevertheless the influence of nonconformity both in the nature of the membership of the Society and of the music it performed is undeniable. It is interesting though that the very same year of the Society's formation saw the opening of the rebuilt Parish Church of St Peter, in Huddersfield — on Thursday, 27 October 1836. On this occasion an anthem composed by James Battye, the Parish Clerk, was sung in the presence of a large congregation. This same James Battye, together with his twin brother Edward, had only a few months earlier been present at the inaugural meeting of the Choral Society. James is in fact recorded on a memorial tablet, on the South wall of the Parish Church, as being himself *the* founder of the Huddersfield Choral Society.

The town of Huddersfield had grown considerably in the quarter of a century or so preceding the foundation of the Society. The population rose from about 7,000 or so in 1801 to something in excess of 20,000 by 1836. At the present day this seems little more than village or small township size, but one must remember that even the largest of towns at that time were small by modern standards. Although village-sized, many a community would no doubt have had features not often associated with our modern villages. The town continued to grow at a steadily increasing rate throughout the nineteenth, and indeed into the twentieth century but during the initial decades of the nineteenth century it advanced from relative obscurity to become, by the mid thirties, an important centre of industry, trade, and commerce, not to mention political activity! This growth mirrored the increasing importance of Huddersfield associated with the changes which were taking place in manufacturing methods, due to the invention of new machinery and the growing use of steam power in factories and mills; the changes which were the very essence of the Industrial Revolution. Huddersfield's most important product being woollen cloth meant that work such as weaving, previously performed in the home, was increasingly being performed in mills and, initially at any rate, by fewer people. Resulting unemployment, or fear of it, and a period of general economic depression led ultimately to the violence of the Luddite Riots of 1812 in which machinery was smashed and mill-owners were violently attacked.

The growth of the town had been accompanied by political unrest which was in contrast to the relative peace which it had enjoyed during the previous century, an unrest which was to bother it for some period to come. Still in the future were the so-called Plug Riots of 1842, the disturbances associated with the Chartist movement, and the activities of the somewhat radical followers of Robert Owen — the new 'socialists' whose presence, as we shall see, was even to make itself felt within the ranks of the Choral Society membership.

Some of the ways in which the Industrial Revolution affected the musical life in England, especially in the growing industrial centres, such as those of the West Riding of Yorkshire, are readily understood. More and more ordinary people were drawn into towns and industrial communities where conditions caused them to seek cheap recreation for themselves. Musical instruments, like other manufactured articles, became more readily available and improved in design and quality; also some industrialists began to provide rudimentary educational facilities in which music played a significant part. Choral singing and the formation of brass bands were encouraged in some areas, and fairly cheap, printed music was soon to be available in quantity — the firm of Novello's was founded in 1811. As the nineteenth century advanced the names of the pioneers of the various sight-singing methods such as Mainzer, Hullah, and Curwen were to become familiar nationwide. In the fiercely debated and, finally, successfully implemented mass education policy of Victorian Britain the subject of music, particularly the teaching of vocal music, was regarded as very important. Its disciplinary and moral influence was regarded as considerable, a view widely held in the nonconformist movement, which was partner to the effects of the Industrial Revolution in the growth in popularity of music, particularly sacred music, among the mass of the people.

Instrumental in the spread of nonconformity in the town, despite his position as Vicar of the Parish of Huddersfield, was the much-admired Revd Henry Venn (after whom Venn Street is named). John Wesley visited Huddersfield on more than one occasion and preached at the old Parish Church during Venn's ministry, which lasted from 1759 until 1771. W. L. Wilmshurst associates the liberation of spirit and energy of the Reformation, which gave rise to the music of the great German masters, with that of the 'democracy that was issuing from the restraints of the old feudal order and straining towards greater liberty', and suggests that, in his Choral Symphony, Beethoven reflected a new spirit of freedom and emancipation. No doubt this is true, but certainly by the 1830s the followers and admirers of Wesley, and of Venn in Huddersfield, in their enthusiasm for Handel, Haydn, and even Beethoven, though they might have been interested in the abolition of slavery in America, were not necessarily wanting more liberty, freedom, and equality for the common man in their own country. Disturbances, and worse, on the continent and the activities of revolutionary elements at home were too recent for the unreserved acceptance of 'the emancipation of society from its old shackles', as Wilmshurst puts it.

Nevertheless there is doubtless a link between the spread of nonconformity and the industrialization of society. Nonconformists delighted in singing simply-learned and harmonized hymn-tunes in community with others, and associated this activity with moral duty and discipline. On the other hand, some pioneer industrialists and educationalists saw music, particularly vocal music, as a suitable vehicle for the beneficial instruction of the new industrial working classes. But this, perhaps, had less to do with a 'straining towards a greater liberty' on the part of the mass of the working folk than on the part of their new industrial masters.

The Huddersfield population was, by 1836, very different from the people whom Wesley described after a visit in 1759, as 'a wilder people I never saw in England'. Despite its political riots, its proportionate share of working-class misery, and its semi-rural character it was a rapidly-developing and increasingly prosperous community, God-fearing for the most part, far from politically inert, and very much alive musically.

This, then, was the background against which sixteen local musicians decided to meet together in the Plough Inn, in Westgate, on 7 June 1836, for the purpose of establishing the Huddersfield Choral Society.

CHAPTER TWO

The Lost Years

THE EARLIEST SURVIVING minutes of the Society's Committee of Management record a meeting held 'at the House of Mr John Gills, the Commercial Inn' on 'Friday evening, the 17 June 1842'. This is almost exactly six years after the Society was formed. Fortunately, in the minute book, covering the period 1842 to 1864, is a printed set of rules and regulations of the Society, a list of committee members appointed for the first year, and a list of performing members as at January 1837. As a preamble to these rules there appears the following declaration:

At a meeting held at the Plough Inn, Huddersfield, on Tuesday, the 7th day of June, 1836; we whose names are hereunto subscribed, agreed to establish a Musical Society, to be called 'The Huddersfield Choral Society'. The first meeting to be held in the Infant School, Spring Street, on Friday Evening, July 15th, at Eight o'clock. The succeeding meetings to be held on the Friday on or before the full moon in every month. We also hereby agree to observe and abide by the following Rules and Regulations.

This bears the following list of signatories:

Edward Battye, James Battye, Henry Horn, John Crosland, John Broadley, John Dyson, Thomas Hartley, Joseph Howard, Joseph Mellor, George Milnes, Henry Wood, William Tattersall, George Wilkinson, Jabez Jackman, George Armitage, and James Lambert.

This same declaration is reproduced, with minor modifications, at the beginning of a revised set of rules, dated 16 December 1842, but printed in 1843, a copy of which still survives, and which contains further interesting information.

The requirement for monthly meetings to be held on days falling 'on or before the full moon' was common in those days, especially if people had to come on foot from a considerable distance to the meeting place. Not that the streets in Huddersfield were unlit in 1836. In fact the town-centre had boasted gas-lighting since 1822. This replaced the earlier use of oil lamps, reported as being of precious little use anyway. But the full moon, on cloud-free nights, would have lighted the way for those members from out of town, who were, by all accounts, numerous. They came from such places as Deighton, Honley, Milnsbridge, Netherton, Outlane, Paddock, and Turn-bridge.

As to the signatories, the Battye brothers have already been mentioned, as also have Henry Horn, Thomas Hartley, and John Dyson, the latter being possibly the Mr Dyson of the Ramsden's Arms Glee Club. He may well also be the same John Dyson whom one finds referred to elsewhere as a flautist, but with this name so common in the locality, then as now, one cannot be sure of this. George Wilkinson, a very well-known, local bass soloist, was for several years choirmaster and principal bass at Ramsden Street Chapel and also turned his efforts to modest composition. At a later date he wrote an anthem, *The Lord is Full of Compassion*, an arrangement and adaptation of material by Friedrich Himmel and Haydn which he 'respectfully inscribed to Mrs Sunderland'. John Broadley was a local tenor soloist of some talent. Both of these men regularly sang solo parts with the Choral Society during its early years. Of John Broadley we have a report of a benefit concert arranged on his behalf when he fell seriously ill in 1840: £40 was raised — a considerable sum of money at that time. He died aged only 45, on Christmas Day of that year, deaths at such an early age being quite common in those days. Mr John Crosland was both a 'cellist and a double bass player, the Society's first Secretary, and its Chairman from 1838 until 1842. William Tattersall's name does not appear often in what records are available, but he was reported as being 'a much-esteemed member of the Society' when, following his death, a memorial concert was given for him by the Society in August 1846. George Milnes sang alto and was one of the Society's very popular principals for years whilst George Armitage, who sang bass in Ramsden Street Chapel choir, was also a Choral Society principal in the early days, and evidently a bit past his prime, coming in for some very outspoken press criticism on that account. At one time he had been one of the town's best bass singers. Mr Jabez Jackman (another of the Society's principal soloists) eventually went to Ely to become a cathedral chorister. He is listed in a volume of glees composed by James Battye, printed at a later date, as one of the subscribers to the volume. This leaves for consideration, Joseph Howard, Joseph Mellor, James Lambert, and Henry Wood, who, with the exception of James Lambert, all appear as members of the Committee of Management at some time or another during the first decade of the Society's existence. Joseph Mellor was the father of Richard Mellor, organist at the Ramsden Street Chapel. Joseph Howard was 'foreman' for the 1837–38 season, but Henry Wood's name appears no later than 1839–40. Unfortunately nothing what-ever has come to light regarding James Lambert.

It would be fascinating to discover more about these founder-members, particularly something of their social background and their means of liveli-hood — assuming they all began as amateur musicians. We know this was not true of Henry Horn who was organist at St Paul's Church, and who was described at the time of his death as a professor of music in the town. In addition to being leader of the Choral Society he promoted public concerts in the locality and both he and his wife were very active in the musical life of the town. We know that James Battye was appointed in 1834 as Clerk at the Parish Church at a salary of 4 gns per annum. Born at Taylor Hill on 6 October 1802 he received his early musical education in Lockwood at night classes costing one penny a week held by a Mr William Sharp, and later, from Thomas Wallace of Elland. This musical knowledge was acquired, it seems, after a long day's work at a mill, though in what capacity is nowhere revealed. His twin brother, Edward, was in 1841, it seems, clerk of St Paul's Church and was elected in that year to be registrar of the Board of Guardians for Lockwood. Thomas Hartley was, as already stated, the landlord of the Woolpack Inn in Buxton Road. Regarding all the other gentlemen informa-tion is difficult to obtain, but they were probably all members of what might now be regarded as a lower middle class, or perhaps of the upper 'respectable' echelons of the working class.

The Rules and Regulations as set down in 1836 have been much quoted in musical histories. The *Huddersfield Chronicle* of 16 October 1858 attributes their authorship to James Battye. They were nineteen in number and made provision for the election of a secretary, treasurer, and committee of seven, one of the members of which was to be selected as 'foreman' to hold office on an annual basis. There were to be quarterly meetings, membership fees of half a crown as half-yearly payments to be made in advance, under pain of forfeiture of membership. Full control over the admittance of members to the Society was to be exercised by the committee, and provision was made for each member to have a stake in the Society's assets, provided he had paid 'his proportionate share (if any) to the property of the Society'. Funds and profits were to be held by members in 'equal and proportionate share' with 'no invidious distinctions'. Monthly meetings were to begin at 7.30 p.m. from October to March inclusive and at 8.00 p.m. for the remainder of the year. There were to be fines of threepence for lateness of up to a quarter of an hour, and sixpence for non-attendance except when due to sickness; these amounts being doubled for the quarterly meetings. The secretary was required to report on the state of the Society at the first meeting in every half year, and the books were to be open to inspection by any who could rightfully claim membership — neglect or refusal to allow such inspection on the part of the secretary cost the latter a fine of half a crown or 'exclusion'.

One rule provided for the transfer to another person of a member's proportionate share of the funds of the Society should he remove from the district and thereby cease to be a member. Another provided for such a transfer should a member die. The recipient of such a transferred share had first to be admitted as a member, according to the appropriate rule. Should he not be admitted then, in the case of the member's removal, the latter would receive his own share 'in money or books', and in the case of his death, his nearest relative would receive his share.

It is apparent that great care was to be taken regarding the suitability of persons seeking membership, and of their conduct, once accepted. Intoxication, use of obscene or abusive language, or calling of any other member or members 'bye-names' at any meeting were regarded as offences incurring a fine of sixpence. This was also the fine to be imposed for leaving a meeting without providing the door-keeper or foreman with an adequate reason, or for failing to be back in one's place at the end of the interval period of twenty minutes between the first and second half of the quarterly meetings. The fine was also to be imposed for not returning a copy of music 'at the next meeting'. Each member was to be allowed one copy only of music and this rule would seem to suggest, at any rate, the arrangement was that music was loaned out only from one meeting to the next. If unreturned music was actually required for performance at the next meeting the fine imposed was half a crown — an amount which at that time must surely have acted as an effective deterrent. The foreman or his appointed deputy was to collect fines which were to be handed over to the treasurer, and the secretary must record their addition to the Society's funds. Should the Committee admit 'too many members who were not duly qualified or any whose conduct may endanger the well-being of the Society' a special meeting of all the members was to be called in order to discuss the matter. If discussion alone failed to produce accord, the matter was to be settled by a vote requiring a two-thirds majority of those present to be in favour of any motion put, in order for it to be carried.

One interesting rule afforded every member the right, in rotation, to select the oratorio to be performed at the next meeting, on the understanding that 'the majority of members think that copies can be procured'. The rule also limited the number of instrumental pieces to be performed by the band to four per meeting. This seems to indicate that 'performances' were envisaged as being, as often as not, readings of works which were not unfamiliar, more for the purpose of personal entertainment than for the benefit of an audience. At monthly meetings members were to be allowed to express an opinion of a piece of music after its performance, provided this was done in a 'respectable, friendly and becoming manner'. Interruption of pieces, however, or disturbances during a performance was to incur the penalty of yet another fine, or else 'exclusion' of the member concerned, the fine again being the high sum of half a crown.

Every member was to be allowed three gills of ale together with bread and cheese at every monthly meeting, whilst at quarterly meetings the refreshment was to consist of 'such other refreshments as shall be agreed by the Committee'. Members were to be allowed to introduce one friend each at quarterly meetings on payment of sixpence for the extra refreshments required, if the friend be an amateur, but no payment was required if the person were a 'female performer'. The latter were also not charged for membership of the Society, although they were to be entitled to the same privileges and subject to the same fines at 'quarterly meetings and the previous rehearsals' as paying members. This reference to quarterly meetings and the previous rehearsals seems to put a somewhat different light on the nature of the monthly meetings. Unless we assume that 'rehearsal' is used in its now somewhat outmoded sense of the reading, recital, or recitation of a piece, it suggests that the monthly meetings were to be regarded as preparatory for the performance of a work at the quarterly meetings. This seems at variance with the rule allowing selection of an oratorio for the next meeting, unless the reference be to the next quarterly meeting, which seems unlikely since then some members would have a long time to wait for their turn to choose!

The revised rules of 1842 are surely a reflection of changes which must have taken place in the organization of the Society soon after its formation, even perhaps as early as 1837. This is indicated by the nature of the activities of the Society during the first six years, as revealed by press reports, though the latter are few in number. Despite the requirements for accounts to be kept of copies of music lent out and of monies received, for six-monthly reports by the secretary, for books to be kept which were to be open to inspection by any member, etc., no records whatever of such matters, and certainly no minute books from the period 1836 to 1842 have survived. It is unlikely that written records of this nature were not preserved, at least for a time, but the fact remains that we have to rely on such sources as occasional reports by the Leeds and Halifax newspapers for any information at all concerning the Society's activities during this period: no regular newspapers were printed in Huddersfield until 1850. The 1843 booklet of revised rules and regulations does, however, provide us with the names of the officers and Committee members for each of those six years and in addition, a list of performing members of the Society in 1842. These are seventy-four in number, exclusive of five 'honorary performing members' (all male), whereas of the seventy-four ordinary members fourteen are female.

In 1837 there had been a total of sixty-two performing members, including eight females. It would seem that there had been no honorary performing members at that time. The name of Thomas Parratt, the organist at the Parish Church, appears on both the earlier and the later list. Miss Susan Sykes's name had, of course, changed to Mrs Sunderland by the date of the later list, and James Peace, the organist at Holy Trinity Church was a member whose name appears, as does that of his wife, on both lists. On the list published in 1843 in addition to the names of Mr and Mrs James Peace there appear the names of Mr and Mrs Lister Peace who were the parents of the famous organist, Dr A. L. Peace, born in 1844. He was organist at Glasgow Cathedral before his appointment in 1897 as organist at St George's Hall, Liverpool, where he remained until his death in 1912. A Miss Milnes is named on the earlier list. She was very active as a principal singer with the Society during the first six years or so and although her name is not on the 1843 list, it appears on a handwritten list at the beginning of the first minute book (June 1842). What relation, if any, she was of George Milnes, the alto singer, is not clear.

John Crosland, the double bass player, was the choir's first Secretary, serving in that capacity from 1836 until 1838 when he became Chairman. From 1838 until 1845 Edward Battye acted as Secretary. James, Edward's twin brother, served on the Committee of Management throughout this period but he was explicitly stated to be the Librarian, in 1842. The Society's first Chairman was George Armitage, appointed perhaps due to his seniority in years, but he was replaced in 1837 by Joseph Howard, and in 1838 by John Crosland, who was elevated from Secretary to Chairman, remaining in that position until 1842 when Henry Horn, the Leader, took over the Chair. The Treasurer from the beginning until 1848, except for the 1844–45 season, was the well-loved Thomas Hartley of the Woolpack Inn.

The first meeting of the Society, scheduled in the preamble to take place 'in the Infant School, Spring Street on Friday Evening, July 15th, at Eight o'clock' duly took place as arranged when, according to reports appearing in the *Leeds Mercury* and in the *Halifax and Huddersfield Express* shortly afterwards 'the oratorio of the *Creation* was performed in very good style'. The meeting was referred to as the Society's first quarterly meeting as was also the next meeting on 30 September 1836, again held in the Infant School Room, Spring Street. Admittedly it could be that the latter referred to the first quarterly meeting of the 1836–37 season (the previous meeting being the first quarterly meeting *ever*, but the last of the 1835–36 season) but the fact remains that this enumeration introduced an error into the calculations of the total number of quarterly concerts performed by the Society, as quoted thereafter, not that it was the only error, as we shall see.

Meetings/performances continued to be held at the Infant School Room in Spring Street throughout that first season. This school (though possibly not the original building) still stands in what is left of Spring Street, and is now the premises of the Huddersfield Plate Glass Company. What a different aspect Spring Street now has compared with what it must have had 150 years ago. The Water Works Building which, as the plaque on its front makes clear, was 'Established by Subscription in 1828', also still stands in Water Street, at the top end of Spring Street. In 1836 it was new and fresh and had pleasant gardens in which visitors to the Infant School are reported to have once walked for pleasure. As to the performance of 30 September 1836, it consisted of a selection from *Judas Maccabaeus* and a 'splendid chorus composed by Mr James Battye', reported the *Halifax and Huddersfield Express* of 12 October 1836.

The Society's first performance of music from *The Messiah* took place in the Infant School Room on 30 December 1836. Although only a selection of items from the oratorio, this nevertheless constitutes the first of a great number of performances by the Society of this work at what was evidently not one of the scheduled concerts. Susan Sykes (the Mrs Sunderland to be) sang principal soprano. She was then still only 17 years old. The concert, in the customary manner of newspaper reports of the time, was said to have been given to a 'numerous and respectable audience' — presumably of subscribers and their friends. We must not entertain any doubts regarding the significance of the reporting of the audience as 'respectable'. There would have been no doubt in anybody's mind in nineteenth-century English society regarding its meaning. An outbreak of typhus fever in Huddersfield in 1847 was reported in the *Leeds Mercury* as being most common in the houses of the poor and destitute although it had 'made its appearance in several respectable families'; this speaks volumes concerning the appreciation of the word.

In August of 1837 the Society gave a performance for the first time in a building which was virtually to be its home, as far as performances were concerned, for the better part of thirty years — the Philosophical Hall. It stood in Ramsden Street on the site later occupied by a theatre (the Theatre Royal) for nearly a century, and now occupied by the shopping and leisure area just below the Public Library. It was first opened for use on 24 May 1837 which was the eighteenth birthday (and thus the attainment of her majority) of the Princess Victoria, who was to ascend the throne less than a month later, on 20 June. This was a somewhat premature opening of the Hall in order to provide a dinner for poor working men in celebration of the occasion of the birthday of the Princess. The following day, 25 May, was the occasion of the first official function to be held in the new building — the Spring Meeting of the Huddersfield Horticultural Society. The fact that it had been used on the previous day was mentioned by the Revd J. C. Franks, the Vicar of Huddersfield Parish Church and the President of the Philosophical Society, in his address on the occasion of the Horticultural Show. He commented that one might say that the building had already been opened under the patronage of the Princess Victoria since nearly 300 persons had dined there the day before in honour of her having attained her majority. This is rather different from the categorical assertion that the hall was opened under the patronage of Princess Victoria and even more different from the report that it was opened *by* Princess Victoria, both of which statements appear in twentieth-century publications concerning the history of Huddersfield. Notwithstanding all this activity, the *official* opening of the Hall is reported as having taken place nearly three months later on Friday, 11 August 1837, which was the day following its use by the Choral Society who provided 'the lovers of music' (reported the *Halifax Express*), with a fine treat on Thursday evening' when they performed 'in the large and beautiful room in the Philosophical Hall'. No details of the music performed are provided in this report but it appears that 'the attendance was the largest ever held in Huddersfield, each member of the Philosophical Hall being furnished with two admission tickets besides two or three hundred tickets having been sold'.

The first quarterly meeting of the Society for the 1837–38 season was also held in the Philosophical Hall. The programme consisted of a selection of airs and choruses from *Solomon*, *Israel in Egypt*, and William Gardiner's *Judah*, with a couple of overtures, one to open each half of the concert. Remarkably, the Society possesses a handbill announcing this concert, and including the details of the programme as given above, which, some years ago, was handed to the then Secretary of the Society, Mr Richard Barraclough, by a person whose identity he cannot recall, if indeed he was ever aware of it. The following statement appears on the first page of the leaflet:

The Committee, in behalf of the Society, return their sincere thanks for the very liberal encouragement they have been honoured with during the past year, and again solicit the patronage of all who feel an interest in this very pleasing and interesting branch of science.

For the information of those who may not already be acquainted with the object of this Society, it may be necessary to state that it was established, and is continued, for the purpose of improvement, in the performance of Modern as well as Ancient Music; should the funds enable them to purchase Modern Compositions.

Details of subscriptions then follow, which are essentially those which appear in the 1843 publication of Revised Rules and Regulations, viz. £1 11s. 6d. entitles a subscriber to 4 tickets to the Saloon 'each Quarter Night', 16s. entitled a subscriber to two such tickets, a guinea entitled him or her to four tickets to the Gallery and 10s. 6d., to two such tickets.

It does seem from this, as suggested earlier, that the revision of rules became necessary almost from the opening of the Philosophical Hall in 1837. Nothing akin to the above subscription charges appears in the 1836 rules. Nothing so bold and self-confident as that quoted above appeared there regarding the object of the Society. This suggests that after only one year the Society had developed a decidedly progressive outlook indicative surely of the quality of musicianship, if of nothing else, of the founder-members. The leaflet asserts that 'upwards of 70 performers are already admitted into the Society'.

Susan Sykes again sang at this first concert of the new season, as did also Miss Milnes, Mr George Armitage, Mr Abel Starkey, Mr Lawton, and Mr John Broadley. The concert was 'well attended', according to a report in the *Halifax Express*, 'considering the numerous attendance at Mr Horn's concert on the previous Wednesday evening'. This is a reference to a concert of vocal and instrumental music promoted and conducted by Henry Horn also held in the Large Room of the Philosophical Hall.

The reference to music as a 'very pleasing and interesting branch of science' in the leaflet quoted above is interesting. The use of the word 'science' rather than 'art' as applied to music may seem strange to us today. Notwithstanding its name, the erection of the Philosophical Hall came about as a consequence of a growing general interest in the promotion of scientific knowledge which in those days had still not yet altogether come to be regarded as a separate thing from philosophy — or at least from natural philosophy — in a way that was to be the case as the century advanced. Indeed, the word 'science', as we use and understand it today, dates roughly from the period which we are discussing.

The next performance of which there seems to be any record is the fourth Quarterly of the 1837–38 season, incorrectly referred to, for the reasons already indicated, as the Eighth Quarterly concert. It took place in the

Philosophical Hall on Friday, 6 April 1838 when a chorus entitled 'Praise Jehovah' (attributed to Mozart in the *Halifax Guardian* report of 17 April 1838) was sung along with excerpts from James Battye's 122nd and 132nd Psalms and a selection of airs, choruses, and instrumental items given by such as Miss Milnes, Miss Sykes, Mrs Peace, Mr Broadley, and with Mr Peace on the violoncello. Whatever the 'Mozart' piece may have been, it was 'admirably managed', according to the *Halifax Guardian* report, in which also, Mr Horn was said to be deserving of 'great praise' for the 'increasing exertions he must have bestowed on the orchestra — which consisted of upwards of 70 performers'. The word 'orchestra' here refers to the body of vocal and instrumental performers numbering seventy in all. Elsewhere one finds it used, as still sometimes nowadays, to mean the place where musicians are located in a concert hall or theatre. Only in this century did its use to mean what was previously known as the 'band' become firmly established. The recorded number of members of the Society quoted earlier, let us remember, was seventy at that date.

Press reports for the 1838–39 season indicate that, in addition to monthly and quarterly meetings, or performances, the tradition was established of giving an annual performance. This was written into the revised rules of 1843 which again lends support to the notion that these revised rules were somewhat overdue by 1842, and that 1837 is the date at which the pattern determining the form of the 1842 revision was established. The annual performance of the season 1838–39 took place in late December 1838 or in early January 1839 when Handel's *Messiah* was performed. According to the report in the *Halifax Express* of 5 January 1839, which gives no date for the concert, the whole oratorio 'was gone through by the performers, which is one of the best and most effective local bands in the kingdom, in very superior style' and gave delight apparently to a 'very numerous and respectable audience'. High praise indeed, and one notices this time that 'band' serves to refer to the entire company of performers, vocal and instrumental. *The Messiah* was repeated at the annual performance for the following season which took place on Friday, 3 January 1840. Other performances up to this date included selections from Haydn's *Creation* and Handel's *Judas Maccabaeus*, Romberg's *Transient and Eternal*, Handel's *Israel in Egypt*, and a March and Chorus of Beethoven.

Most of the press reports of the Society's early concerts were brief but usually very favourable, if not full of praise. The third and fourth concerts of the 1839–40 season were exceptions however, being reported at length, and somewhat unfavourably. Even Mrs Sunderland, as she had now become, was not immune from the adverse criticism; she was 'thought to be rather sharp' in one of her recitative sections. Whether deserved or not, this verbal onslaught was short-lived, and on the occasion of the Benefit Concert given for the ailing John Broadley on 27 November 1840, the reporting reverted to the norm and it was as if it had never been otherwise.

In January 1841 *The Messiah* was chosen again for the annual concert and, with the exception of the performance of Andreas Jacob Romberg's *Lay of the Bell* at the Second Quarterly Concert of the 1841–42 season, it has not proved possible to find any details of other performances either for this season or for the season before it. The *Lay of the Bell* was again given at the Annual Public Concert in December of 1842, together with a selection from other composers. According to a report which appeared in the *Musical Times* of February 1845, the Huddersfield Choral Society performed the *Lay of the Bell* again on 19 December 1844. Thus the Society gave three performances of this work in as many years. It was obviously popular at the time but has long since been forgotten.

It is a pity that the Society's records of its earliest years are largely lost, but fortunately we still have those records, kept since 1842, of the Society's committee meetings. These, however, are not continuous. In the earliest surviving minute book of the Society there are a few unaccountable lapses, during the 1840s and 1850s, when no minutes of meetings (which must certainly have taken place) are recorded. But since 1860 onwards the minutes of committee meetings are all available up to the present day. Needless to say, these have proved to be an invaluable source of information in writing this history.

CHAPTER THREE

Firm Foundations

DURING THE FIRST HALF of the last century the population of Huddersfield may have been small by present-day standards, but the town centre was by no means short of what the directories of the time listed as 'inns and taverns'. According to a contemporary report in the *Leeds Mercury*, there were sixty-one public houses in Huddersfield in 1845, representing one public house to every 234 inhabitants. It was at one or another of these houses that the Choral Society's Committee of Management used to hold its meetings. These took place at the *Cherry Tree* in Westgate, the *Woolpack* (or *Woolpacks*) in Buxton Road, the *Sun* in Cross Church Street, the old *George* in the Market Place, the *Plough* in Westgate, as well as the *Globe* and the *New Inn* which were both in King Street. The favourite — or perhaps simply the most suitable — seems to have been the *Cherry Tree Inn*, which originally stood on the north side of Westgate at the junction with Railway Street until it was demolished in 1868. Subsequently, and until the early 1930s, the *Cherry Tree Inn* was on the opposite side of Westgate, at its junction with Market Street, and next door to the *Plough Inn*.

The minutes of these early meetings are written in a beautiful hand, presumably that of the Secretary, Edward Battye. In 1845 when John Crosland became Secretary the handwriting, though not quite so splendid, still exhibits that old-world elegance which shames the best efforts of most of us today. In 1846 the hand of Edward Battye is again seen, but when he was elected Chairman in 1848 the Secretaryship passed to George Calvert and the quality of the written records deteriorates markedly. In 1849 James Battye became Secretary in Edward's place and from then until 1852 no minutes were recorded at all. Not until 1853, when Edward Battye was again appointed Secretary, did the recording of minutes resume on a regular basis.

The only entry between 1849 and 1853 records a general meeting held at the *Vulcan Inn* on Friday, 22 April 1852 for the sole purpose, evidently, of appointing a new leader following the death, recorded with 'deep regret' of the 'much respected' Mr Horn. The few entries which were made while George Calvert was Secretary are relatively poorly and untidily written. The reason for this, and for the recording of only one meeting during the period 1849 to 1853, is a matter for speculation alone.

During the summer of 1842 several new rules were introduced and it is clear that the need to prepare a new set of printed rules was pressing. A committee of six was appointed to revise the rules at a General Meeting of members on 16 September that year at the *Sun Inn* and at a further General Meeting in December at the *Plough Inn* it was resolved that the revised rules be adopted and printed. This was the set of Revised Rules and Regulations referred to in the previous chapter. Recorded in the minutes of this same meeting is the following interesting resolution 'that the funds of this Society are not in those depressed circumstances [such] as to require a call or demand a payment of Two Shillings and Sixpence per every six months of each of the members for the present'. Thus only six years after the Society's inauguration, came a decision to waive, for an indefinite period it would seem, all subscriptions for continued membership as laid down in the initial rules! However, the revised rule, labelled No. 7, stated that 'if required' this sum should be paid by members each July and January. How envious present-day members might be of circumstances not sufficiently depressed as to require either a call, or demand, for payment of annual subscriptions.

The new rules regularized many practices which had been normal procedure for at least five of the six years of the Society's existence. One new rule required that members should reside within six miles of the Philosophical Hall. Another was designed to deter members from charging any committee member with dishonest or illegal practices. The most interesting of the new rules is surely, however, the last, number 28, which declares 'that no person shall be a member of this Society, who *frequents* the "Hall of Science" or *any* of the "Socialist Meetings", nor shall the Librarian be allowed to lend any copies of Music (knowingly) belonging to this Society to *any* Socialist, upon pain of expulsion'.

The Hall of Science still stands, in Bath Street, where its original name can still be read, though with considerable difficulty, on a stone tablet at the very top of the building. The words were originally written in slate, inserted into the stone, but have long since been removed. The building has had a chequered history of occupation and usage and is now occupied by Ramsey Clay, a firm of painting contractors. It was built in 1839, as were a number of such halls throughout the country, for the purpose of education and enlightenment of the ordinary populace, but the interests of those who patronized and frequented such institutions were predominantly political and certainly secular, if not altogether atheistic. In particular the socialist doctrines of

Thomas Parratt

[Reproduced from *The Musical Times*, 1 April 1902, with the permission of the Bodleian Library, Oxford.]

James Battye

[Reproduced from the *Magazine of Music*, July 1889, with the permission of the Bodleian Library, Oxford.]

The old Cherry Tree Inn

[Reproduced by courtesy of the *Huddersfield Examiner*.]

Cover of the programme for the Society's concert in the new Philosophical Hall, October 1837

Title-page of the Revised Rules and Regulations booklet, 1842

Robert Owen were promulgated in these places, as were those of the Chartists and other radical groups. Owen himself visited the Hall to lecture at public meetings and so did other notable leaders of anti-establishment movements. Ironically, the Hall later became used as a place of worship, first by Unitarians and then by Baptists, but eventually it was acquired by a succession of manufacturers although it was used apparently for a period prior to 1919 as a Railway Mission Hall. It is little wonder that the members of the Choral Society were barred from having anything to do with a place which was regarded as a hot-bed of atheistic socialism. As Wilmshurst says of the guardians of the Choral Society:

They were good Church and Chapel people, orthodox in politics and religion, whereas patrons of the Hall of Science were known to be secularists, socialists, holders of ideas felt to be subversive of the public good and of private morals. Though they sang with the tongues of angels or were qualified to fiddle with the Cherubim, yet, having the taint of infidelity, were they not profaning the music of the Oratory? How should they sing the Lord's song in a Hall of Science?

Certainly, also, the invective showered upon Owen and his supporters by the local press at the time was forceful and relentless.

Not all the Choral Society members shared the abhorence of the Officers and Committee members regarding the Hall of Science, apparently, for at a meeting of the Committee at the *Cherry Tree Inn* on Good Friday, 1843, it was resolved

that Wm Littlewood be sent for into this Committee Room, to state his reasons why he attended to perform at the Socialist Hall a few weeks ago, after having signed the Rule against attending the above place: when he the aforesaid Littlewood, appeared before the Committee and was suitably reprimanded by the Chairman.

Quite evidently there was every intention on the part of those responsible for the affairs of the Society to see to it that members obeyed the rules. Indeed, one is left with a general impression, from all the records and reports of this period, of a society which was disciplined, confident, financially secure, and capable of fine musical performance. With regard to the latter point, however, we can only be satisfied that the performance was considered fine when compared with contemporary performances — and possibly only by local standards, that is to say by the newspaper reporters of the time.

The minutes of the meetings between 1842 and 1849 are nothing if not brief, being confined mostly to the recording of resolutions, of which there was quite often only one per meeting. Meetings took place — or at least, were recorded — somewhat irregularly, although a general meeting of members was held annually either in June or July. At these annual meetings a Committee of Management was elected but its chairman was chosen by the Committee itself at one of its subsequent meetings. Committee resolutions were for the most part concerned with additional regulations or the enforcement of those already existing, with financial matters relating to ticket prices, subscriptions, or with members' holdings in money, property or stock, with music, its purchase, safe-keeping or loan, with choice of music for performances, with selection of soloists, and with the acceptance of new members. It is not clear what regulations, if any, existed concerning the manner in which the Committee was to be satisfied as to the musical competence, vocal or instrumental, of new members. At a meeting of 4 October 1842 we see, for example, the simple resolution 'that Messrs Lister Peace and John Sykes be admitted members of this Society'. In contrast, on the 25 July of the same year it was resolved 'that Mr George Greenwood be invited to attend the next rehearsal — and that Messrs Hall and I. Starkey station themselves on each side of him in order to ascertain whether he can take his part as a Bass Vocalist in a creditable manner'. Evidently a prospective member's reputation went before him, or he had, unknowingly, a single chance of acquiring one in order to avoid rejection.

On 2 December 1842 it was resolved that Mr Luke Liversidge be admitted a member of the Society 'providing Mr John Crosland declines to perform on the violoncello'. At a special meeting held a little later it was decided to admit Mr Luke Liversidge and that he should 'take his place forthwith on the orchestra as a member of this Society'. Luke Liversidge remained with the Society for many years, serving on the Musical Committee from 1865 until 1872, though not before some unpleasant exchanges had occurred, as will be reported in due course.

Occasional resolutions concerned the printing of circulars to inform subscribers of forthcoming performances. One such resolution required that Messrs Crosland and E. Battye should call upon Mr Kemp to ascertain as near as possible the cost of printing 'all the words' in the circulars of each quarterly performance. Mr T. Kemp had owned a printing establishment in New Street since 1821 at least, for in a Yorkshire directory of that year he is described as a 'printer, dealer in music and musical instruments, medical and extensive circulating library, depository to the religious tract society'. The 1843 Rule Book and other printed documents mentioned previously all bear his name as printer. Whether or not a decision was made to include 'all the words' (for the music to be performed) on the circulars is not revealed. Perhaps it proved too expensive even for a society which was sufficiently well-off, as we have seen, to dispense with an obligatory annual subscription, and one, moreover, which was able to reduce ticket prices for subscribers by about thirty-three per cent, as it did in 1845, to a level at which they remained for many years — about a guinea a season for the best seats.

In July 1843 the value of the property of the Society was estimated as £167, £130 of this being the value of 'books and other effects', there being also £17 cash in hand and £20 cash owed. The Committee was vigilant with regard to the payment of membership fees and subscriptions, a fact which no doubt accounts for the financial health of the Society at the time. Two hundred circulars were, for example, printed in 1843 to send out to the subscribers who were in arrears with their subscriptions, and in December of that year it was resolved that legal proceedings should be taken for the recovery of subscriptions from a Mr Jas. Johnson and a Mr S. Tapp, the latter having been previously requested for payment of a subscription owing for the season 1837–38.

The earliest financial statement to be found recorded in the minutebook is for the season 1845–46. This shows a balance in hand at the end of the season of £22 6s. 3d., with an expenditure on refreshments for members of £28 1s. 11d., representing a greater expense than on any other item during the year, as was to remain the case for some years. New members seem now to be making a payment of seven shillings to the Society, and the total income from subscriptions amounts to something in excess of £50. The statement shows that payments were made by the Society in respect of members who died or removed from Huddersfield, in accordance with the rules, but it was later resolved, at a meeting in April 1848, that this practice should no longer apply to members who left the Society. By 1848 the financial state of the Society begins to look a trifle less favourable. Its outgoings were increasing steadily and by the mid fifties an appeal had to be made to the public for increased support.

Both the quarterly and annual performances during the forties concentrated mainly on the works of Haydn, Handel, Romberg, Hummel, and Himmel and selections of works from various other 'authors', as they were termed. *The Messiah* does not seem to have been performed, either in its entirety or in part, during the 1842–43 season but we have a selection from it at the '31st quarterly concert and third of the season' on Friday, 9 February 1844 as reported in the *Leeds Mercury* of 17 February. The soloists were Miss Wood and Miss Wilmington who were making their debut as principals with the Society and received a 'flattering reception from the audience' according to the *Mercury* which described them as 'females of promising talent'. The audience consisting mostly of subscribers was described as more numerous than at the previous concerts of the season and the chorus works as 'very powerfully and tastefully executed'. Wilmshurst wrote that the first recorded performance of *The Messiah* by the Society was on Good Friday, 1844. In fact the statement is wrong on two counts; Good Friday in 1844 fell not on 9 April but on 5 April, when a dinner was provided for the members of the Society at the *Cherry Tree Inn*, and in fact a complete performance of *The Messiah* was given by the Society just after Christmas in 1838 in the Philosophical Hall and as early as December 1836 a selection from the oratorio was performed at the Infant School Room in Spring Street.

The notion that the 1844 performance of *The Messiah* was the first such, has certainly not gone unchallenged but it must also be said that there is insufficient evidence to support the other currently-held opinion that the Society has given an annual performance of the work since 1836. It was certainly not performed at one of the quarterly concerts each season in the early days.

Haydn's *Creation* and *The Seasons* were popular choices for performance at the Society's concerts during this period and of Handel's works there were performances of *Judas Maccabaeus*, *Esther*, *Solomon*, *Israel in Egypt*, *Jephtha*, *Samson*, *Acis and Galatea*, etc., either whole or in part. Works by Beethoven and Mozart appear less often, a March and Chorus of the former being included in a programme in 1839 and a selection from the *Mount of Olives* in 1843 when A. J. Romberg's *Transient and Eternal* was also performed. *Mount of Olives* was given in full at a concert in November 1850 when, at the very last moment, due to unavoidable circumstances, Mrs Sunderland was unable to appear. She was replaced by Miss Whitham, another very popular and talented local soloist. Romberg's *Transient and Eternal* was performed a second time in 1848 and then again on Friday, 2 April 1852 when James Battye conducted due to the recent death of Henry Horn and when, according to report, Mrs Sunderland was not in such good voice as usual, although she sang well and was loudly applauded.

A selection from the new oratorio *The Deliverance of Israel from Babylon* by William Jackson of Masham was chosen both for the first concert and for the annual concert of the 1848–49 season. Jackson is reported to have completed the last chorus of this work on his twenty-ninth birthday in 1845. The previous year the Society had subscribed for two copies, a fact which lends credence to Cudworth's report that Jackson had written a setting of Psalm 103 for the Society back in 1841. Subscribing to his new composition would have been an appropriate way of returning a compliment. It also lends credence to Sutcliffe-Smith's statement in his book *A Musical Pilgrimage in Yorkshire*, written in 1928, that *The Deliverance of Israel from Babylon* had its first performance in Huddersfield in 1845. Scholes says in his *Mirror of Music* that it was first performed in Leeds in 1847, when Novello heard it and later decided to publish it. Reporting this concert in 1847 the *Leeds Mercury* remarked that it gave Mr Jackson the opportunity of hearing his work and 'thereby improving himself in sacred composition'. Cudworth tells us that it also had its first Bradford performance in 1847, by the Church Choral Society there.

Not surprisingly James Battye's works were performed from time to time and as Wilmshurst comments, 'in the Society's minute books one finds this humble parish clerk often enthroned with the immortals of music' such as in a resolution passed at a meeting on 20 November 1848 'that a selection from the works of Handel, Haydn, Mozart, Battye etc. be performed at the fiftieth quarterly meeting'. In 1845 Battye won the Gresham Prize for his anthem *My Soul Truly Waiteth upon the Lord* which he dedicated to Lord Wharncliffe. The Society performed this anthem at a miscellaneous concert in February 1847 along with pieces by Cherubini, Romberg, Handel, and Haydn. In reporting the Gresham award to Battye, the *Leeds Mercury* of 13 September 1845 refers to his 'well known' musical compositions and informs us that 'the umpires on this occasion were Mr Horsley, Mus. Bac., Mr Goss, organist at St Paul's Cathedral and Mr Turle, organist of Westminster Abbey'.

In addition to their appearances at the annual and quarterly concerts of the Huddersfield Choral Society during this period the soloists among the members were often to be heard at other concerts, which were held either at the Philosophical Hall or elsewhere, and which were quite often also organized by Choral Society members. Repeatedly advertisements and reports appear in the press regarding such as 'Mr Horn's Grand Concert' or 'Mr Peace's Annual Concert' or 'Mr George Wilkinson's Subscription Concert', etc., at which leader, soloists and almost certainly instrumental performers, not to mention members of the chorus, were members of the Choral Society. 'Upwards of seventy performers' constituting band and chorus at these concerts is often quoted in the advertisements, leading one to believe that the membership of the Choral Society, under its leader Henry Horn, with its celebrated soloists such as Mrs Sunderland, Mr Milnes, Miss Milnes, Mrs Peace, Mr Broadley, Mr and Mrs Wood, numbering, or having numbered among its ranks, also provided the local musical community with a pool from which the 'orchestra' for many, if not all, of such concerts in Huddersfield might be constituted. Undoubtedly the Choral Society membership represented a major part of the cream of the musical talent of the town. This fact is almost certainly an important reason for the continued success of the Society. By contrast, in a place such as Leeds whose choral society is reported as having given its first public performance in 1839, the situation was different. There the cream of the musical community and the vigour of musical activity was dispersed rather more amongst other organizations which tended to eclipse the choral society, thus we learn of its impending final performance in 1845. By 1849, however, if not before, a new Leeds Choral Society had arisen like a Phoenix, from the ashes of the old, and it was a contingent from this choir which participated along with those from Huddersfield and Hull in the Leeds performance, in 1847, of William Jackson's *Deliverance of Israel from Babylon*.

The Huddersfield Choral Society was also heard outside Huddersfield. Certainly it is difficult to find a concert of any real worth taking place at this time in Bradford, Leeds, or Halifax without the name of Mrs Sunderland appearing on the programme. But other names such as Milnes, Peace, Wood, all from Huddersfield Choral Society, are often to be seen as principal soloists in concerts all over the West Riding. By 1845 it becomes apparent that Mrs Sunderland was in such general demand that dates of Choral Society concerts in Huddersfield were fixed according to her availability. Even so, if there was difficulty with booking the concert hall they might have to do without her. Other soloists such as Mrs Peace would be asked to take her place.

By October 1845 Mrs Sunderland had left the ranks of the Choral Society. The *Leeds Mercury* reports her absence from the first concert of the season and remarks that 'on that account Messrs Wilkinson and Lister Peace and Mrs Lister Peace absented themselves on Friday evening'. Today one can only ponder over the significance of that remark! However, the report goes on to point out that the absence of these folk gave the opportunity for some of the younger members to display their vocal powers. By 1847 Mrs Sunderland was being professionally engaged by the Society and her name appears as soloist at its concerts until 1863, but initially, perhaps, her withdrawal from its membership was not altogether without some ill-feeling on the part of the Society, if the tone of the following letter to her, dated 26 June 1846, which is reproduced in the Society's minute book, is any indication.

To Mrs Sunderland

My Dear Madam

In consequence of two sheets of music having fallen into the hands of the Committee of the Huddersfield Choral Society which are part of Books of accompaniment of Songs, belonging to the Society, and are stated to have come from you, the Committee therefore respectfully request that you will have the kindness to forward the said books of which the two sheets are part to Mr Jas Battye, Parish Clerk Huddersfield at your earliest convenience, or state per return of post how you came into possession of them the aforesaid sheets

by order of the Committee

John Crosland

Secretary.

This is polite but with a hint of reproach. It is certainly formal, as perhaps thought appropriate in the circumstances, but is not, one senses, without irony. Admittedly this lady was by now something of a celebrity who commanded a certain deference, especially at a time when deference was well understood, but she had had very close associations with the Society since its beginning, and since she herself was little more than a young girl. James Battye must have been an old friend of whose position she would have been well aware, without being reminded. Indeed, it would have been more appropriate in the circumstances to address him as the Choral Society Librarian rather than as Parish Clerk, if it was thought that any reminder of address was necessary. It would be fascinating to know the outcome of this little affair, but alas, no further mention is made of the matter. By October 1847 we find a Committee resolution which accords thanks to Messrs Horn and Battye for their promptitude in postponing a quarterly concert so that subscribers may have the opportunity of hearing Mrs Sunderland 'on her re-appearance at the Choral Society' consequent upon her sanction having been procured 'to assist in the public performances of this Society during the whole of the ensuing season'.

According to a report in the *Leeds Mercury* the Christmas Hymn was sung after the performance of *The Messiah* at the Society's Annual Concert in December 1849, the audience participating. It has been such a long-standing tradition for the choir and audience to sing this hymn *before* a *Messiah* performance that the notion of singing it to conclude the concert seems strange, if not almost absurd. Anyway, this appears to be the first reported occasion on which the Society sang the Christmas Hymn at a *Messiah* performance. Huddersfield did not invent the idea, however. The *Halifax Guardian* of 1 January 1842 reported that the Halifax Choral Society sang three verses of the Christmas Hymn before *The Messiah* and expressed the hope that this might be repeated at every Christmas performance. Also in 1849 in the *Leeds Mercury* is a report of a performance by the Huddersfield

Choral Society of Handel's *Samson* on 26 October that year. On the last page of a programme, dating from 2 March 1917, of a concert by the Society when it gave a so-called 'revival' performance of *Samson*, there appear alleged details of what is claimed to be 'the first authenticated performance of *Samson* by the Society' on 13 October 1849. As far as it is possible to judge from the report of the 1849 concert in the *Leeds Mercury*, only the chorus 'Let their Celestial Concerts all Unite' from that oratorio was sung at this concert, the main work being Spohr's *Last Judgement*. In any event, selections from *Samson* had been performed on several occasions before this date, for example in 1843, 1845, and 1846. A selection from *Samson* was again given at the second concert of the 1851–52 season along with a selection of 'airs and choruses' by James Battye, included perhaps because it was he who was conducting in place of Henry Horn as he had been, in fact, since the early part of 1851 because of Henry Horn's indisposition.

On Monday, 8 March 1852 Henry Horn died at the comparatively early age of 51 years. He was buried in the graveyard of St Paul's Church at which he had been organist since 1835. His gravestone may still be seen today near to the North door of the Church, the building being now part of the Polytechnic. It is used, among other things, as a concert hall and is referred to as St Paul's Hall. Henry's wife, Mary, was buried in the same grave in 1868 and she too is described on the gravestone as an organist.

Henry Horn's obituary appeared in the *Huddersfield Chronicle* on 13 March 1852. It described him as having been born into a family resident in the village of Cumberworth for many generations, and noted for musical ability. He became organist at Queen Street Methodist Chapel in 1824 and conductor of the Huddersfield Glee Club in 1829, both of which positions he is said to have retained 'as long as his health would permit him'. He had done much to promote the enjoyment of music in Huddersfield and its environs. His influence both in maintaining the excellent standard of the Choral Society performance, for which it was locally renowned, and in promoting and managing public concerts in the town, should not be underestimated. Some of the leading musicians of the time, from both home and abroad, took part in these concerts. He was clearly much admired and had a wide circle of friends. Although not as locally celebrated as a composer as was James Battye, he nevertheless did write some music — 'a few chants' which possessed 'great melody and sweetness' and displayed 'good taste and expression', according to the *Huddersfield Chronicle* obituary.

At his funeral on Friday, 12 March 1852 the united choirs of the Parish Church and St Paul's (a body of singers no doubt including many Choral

Society members) sang a psalm and an anthem from Spohr's *Last Judgement*, 'Blest are the Departed'. Thomas Parratt was at the organ.

A month or two later, on Thursday, 20 May, the Choral Society sang the Third Part of *The Messiah* which begins with the solo 'I Know that my Redeemer Liveth', in the Philosophical Hall, as a memorial to Henry Horn. The Society possesses a handbill announcing this memorial performance. On this occasion the room was packed with people, including many local dignatories. The choice of music had been Henry's own. The choir appeared dressed in mourning clothes and sang, so it was reported, with great feeling. It was under the leadership of James Battye and the solo items were provided by Mrs Sunderland, Miss Whitham, and Miss Crosland together with Messrs Milnes, Netherwood, and Hirst. The audience, we are told, maintained throughout a profound silence.

CHAPTER FOUR

The Continued Tradition

THE DECISION to appoint James Battye as the new leader of the Society at its general meeting held at the *Vulcan Inn* on 2 April 1852 was, one imagines, an easy one to make. Although no details are recorded, in all probability the decision was unanimous. He had been deputizing as leader during Henry Horn's last illness at several of the concerts over the previous months, his recognized ability as a musician was greatly respected and his personal qualities were much admired. He had, moreover, been very influential in the formation of the Society sixteen years previously when Henry Horn was appointed leader. This was before Battye had earned himself a reputation as a composer of glees and anthems surpassing any, perhaps, to which Horn himself might have aspired. But at that time Horn was already an established professional musician and this would have rendered him a more obvious choice as leader. By 1852, however, James Battye's standing, in local musical circles at least, was considerably enhanced and the Society turned to him as Horn's natural successor.

It was at the beginning of the period 1849 to 1852, during which scarcely any minutes of meetings are recorded, that James was elected as Secretary. If he remained Secretary throughout this period it might explain why no records were kept. Because of increased musical activity on his part, of which there is much evidence, he may have been too busy to transfer notes, scribbled at meetings, into the minute book. Whatever the reason, we have to rely on sources other than minutes of Society meetings for what occurred between September 1852 and June 1853.

The *Huddersfield Chronicle* of Saturday, 3 April 1852 reports that the first of the Society's quarterly concerts to take place after Henry Horn's death was the fourth and last of the 1851–52 season and took place in the Philosophical Hall on the previous evening. This was the same day as the meeting in the *Vulcan Inn*, although the report mentions nothing regarding the appointment of James Battye as leader. On this occasion *Spring* from Haydn's *Seasons* was performed along with Romberg's *Transient and Eternal*. The soloists were named as Mrs Sunderland, Miss Whitham, Miss Crosland, and Messrs Netherwood, Milnes, and Hirst — a group whose names were invariably to appear together as soloists at the concerts, with occasional additions and subtractions, for several years to come. It had been Haydn too at the previous concert at the end of January when his *Creation* was performed but for the annual concert held at the beginning of January, there is no report of what was sung; the *Chronicle* of 10 January 1852 commenting only that the concert took place, that it was well attended, but adding that 'the usual courtesy hitherto shown was not extended on this occasion and we were not present'. A similar circumstance may also account for the fact that there is no press report of an annual concert for the previous season (1850–51), nor for the following two seasons, that is 1852–53 and 1853–54. The minute book nevertheless does record a receipt of £12 3s. 2d. for an annual concert during the 1852–53 season although not for the one which was reported by the *Chronicle* as having been given during the previous season. There is a report of a performance of *The Messiah* at the annual concert on Friday, 5 January 1855, and a programme survives of what is announced categorically as the twenty-second annual concert held on 22 January 1858 (again a performance of *The Messiah*) but there are no further records of annual, as distinct from quarterly concerts thereafter. Since an annual performance is provided for in the rules, as revised in 1842–43, this suggests that a revision of the rules took place in 1858. Indeed, there are clear indications here and there that the rules had been modified at least once before this date. However, since no rule book of the Society survives which dates before 1909, apart from the very early one of 1843, it is difficult to know for certain when the provision for an annual concert was removed from the rules, but it seems likely that the *Messiah* performance of 1858 could have been the last so-called annual concert of the Society.

The minutes of the general meeting of 24 June 1853 consist only of the recording of the names of committee members elected at that meeting but a point of interest is that James Battye was styled 'leader and conductor'. This would seem to be the first use of the word 'conductor' in the Society's records. Edward Battye is named as Secretary and, although not very evidently in his hand, the minutes are once more written up fairly regularly until 1856, albeit at somewhat lengthy intervals. Details of the Society's financial affairs are given from time to time which indicate that among the costliest items of annual expenditure were those for rent and gas, for printing and for the purchase of new music. Rent and gas accounted for about £14 per annum, £12 being for rent, printing cost about £10 per annum whilst the purchase of new music (which decreased during the period under consideration) never accounted for more than about £10 in any season. The item of greatest annual expenditure remained that of refreshments, amounting at times to over £30 for the season. In his *History of the Bradford Festival Choral Society*, G. F. Sewell comments on a similar disproportionate expenditure on the part of that society on coffee and buns in 1860, over £40 being spent on such delights and less than £35 on two concerts! Smaller items of expenditure by the Huddersfield Choral Society concerned the carriage and collection of books, postage, repairs to drums, payments to doorkeepers, and a regular 'percentage to John Shaw' who, it seems, looked after books and collected subscriptions. Whereas the stock of the Society was valued in 1843 at about £130, by 1853 it was only valued at about £80, suggesting that the Society may have been in decline to some extent.

It is difficult to discover the extent of any such decline, if indeed it occurred at all, or to discover precisely what *was* going on during the period between 1853 and 1858, when James Battye died. Press reports, especially during the latter part of this period, seem to be concerned much more with the affairs of newly-formed or emergent musical societies in the neighbourhood than with the Choral Society, which was occasionally, even at that time, referred to as 'this old society'. But when an item concerning the Choral Society does appear in the columns of the local newspapers there seems never to be any serious suggestion of a lessening of its musical standing or of its musical competence. It is almost as if the local recognition of excellence of the Choral Society is accepted without need for continual comment, and as if failure to mention its every performance is less an indifference and more a compliment.

A Special General Meeting was held at the Queen Hotel on 16 December 1856, called (to quote the minute) 'for the purpose of discussing matters of great importance relating to the present state of the Society'. This *was* reported in the *Huddersfield Chronicle* (of 20 December 1856) though not with the same apparent sense of importance that the Society itself would seem to have attached to it. According to the press report the principal subject for discussion at the meeting was the best means of strengthening the Society by uniting with it the different village choral societies of the neighbourhood so as to bring out and encourage the native musical talent of the Huddersfield district. The minutes of the meeting record the resolution that 'J. C. Fenton Esq., Messrs Battye, Edgar Fenton and Edward Battye be requested to prepare an address to the subscribers and public generally setting forth the objects of the Society and urging its claims for support and patronage on the inhabitants of Huddersfield and surrounding districts thereof'.

Assuming that the address was in fact prepared and propagated, it is a pity that no copy of it seems to have survived for it surely would shed some light on a somewhat obscure, but fascinating, period in the Society's history. All we have, apart from that reported above, are the other recorded resolutions of the meeting which were intended to assist towards achieving the overall improvement in the Society's fortunes. They were concerned with the modification of certain rules regarding recruitment of new members, the apportioning of rehearsal time as between instrumental and vocal practice and performance, and disciplinary measures concerning members' attendance. These rules are referred to by numbers not appropriate to the 1843 rules, affording a further clear indication that there had in fact been a revision since that date. Of particular interest is the resolution of the meeting resulting from a unanimous agreement to elect J. C. Fenton Esq. to the hitherto non-existent office of President of the Society. Previously there had been a Leader, a Secretary, Treasurer, Librarian, and a Committee of seven persons invested with the responsibility for the management of the Society, according to the requirements of the 1843 rule book.

The name J. C. Fenton appears at the head of the list of five Honorary Performing Members which is given at the end of that book. He is also named in the minute book once during the intervening years in connexion with a resolution, already quoted in the previous chapters, concerning Mrs Sunderland. It was he who, in 1847 'procured the sanction' of that lady 'to assist in the public performances of this society during the whole of the ensuing season'. He was also named in the newspaper report of Henry Horn's funeral in March 1852 as one of the pall bearers. John Crosland Fenton was the leading partner in the Huddersfield firm of solicitors, Fenton, Jones, and Rayner and was also steward of the Manor Courts. He was the son of a Colonel Fenton of Sheffield and the adopted nephew of Joshua Crosland who was Colonel Fenton's brother-in-law and who established himself in Huddersfield as a solicitor. John Crosland Fenton succeeded Joshua to the practice when the latter died in 1825. J. C. Fenton had no children of his own but he in his turn adopted two nephews, the younger of whom was Edgar Fenton, who also entered the legal profession and served the Choral Society. Remembering that Fenton was the name of Huddersfield's first MP — a Captain Lewis Fenton — it is interesting to note that D. F. E. Sykes in his *History of Huddersfield and its Vicinity* states that he believes him to have been the father of 'that Edgar Fenton, solicitor of the firm of Heap, Fenton, and Owen, who so endeared himself to his professional brethren by his courtesy'. If this were true it would surely mean that Captain Fenton was another of Colonel Fenton's sons and therefore John Crosland Fenton's brother. In this case it is strange that no mention of it was made in the obituary to J.C. which appeared in the *Huddersfield Chronicle* of 10 April 1858 the week following his death at Torquay only sixteen months after his election to the presidency of the Choral Society. He was well known for his interest and activity in the world of music, for his wit, kindness, freshness, and his keen relish for a lively joke. For over 30 years he was the patron for anything which advanced the science of music, holding private concerts in his home at Lockwood which gave unforgettable pleasure to all who attended. 'To the end', says the obituary 'he was a patron and performer with the Huddersfield Choral Society. Seated at the orchestra with his double bass his countenance betokened a measure of enjoyment which diffused itself to the audience. It was generally thought that if Mr. Fenton was not at a Choral concert, it went off heavily'.

His place in the President's chair was taken by John Brooke, Esq., J.P., who was the first officer of the Society to be entitled 'J.P.' in the records, but one of a long line of such reaching to the present day. Edgar Fenton, J. C. Fenton's adopted nephew, was appointed as Vice-President and, also for the first time, two secretaries were appointed, Edward Battye and William Fitton. The latter was to remain as Secretary until 1870. James Battye was re-elected 'Conductor', his title since Mr Henry Hartley was appointed as 'Leader' in 1854. These appointments were all made at the Annual Meeting of the Society on 25 June 1858, the first meeting to be recorded in the minute book since the one in 1856 when J. C. Fenton was appointed President, and the meeting at which his death was now recorded. Almost as if the only meetings worthy of report were those occasioned by the death of a prominent member, the very next entry in the minute book refers to a Special General Meeting held on 12 November 1858 'for the purpose of electing a conductor in the place of the late Mr James Battye'. But this is to anticipate unduly. Much of interest and significance had been taking place since 1852 which played a part in the subsequent development of the Society.

When Henry Hartley was appointed Leader in 1854 it was not long after his father, Thomas, had died. Thomas, it will be remembered, was a founder member of the Society and its first Treasurer. Most of the members of the Choral Society were reported as having been present at St Paul's Church where the funeral service for Thomas was conducted in March 1854. J. C. Fenton and his nephew, Edgar, headed the funeral procession and Henry Parratt played Handel's 'Dead March' in *Saul* on a horn during the service.

Henry Parratt had taken over as organist at St Paul's after Henry Horn's death in 1852. He had previously been organist at Armitage Bridge where, announced the *Huddersfield Chronicle* of 3 April 1852, 'he will be succeeded by his younger brother, Master Walter Parratt'. Thus were reported the humble beginnings of one who was later to be appointed master of the royal music. In the somewhat lengthy report of Thomas Hartley's funeral which appeared in the *Huddersfield Chronicle* of 1 April 1854 we find the interesting comment that 'almost every Cathedral Choir in England numbers some one or more who have been connected with the Huddersfield Choral Society'.

The year 1853 was an important year for music in West Yorkshire for it was in this year that St George's Hall was opened in Bradford. The opening was celebrated by a three-day festival of music, under the patronage of many eminent people headed by Queen Victoria and Prince Albert. Of the two hundred choristers comprising the festival choir, Huddersfield provided thirty-one, most of whom were members of the Choral Society. In addition there were Jabez Jackman who came up from Ely for the occasion to sing with the festival choir and Mrs Sunderland who was engaged as a soloist, a fact which was not without interesting consequences, as we shall see. The Chorus Master was William Jackson and the conductor was that of the Royal Italian Opera at Covent Garden, Michael Costa. The soloists included the eminent sopranos Clara Novello and Louisa Pyne, the contralto Jeanne Castellan, the tenors Sims Reeves, Charles Lockey, and Signor Gardoni and the bass Herr Karl Formes. Among this glittering galaxy no doubt Susan Sunderland could, and did shine as brightly as the rest but her contribution was limited to the singing of 'If God be for Us' in the Thursday morning performance of *The Messiah* and an 'air' sung at a Miscellaneous Concert on the Wednesday evening. G. F. Sewell, in his *History of the Bradford Festival Choral Society*, tells us (unlike the official programme) that the title of this air was 'I'm Alone'. He says that Mrs Sunderland's scanty recognition at the Festival caused disappointment on the part of her numerous admirers. She was loudly cheered, sang the song again as a furiously demanded encore, in even better style than the first time when, Sewell submits, the concluding words of the piece seemed to indicate to the audience her sense of apparent neglect by the promoters of the Festival.

The Festival opened with a performance of Mendelssohn's *St Paul*, the remainder being devoted to Haydn's *Creation*, Handel's *Israel in Egypt* and miscellaneous items including excerpts from Italian Opera by such as Rossini, Mozart, Donizetti, etc. The chorus received high praise in the London Press and Jackson was said to be entitled to every credit. The first performance in England of *St Paul* was in 1837, in Liverpool, but it was not performed by the Huddersfield Choral Society until 1854, the year after the Bradford Festival performance. This was the Society's first real attempt to tackle Mendelssohn, but they repeated *St Paul* in December 1855 and again in 1857 when it was erroneously reported as being their first performance of the work, along with the comment that it needed much practice to pass muster with the musical public. Maybe it merely sounded to the reporter like a first performance!

Another music festival was held in Bradford in 1856 which occasioned a major row concerning the non-appearance of Mrs Sunderland as one of the soloists. As a consequence, a decision was made in Huddersfield to hold a special festival in her honour which in fact took place in the Philosophical Hall only six weeks after the one in Bradford. This Huddersfield Festival was not organized by the Choral Society but the part played by members of the Society in the event was undoubtedly considerable. The man who was soon to be elected its first President, Mr J. C. Fenton, chaired a meeting held at the George Hotel on 1 September 1856 when the decision to hold the festival was made, and he was elected Chairman of the Festival Committee, the members of which included James Battye, Edgar Fenton, and Thomas Parratt. The Festival was planned on a modest scale and was to consist of a morning performance of *The Messiah* and a Miscellaneous Concert to be held on the same evening. The local determination to do honour to Mrs Sunderland was, however, tremendous. No printed programme of the Festival seems to have survived although some details are preserved in press reports. It may safely be assumed, nevertheless, that a large percentage of the chorus and instrumentalists consisted of Choral Society members. As to the row concerning the second Bradford Festival which sparked it all off, one gets only a modest indication of its nature from G. F. Sewell's comments in his book on the Bradford Festival Choral Society. He writes:

The name of Mrs Sunderland was again included in the list of principals at this festival, but was subsequently withdrawn. It was originally intended that she should sing the solo 'If God be for Us' in the latter part of *The Messiah*. This air, along with several other numbers in *The Messiah* is generally omitted; yet, not withstanding these excisions, the performance of the oratorio is felt to be too long for modern audiences. It was decided therefore to omit the song, beautiful as it unquestionably is, and to give Mrs Sunderland the choice of another song in one of the evening performances. The 'Yorkshire Queen of Song', however, felt that she was not treated with the consideration due to the position to which her talents entitled her, and declined, under these circumstances, to take any part in the festival. Much sympathy was felt for Mrs Sunderland, and an angry feeling was aroused, which found expression in an acrimonious newspaper correspondence. It must, however, be admitted, that the Committee of the festival had an exceedingly delicate and difficult duty to discharge, and one which only those who have had experience in matters of this nature can properly appreciate.

The case of Mrs Sunderland was taken up by the celebrated baritone singer, Henry Phillips, who had recently formed a *New English Glee and Madrigal Union* of which she was a member. Mrs Sunderland was responsible for the publication in the press of the correspondence between herself and Mr Sam. Smith, the Chairman of the Bradford Festival Committee, and won much public sympathy thereby. The *Illustrated London News* commented some months later, however, that they felt that her outburst had little foundation. This comment was included in a report of her singing with the Sacred Harmonic Society in the Exeter Hall in London concerning which the report was more sympathetic. She was 'well worthy of the fame she had acquired in the most musical district of all England and among people not likely to be deceived on such a subject' it said. Such was the opinion concerning the musical pre-eminence of the West Riding expressed in a celebrated London journal.

The Huddersfield Festival was held on Thursday, 9 October 1856 in a repaired and newly-decorated Philosophical Hall. The morning performance of *The Messiah* went well apart from a rather unfortunate difference of opinion regarding tempo as between soloist (Henry Phillips) and the band (the London Orchestral Union) in the aria 'The People that Walked in Darkness'. The conductor was reported as having been unable effectively to slow the players down to the soloist's pace but the latter as having made the best of a bad job. Mrs Sunderland sang brilliantly, it seems, and the adoration of all her devotees in the audience was given full expression. Her oft-times deputy, Miss Whitham, sang 'There were Shepherds' and was warmly appreciated. This local soloist had also recently sung in Exeter Hall with the Sacred Harmonic Society and was regarded as a promising solo performer of top rank, although she never rose to national prominence. The evening performance of miscellaneous items was criticized for its length but was otherwise highly praised.

A correspondent complained in the *Huddersfield Chronicle* of 16 October 1858 that only about thirty members of the festival chorus in Bradford in 1856 were members of the newly-formed Bradford Festival Choral Society which was, he said, 'using the name and the prestige of the Festivals to puff themselves up'. 'Costa', added the correspondent, 'may have conducted and praised the Festival Chorus, but he never heard a performance of the Bradford Festival Choral Society'. Such a charge could never be made against the Huddersfield Choral Society which, in the event, would appear to have carried on (though perhaps it did not) as if there never had been a Huddersfield Festival. The refurbishing of the Philosophical Hall and the incidence of the Festival in October 1856 did have one obvious effect on the Society, however. It resulted in the first quarterly concert of the 1856–57 season being delayed until the January of 1857, when Haydn's *Creation* was performed. The second concert of the season was given in February with a selection from Handel's *Judas Maccabaeus*. His *Samson* was performed at the third, in March, and his *Israel in Egypt* as the final one in April. This is all very much the mixture as before and, indeed, with the exception of the introduction to the repertoire of Mendelssohn's *St Paul*, as already mentioned, nothing musically very new seems to have taken place during James Battye's period of conductorship. It was left to the Leeds Choral Society to perform Mendelssohn's *Elijah* in the Philosophical Hall in Huddersfield! This took place in March 1853 and was conducted by R. S. Burton, who was to succeed James Battye as the conductor of the Huddersfield Choral Society in 1858. Burton had also conducted the work in Bradford in 1849 but it was not performed by the Huddersfield Choral Society until 1859 when, no doubt, Burton was responsible for importing it. This was as many as thirteen years since its first performance in England at the Birmingham Festival of 1846. Leeds had heard it last in 1858 when Sterndale Bennett conducted a performance of it at the opening of the Leeds Town Hall that year by Queen Victoria.

The musical scene in Huddersfield during the 1850s was not, however, altogether static. James Battye had formed a Glee and Madrigal Union in 1855, an Amateur Vocal Union was started in 1857, which performed quite frequently and numerous concerts of various kinds were given locally. The Drury Lane Opera Company were at the Theatre Royal in Ramsden Street from time to time and Huddersfield did try, but failed, to get Jenny Lind to come and sing there after an appearance in Wakefield in 1856. Charles Hallé played the piano at a concert in the Philosophical Hall in October 1858 and John Curwen could be listened to when he gave a lecture in the same place in October of the previous year on his Tonic Solfa singing method. But by 1858 the Choral Society was beginning to change. Many of the old people had died or were soon to die. Two founder members died in the autumn of 1857, John Crosland, the 'cellist and double bass player, and George Wilkinson. The latter had promoted many concerts in the town including the Leeds Choral Society's *Elijah* concert in 1853. Then came the death of John Crosland Fenton, as noted earlier, in April 1858 followed in October of the same year by James Battye on the tenth day of that month at the beginning of his 57th year.

James Battye had been very active as a teacher, composer, and conductor of music for most of his life. Miss Whitham had been one of his pupils. 'He owed most of his knowledge of music' stated the *Huddersfield Chronicle* in an obituary, 'to his own patient study and continual practice and perseverance [rather] than to any tuition by masters in the art'. James had, for twenty-six years it seems, been a frequent guest at J. C. Fenton's private instrumental concerts at his home in Lockwood where James's musical abilities were held in high esteem. Reference has been made already to his musical compositions and the honours they brought him. He was remembered too for his conducting of a choir of six hundred vocalists in St George's Square at a Peace Demonstration celebrating the end of the Crimean War in 1856. They gave him a public funeral in 1858 which took place on Thursday, 14 October at the Parish Church, where he had remained Clerk until his death, and where he now lies buried. Members of the Choral Society, other friends and a number of Freemasons (to which organization he belonged) formed a procession from his house to the church where his setting of Psalm 90 was sung, as it had been at Henry Horn's funeral for which it was written. Spohr's 'Blest are the Departed' was also sung again. A memorial tablet to him is to be found on the South wall inside the Church where it is inscribed that 'he did much towards the development of that love for music which has rendered this district so justly celebrated'. We, in this generation and who are of this town, either by birth or by adoption, would do well to be reminded more often of this gentle man of music who grew to manhood and maturity during that period when the town itself, to which he gave so much, grew from relative obscurity to some measure of importance and prosperity.

The Society gave a memorial concert to Battye on 12 October 1858 at the Philosophical Hall which was crowded with attenders. Again Spohr's 'Blest are the Departed' from the *Last Judgement* was sung, as was also Battye's prize anthem *My Soul Truly Waiteth Upon God*. Miss Whitham sang 'I Know that my Redeemer Liveth' and Miss Hirst, 'If God be With Us' from *The Messiah*. The choruses 'Worthy is the Lamb' and 'Amen' also from *The Messiah* ended the performance. Surprisingly, Mrs Sunderland's name is not mentioned among those of the solo performers.

On Friday, 12 November 1858 at a Special General Meeting of the Society held at the Queen Hotel, Mr R. S. Burton, organist of Leeds Parish Church was proposed as the Society's new conductor for a period of twelve months. Mr Luke Liversidge was required to wait upon Mr Burton and ascertain on what terms he would attend as conductor. It was also proposed that either his services should be paid for by an annual concert, or else by direct payment, as he should think proper. These propositions were carried unanimously, although, according to the *Huddersfield Chronicle* report of 20 November 1858, it was a proposition that Mr R. S. Burton be *elected* as conductor which was carried unanimously. In the event however, whatever the form of the proposition, Burton was elected as the conductor to succeed James Battye and the Society entered upon a new phase of its development. What might be regarded as its age of innocence was over and things were never to be quite the same again.

CHAPTER FIVE

Fresh Fields

ROBERT SENIOR BURTON was a man of considerable musical reputation who, by 1858, had already played a distinguished part in the musical life of Yorkshire, and was to continue to do so. Born into a musical family at Dewsbury in 1820, he had studied under Cipriani Potter and succeeded Dr S. S. Wesley as organist at Leeds Parish Church in 1849, where he stayed until 1880. There, says G. F. Sewell, 'he succeeded in bringing the choral services to a state of great perfection, and his perfect mastery of the fine organ was a theme of universal admiration'. He was to be conductor of musical or choral societies in over half a dozen Yorkshire towns apart from Huddersfield at one time or another. The fact that he was Chorus Master at the Leeds Festival of 1858 may have influenced the Society in its decision to seek his appointment, in that same year, as its conductor.

Burton's undoubted musical talents were evidently coupled with a less than amiable temperament. Though possessed of a brusque manner at times, among his intimate friends he was said to have been most genial. His association with several societies, including the Huddersfield Choral Society, was terminated in rather unhappy circumstances. Yet Henry Coward wrote that he regarded it as an honour to have succeeded Burton as conductor of the Barnsley and Huddersfield Societies, as well as those at Leeds and Sheffield. 'I am sorry that I have never spoken to him', he remarks in his book, *Reminiscences.* In fact it was more than a quarter of a century after Burton's departure from Huddersfield that Coward took over the conductorship of its Choral Society, by which time Burton had been dead for nine years. But Coward was well aware of Burton's temperament, describing him as of strong will and firm convictions with a large share of combativeness. This aspect of his personality brought him into conflict both with individuals and organizations, and it is evident that his musical standing redeemed much. He was direct and outspoken, and not to be thwarted even when the occasion denied him speech, as when, according to a story told by Coward, he played the well known chorus from *St Paul,* 'Now this man ceaseth not to utter blasphemous things' as a concluding voluntary at the end of what he considered an unacceptably unorthodox sermon. Although, according to Sewell, he could not have claimed to be numbered among the country's foremost conductors, his musical talents were of a very high order. He describes Burton as an accomplished pianist as well as an excellent organist who, having by his own admission, nothing in the way of a voice, used the piano to convey his wishes most effectively at choir rehearsals. This notwithstanding, Sutcliffe Smith asserts that through his uncompromising attitude Burton was 'practically dismissed' as Chorus Master of the Leeds Festival Chorus in 1873, and that his musical ability seems to have been far in advance of his discretion as a man. His successor in Leeds was James Broughton whom, ironically, Burton succeeded as conductor of the Bradford Festival Chorus in 1879.

Burton stayed with the Huddersfield Choir until 1874, when relationships had become such that a resolution of the Annual Meeting of 24 July 1874 was no warmer in expression than 'that the best thanks of the members of the Society be given to Mr R. S. Burton for the efficient manner in which he has conducted the concerts and rehearsals for a number of years'. The 'number of years' was, in fact, sixteen, a period of service as long as Henry Horn's and considerably longer than James Battye's. His influence during that period was evident and some of it, according to his critics, not to the benefit either of the Society or of the musical life of Huddersfield. According to Wilmshurst, 'Burton struggled hard to advance the Society's progress, often in the teeth of opposition from its members, and to his broadening influence much more was due than was recognized or compensated for at the time though that influence bore good fruit later'. Perhaps this is true, but less readily acceptable is Wilmshurst's contention that the end of what he calls the Society's 'primitive period' coincided with Burton's retirement. The latter's introduction of new methods, new musicians, new works, and new ventures was accompanied by a new style of management. Ambition, whether on the conductor's part alone or whether shared by the Society, ran it into financial difficulties. There were also accommodation problems but musically the Society remained sound, if not considerably improved. Any 'primitive period' surely ended with Burton's arrival, not with his departure.

Despite a steady stream of new members to the Society, its total membership grew only slowly following Burton's arrival. In 1866, at a concert given in the Philosophical Hall (already converted at that date for use as a theatre) when Mozart's *Twelfth Mass* and Handel's *Acis and Galatea* were performed, it was reported that band and chorus together numbered one hundred performers. This was only twenty or thirty more than in Battye's time. The number of the subscribers to the Society also increased, as did the general level of their social standing. At this time the Choral Society began increasingly to develop from being merely a modest musical society and began to acquire distinctive social status. The executive body was manned to an increasing extent by civic dignitaries and professional men whether or not they had any competence in music. Subscribers began to be recruited in increasing numbers from the ranks of the 'very respectable', however humble (though undoubtedly respectable) might have been the background of performing members, and this pattern has largely survived until the present day.

At about the time of his appointment to Huddersfield, Burton founded the Yorkshire Choral (or Vocal) Union consisting initially of singers from the Leeds Festival, Huddersfield, and Halifax Choral Societies. This Choral Union was commanded, in the late spring of 1860, to sing at Buckingham Palace before Queen Victoria and Prince Albert. The Bradford Festival Choral Society had sung at Buckingham Palace in 1858, doubtless in consequence of their successes at the Bradford Festivals of 1853 and 1856 in their own St George's Hall. The fact that the majority of the vocal members of the Huddersfield Choral Society (forty or fifty, according to contemporary reports) sang at Buckingham Palace in 1860 seems to have been forgotten. Wilmshurst made no mention of any visit to London before 1862, and certainly no mention of a visit to Buckingham Palace, although he does quote from a letter which appeared in the *Huddersfield Chronicle* on 24 March 1860 from 'A Friend to Native Talent' which hints at the possibility of such a visit.

This letter complains of the employment (often preferential) of non-local musical talent, particularly instrumental talent, by the Society and of the fact that some performers receive payment for services. This, it claims, represents a departure from the worthy aims of the founder-members. It asks if *native* performers are incapable of recognizing the 'meshes of the treacherous snare spread to entangle them, in the adroit hope held forth that at some future day they may be admitted into the presence of royalty at Buckingham Palace'. It was either a well-informed correspondent or one possessing prophetic powers who wrote this only a month or two before the Royal Command was made known publicly.

On 1 June 1860 R. S. Burton conducted a choir of some two-hundred voices at the Palace in a programme revised and approved by Prince Albert. The soloists included the popular local Huddersfield performers Mrs Sunderland, Miss Crosland, Miss Whitham, Mr Inkersall, and Mr Garner. The second-named of these, who won for herself considerable acclaim over the years, was the daughter of John Crosland, the Society's first secretary. Burton received personal congratulations from the Queen after the performance and 'the chorus enjoyed the generous hospitality of Her Majesty in one of the adjoining rooms' says the *Huddersfield Examiner* report of 9 June 1860. The following day saw the choir at the Crystal Palace where they presented an entirely different programme. Sterndale Bennett was there and attested, as he had done in Leeds in 1858, to the excellence of Yorkshire Choristers.

Despite some local opposition to Burton, it was unlikely that a man of his musical ability and standing would be too readily rejected. One who had, moreover, within a year or two of his appointment taken over half the choir to sing in London before royalty and who soon began, apparently, to improve the standard of the Society's quarterly concerts in Huddersfield, would be forgiven if his manner was at times somewhat abrupt and forthright.

The management of the Society began to change markedly after 1858. Re-elected in 1859 were John Brooke as President and Edgar Fenton as Vice-President but this year a second vice-president was elected. This was Samuel Howell, elected to the Committee for the first time in 1858. In 1862 James C. Laycock, a local solicitor and clerk to the magistrates, succeeded John Brooke as President. With the exception of the 1863–64 season, when Samuel Howell was President, he was to remain as President until 1872 and was then succeeded by Howell. The latter was a 'cellist but an artist by profession. Mrs Sunderland had commissioned him in 1856 to paint her full-length portrait in pastels which was 'executed in Mr Howell's best manner — true to the life — the expression of feature being admirably caught and rendered' said the *Huddersfield Chronicle* of 12 April 1856. Almost without doubt this is the same portrait of which a black and white lithograph copy now hangs in the Town Hall and of which there are two further copies, signed by Mrs Sunderland, at the Huddersfield Public Library. It is the picture of Mrs Sunderland which has been repeatedly reproduced over the years and if it was indeed true to life, she was, in her middle years, a very handsome woman.

In 1859 the Society again appointed Edward Battye and William Fitton as joint secretaries but in 1860 Edward Battye's resignation from the Society was accepted with much regret at the Annual Meeting and a vote of thanks was tendered for his services over a long period. He continued to be musically active locally and one is left to speculate about his reasons for leaving. To William Fitton fell the task, in 1859, of writing to Sir John William Ramsden, the local Manor Lord, to ask for patronage on behalf of the Society which, it was said, was put to great and increasing expense. Support and encourage-ment were asked for in the Society's endeavours to place itself in an equal position with other provincial choral societies. John Brooke and Edgar Fenton were named in this petition as patrons and subscribers, being 'most influential gentlemen in the Town'. The letter, which is among others in a local collection of Ramsden's papers, was dated 26 October 1859. There is no record of a reply, nor is there any reference to the correspondence in the minutes of the meetings of the Society's Committee, which, as Fitton says in the letter, had instructed him to write it. But Sir John William did not neglect the Society. He is reported to have donated £10 towards the expense of the trip to London in 1860 in response to further request from the Committee. Local patronage of this sort was surely sufficient to set the seal of approval on any society, affording it a status of utmost respectability.

The minutes of the Annual Meeting of July 1860 record that a Committee of Management was set up 'in addition to' a so-called Musical Committee, the former thus being made to sound like an appendage to the latter, which retained many members of the former Committee. Predictably, in time, the additional Committee assumed supremacy — managers were no longer necessarily musicians and vice versa. The chief officers were *ex officio* members of both committees and it was not long before the executive committee (i.e. the Committee of Management) was given power to add to the number of its members, which it did to the extent of five members in 1861.

The money spent on outsiders, both instrumental and vocal, resulted in financial difficulties and extra concerts were sometimes given, and some musical festivals suggested which do not always seem to have come to anything. At one such, it was hoped that Sims Reeves, the celebrated British tenor, would be engaged for a sum not to exceed 75 gns. He was not new to Huddersfield when, in 1864, he did come to sing at a one-day festival in the town at which the Choral Society added its strength to a choir of 250 voices with Burton as conductor. In 1861 Reeves had appeared in Bradford singing in *The Messiah* with Jenny Lind, the so-called Swedish nightingale, on the same day, 13 December, as the Huddersfield Choral Society was performing *The Messiah* in the Philosophical Hall in Huddersfield. A correspondent to the *Huddersfield Chronicle*, requesting a postponement of the Choral Society *Messiah* in order not to miss attending the Bradford concert was replied to promptly by William Fitton. The latter, after providing all the fairly obvious reasons why postponement was not possible, added somewhat acidly that when Madam Lind had sung recently in Leeds no more than about twenty people went from Huddersfield to hear her.

The previous season's *Messiah* performance (postponed from 28 December 1860 to 4 January 1861) was announced, incorrectly, as the Society's hundredth quarterly concert. This error resulted from a mistake at the beginning of the 1858–59 season when the first quarterly concert was numbered 91 instead of 89. Incorrect numbering persisted until 1894 when a further mistake occurred. Mercifully, the practice of numbering concerts was eventually abandoned. The ranks of the Society's membership at this supposed centennial concert were swollen by additions of both vocalists and instrumentalists, the latter in particular from the Yorkshire Orchestral Union. Burton's critics could not have been at all pleased that the *Huddersfield Chronicle* advertised the next concert of the Choral Society as being *Elijah*, on 1 February 1861 when in fact it was to be *The Creation* on 22 March. *Elijah* was the next concert to be given by Burton's Yorkshire Choral Union and Orchestral Union — albeit under the same conductor and including the Huddersfield Choral Society. The Choral Union, incidentally, sang in an end-of-season, and consequently badly attended, concert in London in June 1861 where Mrs Sunderland and Sims Reeves were the soloists.

Only a few Huddersfield singers were invited to the Handel Festival in London in June 1862 to sing in performances of *Israel in Egypt* and *The Messiah* but the month before this a score of the Society's members went to London to sing at the opening musical festival at the Great Exhibition at the Crystal Palace on 1 May. For this occasion Sterndale Bennett had composed music to a specially-written Ode by Tennyson, a work which the Huddersfield Choral Society were quick to bring to Huddersfield, performing it at the first quarterly concert of the 1862–63 season along with *Hymn of Praise* by Samuel Howell, their Vice-President, and Haydn's *Spring* from his *Seasons*. Bennett's *Ode* was 'really a fine piece of choral music', reported the *Huddersfield Chronicle* after the local performance. It contained a few lines which Tennyson had especially written into it in recognition of the recent loss of the Prince Consort who died at the close of 1861.

It was another work of Sterndale Bennett, himself a Yorkshireman born in Sheffield in 1816, that was chosen for the second quarterly concert of the 1862–63 season in Huddersfield. On this occasion the Society performed his Pastoral, *The May Queen* which he had written for the Leeds Festival of 1858. Burton's regard for Bennett (of whose piano playing he is reported to have declared 'I have never heard a piano sound like it') may have influenced the choice of the latter's *Woman of Samaria* for the Choral Society's last quarterly concert of the 1869–70 season. This work was written in 1867 and performed that year at the Birmingham Festival. Its performance in Huddersfield was in replacement of a previous unanimous choice by the Committee of Barnett's secular cantata, *The Ancient Mariner*, also first performed in Birmingham in 1867, which was never subsequently performed by the Society.

Mrs Sunderland

Robert Senior Burton

The Armoury, and adjoining Zetland Hotel, *c.* 1900
[Reproduced by courtesy of Mr Jim Allen of the Zetland Hotel.]

Something of a novelty was the performance of Joseph Barnby's choral work *Rebekah*, at the first concert of the 1870–71 season, along with Spohr's *Last Judgement*. *Rebekah* was conducted by the composer himself, gratuitously be it noted, copies of the work being loaned to the Society by him. Barnby, who wrote the popular *Sweet and Low*, succeeded Gounod as conductor of the Royal Albert Hall Choral Society, spent much time conducting oratorios but himself composed only three large-scale choral works, *Rebekah*, *The Lord is King*, and *King All Glorious* in addition to forty-seven anthems.

Before the end of the 1860s the Society had lost its concert hall. The Riding School in Ramsden Street reverted to its originally-intended purpose as a drill hall late in 1862 and henceforth became known as the Armoury. There is now a cinema where it stood, adjoining the Zetland Hotel which is no longer in what survives of Ramsden Street today. The proprietors of the Theatre Royal which had occupied the building for some time prior to 1862, sold it to the Sixth West Yorkshire Rifles and subsequently began to make use of the Philosophical Hall, which in 1864 was internally remodelled as a theatre, being fitted with a stage instead of a simple platform, boxes, and a rebuilt gallery. It was variously known as the Philosophical Hall or the Theatre Royal for some time but the Society was finally ousted in 1867 from what had been its concert hall and meeting place for thirty years. The newly- erected proscenium was nevertheless taken down and an orchestral gallery erected in early June 1864 to do honour to Mrs Sunderland on the occasion of her farewell concerts. Rumours of her retirement date from 1862 but in 1863 she had decided to retire from public singing and had toured Yorkshire giving farewell concerts when she was at the height of her powers. A two-day festival was arranged, though not by the Society, for early June, although many Choral Society members took part in it. The Society declined to have any part in the arrangements after receiving no response to their efforts at amalgamation with the 1856 Mrs Sunderland Festival Committee for that purpose.

The Festival began on Thursday, 2 June with a performance of *The Messiah*. On the Friday there was a miscellaneous concert which began with a performance of James Battye's glee, *Hail, Memory*. The conductor was Alfred Mellor, conductor of the Covent Garden Opera, and the chorus master was reported as having been Mr Edward Battye. The *Huddersfield Chronicle* of 4 June 1864 reported that the Festival was accompanied by 'the warmest demonstrations of esteem and admiration from the principal inhabitants of Huddersfield'.

Things did not always go well for the Society. Its performance of Handel's *Samson* at the first quarterly concert of the 1864–65 season was slated by the critic of the *Huddersfield Chronicle*; the musical talent of the Society being described as 'crude' and 'mediocre'. The evening was also the occasion of unpleasantness within the Society's ranks. Luke Liversidge (who had been with the Society since 1842) a member of the band as well as of the Committee, had used insulting language to the conductor and to the leader, Mr Thomas. The President was obliged to write to Liversidge with instructions to apologize to both gentlemen concerned or else face exclusion from the Society. There is no record of how the matter was resolved but sufficient to say that Luke Liversidge's name appears again as a member of the Musical Committee in 1865 and also in later seasons. In 1866 another difference of opinion arose between Liversidge and Burton whose manner was clearly not always to the liking of Luke. This time Burton wrote to the Secretary concerning the matter of which neither the substance nor the resolution is revealed, but the effect of such incidents could certainly have been of no benefit to the Society.

In 1865, for the first time since the Society's inauguration, the need for more rehearsals on a regular basis was considered and fortnightly rehearsals were finally proposed in 1866. The days of meeting only when the moon was full were past and there evidently was to be no repetition of an experience back in 1856 when a new oratorio, *Winter* by a John Hanson was performed on a Monday evening without a rehearsal of any sort! Even the conductor had seen the music for the first time only on the previous Saturday. Not surprisingly, the concert was reported as reflecting no credit on those who consented to give it. Only the soloists earned a little approval. An increase in the number of rehearsals may have been provided for in one of the revisions of rules which occurred at this time. Reference was made to several of these between 1860 and 1880 in committee meeting minutes. One revision in 1876 concerned the issue of tickets to the orchestra for members. These tickets were to be issued only at rehearsal and only to those members with sufficient number of rehearsal attendances.

The problem of a suitable concert hall for the Society's performances was a preoccupation from 1865 onwards. With the conversion of the Philosophical Hall for use as a theatre, the Society moved either into the Gymnasium Hall, virtually next door in Ramsden Street, as in 1866, or to the Queen Street Assembly Rooms where, by 1870, it had established its headquarters. The days of Committee meetings in hotels and public houses were over. Today, more than a century later, with both the Philosophical Hall (gutted by fire in

1880) and the Gymnasium Hall, long since gone, and most of the old Ramsden Street with them, the centre of Huddersfield, though very different, is still not totally changed from its appearance in 1870. The Railway had, of course, come to Huddersfield by this date, facilitating travel to and from the Town. Increasingly, leading solo artists, both vocal and instrumental, from home and abroad, were enticed to come to Huddersfield by local concert organizers, the Choral Society included. The Railway excursion had arrived too and in the 1860s the Choral Society started to organize day trips during the summer months for members to such spots as Hollingworth Lake near Littleborough, Wharncliffe Rocks en route to Sheffield, or further afield to York. The summer air sounded to their glees, by waterside and woodland, which was, and indeed still is, to be found not far from the centres of industrial development in the region.

With the exception of *The Messiah*, the quarterly concerts of the 1866–67 season all took place at the Gymnasium Hall, as did also an extra concert in March 1867 held to meet what is described in the minute book as 'extra expenses incurred by the Secretary'. The nature of these extra expenses were not identified, but an anonymous correspondent to the *Huddersfield Chronicle* in November 1867 wrote complaining of the poor performance of Mendelssohn's *Walpurgis Night* at the previous month's concert, and asked where all the Society's money was going, accusing the officers at the same time of improper procedures at the previous Annual Meeting. The chorus and band had made a perfect burlesque of *Walpurgis Night*, the Society was going down hill, it was all the fault of *foreign* importation to the town — and hadn't Burton refused to conduct if the person who threatened violence was allowed in the orchestra again? A clear reference this, surely, to the Burton–Liversidge row. The Secretary replied promptly, refuting the charges and, with reference to the last point, said that the Committee preferred to heal rather than to foment quarrels. This elicited a vehement response from the correspondent accusing Burton of using the Society for his own ends, running it into debt and into musical mediocrity. The Society resolved to ignore this but in a last fling from the correspondent he declared that the Society's silence was 'clearly indicative of a desire to suppress the truth' and that he took satisfaction from learning of the Society's intentions to rehearse *The Messiah* before the next performance, which it had not done for years, and that everybody knew that the performance last year had been far worse than that given at Mr Wood's Christmas Concert.

This was an isolated criticism, but it may have had some validity. It is difficult to judge fairly after the long lapse of time but it might have seemed that Burton was using the Huddersfield choir for his own ends rather than for the nurturing of Huddersfield's music and musicians.

In 1869, for the first time, an assistant conductor was appointed. This was the Revd John Thomas, M.A., who had been leader of the band and a member of the Musical Committee almost from the time of his arrival in Huddersfield in 1862. He was the Minister at the Unitarian Church in FitzWilliam Street from that date until 1884 and founded the FitzWilliam Street Philharmonic Society in 1875, a forerunner of the present Huddersfield Philharmonic Society and Orchestra. Earlier, in 1874, the Choral Society's minute book records that he was to be allowed 'not more than £5' to purchase music for 'an intended local band'. In 1871 he seems to have withdrawn his membership of the Choral Society despite attempts to dissuade him, but by 1873 his name again appears as a Committee member. One wonders whether he had his differences with Burton over the employment of local instrumentalists in the Choral Society's band. Nevertheless it was he, Thomas, who proposed Burton as conductor for the 1873–74 season when the latter was giving the Society a little trouble over the matter of his salary and it was also he who proposed Burton as conductor for the following season when there was a counter-proposition in favour of Joshua Marshall. Thomas's proposition was lost but it was Thomas again whose proposal had led to the resolution, referred to at the beginning of this chapter, that Burton should be given the members' best thanks for his services to the Society 'for a number of years'.

In 1873 Burton wrote to the Society virtually refusing to continue as its conductor unless he was paid more. He argued that the Society's publication of its accounts, revealing as a separately listed item the amount paid to its conductor (£20 per annum), had affected his position with other societies — from which he evidently received more than this. The Society refused to agree to his terms, he relented, and was re-elected as conductor for the season. The *Huddersfield Chronicle* records that at the Annual Meeting of the following year the Revd Thomas alluded 'in favourable terms to the talents and abilities, musically considered' of Burton before proposing him as conductor for the ensuing season, but failed to carry the meeting with him. Also we read that a Mr Bradley, member of the band, complained of too few rehearsals, failure on Burton's part to use and foster local talent and his preference for using *foreign* talent 'from Leeds, Bradford and other places'. Indeed, the minutes of a Committee meeting held the previous November make it clear that Burton had not been prepared to comply with a request regarding the 'nurturing of a local band'.

Thomas, being himself engaged in fostering local instrumental talent, must surely have shared some of Bradley's sentiments, but his regard for Burton's abilities 'musically considered', combined perhaps with the exercise of a little Christian charity may account for his behaviour in respect of Burton. Nevertheless he opposed a proposition to include the Conductor's fee along with those of other musicians as a single item in the published accounts of the Society, counter-proposing that this fee be continued to be listed separately. Though never again the Society's Assistant Conductor, Thomas continued as an active member of the Committee until he fell ill in 1884. He died of a brain tumour in October of that year.

By 1873 accommodation problems again beset the Society. The Queen Street Assembly Rooms were to be closed and pressures were mounting for the provision within the town of a suitable concert hall. The Society played a prominent part in this campaign. A concert hall committee was set up which set out to raise money by issuing shares to build such a hall in Queen Street South, plans having been prepared by W. H. Crossland, a London architect, for a hall to seat seventeen-hundred people and with room for three-hundred performers in the orchestra. In 1868 Huddersfield had been granted its Charter of Incorporation and in November 1872 the *Huddersfield Chronicle* carried a leading article expressing the need of the new municipal borough for a Town Hall and its lack of a hall of any suitable size for lectures, meetings, and musical performances. It was not for nearly a decade that the need for a hall was satisfied and in the meantime the Society secured the Armoury as a new home; but it lacked cloakrooms and waiting rooms for audiences, an ante-room for performers, and had to be fitted out with seating accommodation and an orchestra. Instrumental in obtaining the Armoury was Joe Wood of Kirkheaton, Bandmaster of the Sixth West Yorkshire Volunteers and solo trumpet player on many an occasion in the Society's *Messiah* performances.

The Society's first concert in the Armoury consisted of a performance of Mendelssohn's *Midsummer Night's Dream* music and his *Hymn of Praise* in October 1873 with the soprano, Miss Tomlinson from Leeds, the tenor, Mr William Coates from London and the local soprano, Mrs Barras as soloists. The *Chronicle* reported that the Society seemed to be 'fired with a new spirit' but it is significant, surely, that there were only reported to be 'upwards of about sixty performers'.

In 1874 a rehearsal room for the Society was procured in Byram Buildings, Station Street. This became an official address of the Society, listed in the local Directory, where the annual general meetings were held until 1882 and where rehearsals continued to be held until that date. From 1882 right up to the beginning of the second world war in 1939 these were held in the High Street School Buildings which occupied the site of the present Gas Showrooms in High Street.

One is tempted to believe that Burton's rejection as Conductor at the end of the 1873–74 season was anticipated, if only because the last concert of that season was a performance of Handel's *Samson* in place of the previously proposed *Joshua*, 'in deference to Mr Burton's wishes' — as it was put in a resolution of the Committee on 6 February 1874. This sounds rather like a sop: the granting of what was calculated to be a final request. A few years later, after the resignation due to ill health of James Broughton in 1877, Burton was chosen to conduct the Bradford Festival Choral Society, but he was only officially appointed as its conductor in January 1879 at a salary of £50 per year. There he lasted until 1887 but left after a dispute concerning the discharge of his duties. Shortly after this he retired from his post as organist at Leeds and went to live in Harrogate where he was organist for some years at St Peter's. He died in Harrogate on 2 August 1892 and lies buried at Harlow Hill cemetery.

His successor in Huddersfield in 1874, Joshua Marshall, was a local man, described by Wilmshurst, writing in 1936, as a 'brilliant musician'. He certainly played a significant part in the musical life of Huddersfield. He was associated with the music business of Wood and Marshall in Huddersfield and founded the music firm of Joshua Marshall and Co. which had branches in Bradford, Wakefield, and Dewsbury. At the age of sixteen he played the organ at St Patrick's Roman Catholic Church, New North Road, became a teacher of the pianoforte and of singing, choir master of the Parish Church in Huddersfield, and the conductor from its beginning in 1875 of the present Huddersfield Glee and Madrigal Society. His daughter was Mrs Edward Haley, the eminent pianist whose daughter, Olga, became a singer of some reputation in Yorkshire. Another of his daughters, Florence, was also a singer whilst his brother, Charles Marshall, who was a professional musician in London, can claim some measure of fame as the composer of the popular song, *I Hear You Calling Me*.

Joshua's musical renown seems to have been limited to local musical activities, but the effect on the Choral Society of his assuming the Conductorship was immediate. At the Society's Annual Meeting of 1875 the Secretary, John Eagleton (who deserves, and will receive, special mention later) was able to report that it had reached its highest point of prosperity since its formation. The list of subscribers was never so large, in some measure due to Marshall's own personal recruitment, and the band and chorus were never so efficient.

The old debt had been cleared, new works added to the library, there were thirty-four new instrumentalists as members of the Society and there had been no less than thirty-five rehearsals during the season. Marshall was unanimously elected Conductor for the next season.

Marshall's first concert at the beginning of the 1874–75 season had been a performance of Michael Costa's oratorio, *Eli*, described by the *Huddersfield Chronicle* report of 24 October 1874 as 'splendid'. 'Although it does not rank in the highest class' said the report, 'it is one of the finest compositions of the present day'. When Costa died in 1884, the *Musical Times* said of the work, after listing its merits, that it was 'only wanting perhaps in a full measure of the indefinable quality known as genius'. This oratorio waited another nine years for its next performance by the Huddersfield Choral Society when the celebrated singers, Charlotte Thudichum, soprano, and Hilda Wilson, contralto, made their first appearance in Huddersfield as the soloists.

About this time the band was usually augmented by members of Mr Hallé's band and others, and the chorus numbered in excess of a hundred singers. Increasingly the audience came to be described in the press, no longer as 'numerous and respectable' but as 'large and fashionable'. Marshall was clearly greatly appreciated by the Society, public and press, and especially by the Society no doubt, since he gave his services gratuitously! This must have provided a welcome relief from the problems set by Burton with regard to his salary. At the *Messiah* concert of 1875, which was reported in the *Huddersfield Chronicle* as one of the best concerts ever of the Society, Marshall was presented with a gold-mounted, ivory baton in a blue, silk-lined, Morocco leather case by the Vice-President, and President-elect, Mr J. J. Grist, on behalf of the Committee. On the following evening a special *People's Messiah* performance was given, but it was to be a long time before this was to become a set tradition, as it is now.

For the next few years, with the exception of the introduction of MacFarren's *Joseph* at the first concerts of both the 1878–79 and 1880–81 seasons, and his *St John the Baptist* in 1875 and again in 1880, there was the usual diet of Handel, Haydn, and Mendelssohn, although Rossini's *Stabat Mater* was given in 1877. *Joseph* was well received, as indeed it had been at its first-ever performance at the Leeds Festival in 1877 but its second performance by the Society in 1880 was reported as having been not as good as its first.

A milestone in the Society's history was the decision at the 1876 Annual General Meeting to reduce the number of regular subscribers' concerts from four to three per season in an attempt to reduce costs, since the Society was again running into debt. For a time the result of this was beneficial, but by

1879 a reduction in ticket sales and the expenditure on new music both adversely affected the annual balance sheet. The subscription list remained strong, however, and a trade recession was blamed for the falling off of ticket sales.

During the seventies an increasing number of principal soloists were engaged from London and elsewhere and at increasing cost. These included the soprano, Edith Wynne, and the tenors, Edward Lloyd and Bartin McGuckin. At this time the celebrated tenors, Joseph Maas and James Turner proved too expensive and the Society had to wait until 1881 before sharing the concert platform with Maas. To ensure the quality of the chorus itself, which continued to grow, there is the first indication, in 1874, of a definite policy of testing the vocal capabilities of its new recruits. A sub-committee consisting of Joshua Marshall, the Revd J. Thomas, and Ben Stocks was set up to do this in September that year. Ben Stocks had been a Committee member since 1864 and was a bass soloist with the Society from the same date. He was a local architect whose offices in 1881 were listed as at No. 7, Union Bank Yard, New Street, by which date he had been elected one of the two Vice-Presidents of the Society. He was its President for the 1884–85 season and again between 1899 and 1902. In 1875 he had invited Joshua Marshall to conduct a choir which became the Glee and Madrigal Society of which Ben Stocks himself was first Secretary, Treasurer, and Librarian.

Stocks managed to combine his talents in the service of the Choral Society in quite a special way, for it was he who, at the time of the completion of the new Town Hall in 1881, had become the consulting architect when John Abbey, the Borough Surveyor, died. Earlier attempts by the Society to provide the town with a concert hall had come to nothing, as we have seen, and conditions in the Armoury, meanwhile, were a continuous problem. At the Annual General Meeting in 1880 the President, William Harrop, described it as 'a hole' with which they would need to make do until the new hall was ready at the end of the following year. The necessity for a Town Hall was urged by the Committee of the Society upon the Town Council in 1875 by a deputation consisting of President, Vice-President, Conductor, Leader, Treasurer, and Secretary. By 1877 a decision had been made to provide a hall and its dimensions were approved by the Society and its speedy erection urged. In fact the hall was completed by the autumn of 1881 at a cost approaching £60,000. It was designed to accommodate 2,250 people. The Society was influential in a decision to hold a Musical Festival to mark its opening. In March 1881 a meeting was called by a circular signed by Messrs Harrop, Albert Wrigley, and Joseph Woodhead, for the purpose of holding discussions with the Mayor and other civic dignatories and interested parties with a view to setting up a committee charged with organizing this festival. The three signatories to the circular were respectively the Presidents of the Choral, Orpheus, and Glee and Madrigal Societies.

The meeting, duly held, was reported in the *Huddersfield Chronicle* of 5 March 1881. 'The gentlemen present', it said 'had put down their names as guarantors for nearly £600' to provide a fund for the provision of a Musical Festival. The *Chronicle* was able to report on 9 April 1881 that the executive committee for the Music Festival had arranged for it to take place on 20, 21, and 22 October of that year. The works to be performed, the band, conductor, soloists, and chorus master had all been chosen. The chorus was to be one of 250 voices and 500 applications to join it, some from members of the Leeds Festival Chorus, had been received; 116 local people having already been selected. The guarantee fund already stood at £3,000. The members of the Committee were named, many of whom were officers and committee members of the Choral Society. The Choral Society had circulated its members requesting that those who wished to should apply personally to the Festival Secretaries for admission to the Festival Chorus.

The Choral Society gave a performance of Haydn's *Creation* on 4 March 1881 at the last concert which it was obliged to hold at the Armoury, which was no doubt cause enough for celebration. It would appear, however, that there was a greater cause for thanksgiving. In reporting the concert the next day, the *Huddersfield Chronicle* observed that the public had rejoiced over the non-fulfilment of Mother Shipton's prophecy of the end of the world on the morning of Thursday, 4 March, 'expressing their sense of survival by celebrating the world's creation' at the concert in the evening.

CHAPTER SIX

In from the Cold

ALDERMAN WOODHEAD, Vice-President of the Festival Committee, in his address on the occasion of the official opening of the Town Hall on Tuesday, 18 October 1881, said that he hoped Huddersfield men had at heart not only the welfare of the town's people in their own time but also that of the people in years to come, for if so, the hall had not been built in vain. We can surely attest to the fulfilment of such hope. In a foreword written in 1944 to Robert Elkin's book on the Queen's Hall, Dr Malcolm Sargent tells of being taken round its ruins on 12 May 1941. 'One felt the spirit of the building breathing echoes of past beauty as an empty cathedral whispers sanctity' he wrote. Though perhaps not to be compared in fame and grand function with the Queen's Hall, the Town Hall in Huddersfield, like all concert halls, ruined or otherwise, may too be said to be possessed of a breathing spirit. Many echoes of past beauty ring around its richly-ornamented interior and many of these are associated with Huddersfield Choral Society performances. Moreover, many other choirs, orchestras, organists, conductors, and celebrated vocal and instrumental solo artists have performed in the hall, and long may this continue.

The 1881 Musical Festival proper, promoted in aid of the Huddersfield and Upper Agbrigg Infirmary, began on Thursday, 20 October with a morning performance of Mendelssohn's *Elijah* given, said the Book of Words printed for the occasion, by a 'band and chorus of 350 performers'. The conductor, Mr Charles Hallé, came with his band from Manchester and the following day's *Manchester Examiner* commented that 'in listening to such splendid choral singing one naturally inquired under whose care so excellent a result has been gained, and certainly the Committee and the town have good reason to be proud of the chorus master, Mr Joshua Marshall'. The soloists, Marie Albani, Mary Davies, Janet Patey, Edward Lloyd, Joseph Maas, Frederick King, and Charles Santley, all of considerable eminence, were engaged for the entire Festival at a cost approaching £1000 — as much as was finally handed over to the Infirmary. There was a Miscellaneous Concert on the Thursday evening, a performance of Spohr's *Last Judgement* and Rossini's *Stabat Mater* on the Friday morning and a performance of *The Damnation of Faust* by Berlioz on the Friday evening which drew the largest audience. Hallé was largely responsible for the popularity of *Faust* in England. He conducted another performance of it in 1881 at St James's Hall, London and had in 1880 conducted its first performance in England in Manchester when Mary Davies and Edward Lloyd had also been soloists.

In a letter dated 23 October 1881 from Hallé to his daughter, he writes

The Huddersfield Festival was really a great success, and the people most enthusiastic. *Faust* never went so well yet. Lloyd sang better than ever, and so did Miss Davies; Santley was splendid too although a little fatigued at first . . .

I send you two Huddersfield and one Bradford papers which will tell you the whole story. How things grow! I cannot help thinking now often of the evening when I asked you if you could not help me by translating *Faust*, and now people have actually come from Ireland to Huddersfield merely to hear it. I have seen them with my own eyes. They had been ruefully sea-sick, and said they would not mind being so again the next day if they could hear *Faust* once more.

Hallé departed with his band immediately after the *Faust* concert but the Miscellaneous Popular Concert on the Saturday evening which Joshua Marshall conducted went very well. J. E. Ibeson accompanied the choir on the piano and Henry Parratt is reported as having played the organ although his brother Walter's name alone appears on the programme, as organist at the previous concerts. The soloists stayed on, and with a chorus of 280 voices, the concert brought the Festival to a splendid finish. The Festival Committee's balance sheet published in January 1882, indicates a sum of £60 paid in respect of the chorus master but there seems to be no record anywhere of the presentation to him of a gold pocket watch, engraved in recognition of the Committee's appreciation of his services as Festival Chorus Master. This watch is still in the possession of Marshall's great-grandson, Charles Marshall of Cullingworth.

The Town Hall organ, installed by the local organ builders, James Conacher and Sons, had been built originally for the Albert Hall, Newport, Montgomeryshire by Henry Whittle and Sons of London. After some modifications by Conacher's it was regarded as likely to be unequalled in Yorkshire by those, qualified to judge, such as Joshua Marshall, who was appointed Borough Organist. A player of eminence was soon to perform on it, for in February 1883 the great French organist and composer, Alexandre Guilmant came to Huddersfield to take part in two concerts arranged by the Choral Society to help clear off its debt. Mr Allen Haigh of the Choral Society Committee was responsible for the engagement of M. Guilmant and also personally guaranteed the Society against loss from the two concerts.

Huddersfield Town Hall in the 1880s

Ben Stocks

J. Edgar Ibeson

Joshua Marshall (*top left*), Charles Hallé (*top right*) and others, sketched at the 1881 Music Festival marking the opening of the Huddersfield Town Hall

On 23 February 1883 a well-filled Town Hall listened to Guilmant's *Grand Mass No. 3* performed by the Choral Society joined by local soloists and with the composer at the organ. The *Huddersfield Chronicle* report was full of praise for M. Guilmant, observing also that the fine power of expression of the chorus was sufficient to prove that the members of the Choral Society were capable of doing most excellent musical work. The following evening's concert, consisting of an organ recital by Guilmant including some of his own works, was poorly attended despite a reduced price for seats, but the enjoyment of those who did go made up in part for the poor attendance. Whether or not Mr Allen Haigh was obliged to make good any loss is not known.

By this date Henry Parratt was playing the organ regularly for the Society but only in 1884 was he officially elected as its organist. In May the following year his resignation, due to failing eyesight, had regretfully to be accepted and the 1881 Festival accompanist, Mr Edgar Ibeson, was appointed to replace him. Ibeson stayed until 1915, when ill-health forced him to retire, serving in that long period variously as organist, accompanist, and deputy conductor. He had also served as conductor of the Glee and Madrigal Society between 1894 and 1903.

The new concert hall was not without its teething troubles. Initially, after the removal of platform extensions used for the Festival, the chorus, which was growing in numbers considerably at this time, was too cramped. Fortunately the extra fittings were able to be retrieved and re-erected for the start of the 1883–84 season. Seating accommodation for the audience was also a problem and negotiations with the Town Council took place regarding this matter together with that of off-platform accommodation and facilities for band and chorus. The rules of the Society were revised in 1881 and, though we have no record of these changes, perhaps they were necessitated in part by the facilities which the new concert hall afforded. After various initial changes seat prices were fixed at six shillings each for the best seats in the balcony (thirty shillings per season; two tickets each concert) whilst unreserved seats sold at half a crown each. It cost a shilling just to stand — presumably at the rear of the area. These were no paltry amounts in those days, indicating the Society's highly 'respectable', if not always 'fashionable' patronage.

Rehearsal accommodation was something of a problem at the beginning of the eighties, and the move in 1882 from Byram Buildings, with the library and all the other effects of the Society, to High Street Chapel School Rooms must have been a welcome one. No rental was charged at High Street but the

Society made annual donations to the Sunday School, though the recipients, not averse to looking a gift horse in the mouth, asked that the donation be doubled. The request was not granted and, either due to resulting embarrassment, or simply to the need for more room, attempts were made to secure alternative accommodation. In the event this did not come about until 1890, and then only temporarily.

By the beginning of 1884 Marshall's health was creating difficulties. Although he had conducted the *Messiah* concert before Christmas in 1883, he was scarcely well enough to do so. The Revd J. Thomas was also very ill at this time and the Society gave him a benefit concert in June of 1884. It was a Miscellaneous Concert which raised £127, the Town Hall having been made available gratuitously. One person who had expressed the wish for the success of this concert, and a man ever ready to help needy musicians, was Mr Joe Wood, senior partner of Wood and Marshall's music business. As was common in those days with local music dealers, Mr Wood promoted many a concert in and about the town. In the event he did not live to witness this one. He caught a severe chill and died from its consequences in early June, aged 58 years. Joshua Marshall, his business partner, had been his pupil and had married into his family. Wood, a pupil of the organ under Henry Horn, went to High Street Methodist Chapel in 1845 as organist and stayed there until 1861 when he succeeded Walter Parratt at the organ of St Paul's, Horn's old post, remaining there until 1883. He was an accomplished musician who had done much for the cause of music in the neighbourhood and his passing was a sad loss.

Joshua Marshall was sufficiently ill at the beginning of the 1884–85 season for a letter of condolence to be sent to his wife from the Society expressing regret at his inability to take his post as conductor, and to inform her of the decision to ask Mr John North to assume the appointment temporarily, in his place. North (of whom more later) conducted the performance of *Elijah* on 24 October and *The Messiah* on 19 December 1884. By the new year Marshall's health was sufficiently restored for him to resume his duties. He attended rehearsals for *The Creation* and conducted its performance on 20 March 1885 when as many as 400 performers took part. A good report in the *Huddersfield Examiner* the following day included a plea for a new work to be performed next season, and a couple of works were suggested for consideration. Since smaller towns had done them, it commented, then so excellent a society as the one at Huddersfield should also move with the times.

Pressures for the replacement of Marshall by North, favoured by the Secretary, John Eagleton, were finally effective at the Annual Meeting in

John Bowling   John North

1885. The precise nature of Marshall's affliction is nowhere made clear, but there is evidence to show that he was subject to periodic mental instability and was the victim of some sort of breakdown. A special complimentary benefit concert was arranged for 15 May 1885 when *Elijah* was again performed with John North conducting. This raised over £80 which was passed to Mrs Marshall but not until April 1886 was Marshall able to write and thank the Society for it. He wrote from the South Shore Hydropathic Estate, Blackpool expressing great appreciation both from himself and his family who were anxious, he said, that he should 'not again take an active part in the association' until his health was thoroughly restored. But despite some attempt to bring him back after North died, he never again conducted the Society, although in 1888 the *Yorkshire Musician*, in reporting his silver wedding anniversary celebrations, described him as 'fully recovered'. Indeed, in 1896 he was back at his post of Choirmaster at the Parish Church, and in October 1897 he conducted a Glee and Madrigal Society concert when J. E. Ibeson was ill.

Apart from Sullivan's *Martyr of Antioch* and a second performance, referred to in the previous chapter, of Costa's *Eli*, nothing very new had been given between 1881 and Marshall's departure. The *Martyr of Antioch* was dedicated to the Prince of Wales and written for the Leeds Festival in 1880. It was given by the Society at the final concert of the 1881–82 season using mostly the same soloists as at Leeds, namely Mdme Patey, Edward Lloyd, and Fredrick King. For the first time the printed programme of this concert provided details of specially-run late trains instead of giving details of carriages for homebound concert-goers. The work has been described by one critic as alternating between dullness and vulgarity, lacking in dramatic expression, although lyrical in parts, but this did not prevent the Society from performing it on several occasions subsequently right up till 1920.

John Eagleton, who championed John North as Conductor in 1885, had served as Secretary continuously since 1873 and had been in partnership in that capacity with William Dawson since 1878 when the latter was appointed Assistant Secretary. This partnership was to continue until 1915, Eagleton himself remaining as Secretary until 1917. 'The one and only J. Eagleton' as Henry Coward calls him in his *Reminiscences*, had joined the Society as a vocalist in 1862 but turned to playing the bassoon in the band when he was elected Secretary in 1873. He also played the violoncello, as had his father, one of the earliest members of the Society and also named John, whose name appears in the 1837 list of members. J. Eagleton junior was elected to the Musical Committee in 1869 and, in his time, was secretary of the Philharmonic Society as well as serving as its president. By profession he was a traveller for the Honley firm of Joshua Beaumont & Co. As such he was often in London on business and, says Wilmshurst, was instrumental in linking the musical life of the capital with that of Huddersfield by helping to bring leading composers and soloists to perform at the Society's concerts. Wilmshurst adds that the Society is perhaps indebted to no other single member's efforts more than it is to his. After over fifty years of membership and forty-four years as Secretary this could well be true. He is said to have played the bassoon at every Handel Festival in London from 1878 until his death. The *Musical Times* of April 1902 reports him as having been one of only two amateur double bassoon players in the country. He died in 1918 in his seventy-first year.

The new Conductor, John North, about thirty-two years old at the time of his appointment, was apparently a man of considerable talent and attractive mien. At the age of nine he had started work at Wood and Marshall's where he rapidly developed his musical talent. He turned eventually to teaching and conducting and for a time conducted the band at the Huddersfield Theatre Royal but relinquished this in favour of training and conducting choirs. When Joe Wood, of Wood and Marshall's, died in 1884, North joined with

Wood's son in running the business. He followed Joshua Marshall as conductor both of the Choral Society and of the Glee and Madrigal Society and, in 1887, as choir master at the Parish Church. He was appointed conductor of the Philharmonic Orchestra and was also in his time conductor of Holmfirth, Skipton and Todmorden Choral Societies. He was a competent organist and violinist, which latter instrument he had played in the Huddersfield Choral Society band since 1882. He was soon to prove his worth.

The Choral Society had declined to take part in a vocal contest in Liverpool in 1886 where John North carried off two prizes with the Glee and Madrigal Society in August, one of £50 for the best mixed choir and one of £40 for the best male voice choir. The following year North came home in triumph again, this time from London where he had again taken both a mixed and male voice choir to the Welsh National Eisteddfod held in August of that year at the Royal Albert Hall. This time both the Choral and the Glee and Madrigal Societies participated, each contributing vocalists to both the mixed and the male voice choirs. The mixed choir of 246 voices shared the first prize with a Welsh choir from Bangor, and the male voice choir shared the first prize with a Rhondda choir. For these successes North received two gold medals. The judges decisions proved controversial, some regarding it as indicating a reluctance to award first prizes to a Yorkshire choir at a Welsh Eisteddfod, it being fairly generally believed that the Huddersfield choirs were the better. All this did not diminish the welcome received by the victors, when they emerged from the Railway Station, from the large crowd assembled in St George's Square. Such was the general approbation that the winners were later to receive the gift of a grand piano from Archibald Ramsden of Leeds. In recording the history of the Glee and Madrigal Society in 1975, Sydney Crowther wrote that it was the Glee and Madrigal Society that was given the piano which 'they allowed the Choral Society to use for its rehearsals — the Choral Society giving for many years a subscription to the G. & M. in return'. The minutes of a Choral Society Committee meeting of 15 October 1887 however, indicate that the Choral Society regarded both itself and the G. & M. as the joint recipients of the gift and arranged to keep the piano at its rehearsal rooms in High Street, offering to pay half the cost of hire of 'a cottage piano for use of the Glee and Madrigal Society at their rehearsals'. The question of the ownership of this piano was the cause of contention many years later.

As if in response to Press criticism for not performing many new works, the Choral Society performed Ebenezer Prout's cantata *Hereward* in October 1885 at the first concert after North's appointment as conductor. Prout, who was Professor of Composition at the Royal Academy of Music, came up to Huddersfield and conducted the work himself. He had written it in 1878 for the Hackney Choral Association of which he was conductor. Now chiefly remembered only for his writings on musical theory and for his revision of the score of Handel's *Messiah* commissioned by Novello's in 1902, in his own day Prout was highly regarded as organist, conductor, critic, and composer. The Society's performance of his *Hereward* was enthusiastically received by both public and press. No modern work since *Faust*, heard at the 1881 Festival, had given such delight in Huddersfield, according to the *Huddersfield Examiner* of 17 October 1885 and although *Hereward* had not been especially written for the Society, such an event was 'not beyond the range of possibility' for the future. Prout was quoted as saying, regarding *Hereward*, that he had 'never heard it better' and, except in Yorkshire, did not expect to again. Despite its apparent success musically, the concert resulted in a loss of £29. *Hereward* was given again at the end of the following season with Prout in the audience this time. Again the reception was enthusiastic, the *Huddersfield Examiner* asking why Prout had not been commissioned more often to write works for great English Festivals.

Encouraged by all this, Prout wrote *The Red Cross Knight* especially for the Society, which resolved at a meeting on 8 January 1887 to put it on as 'the special Jubilee performance by the Society, to be given in October 1887'. This was not the jubilee year of the Society but of the Queen. However, the report of the October performance in the *Huddersfield Examiner* unequivocally describes the concert as being in celebration of the Society's jubilee. Scholes too, in his *Mirror of Music*, says that Prout wrote the work for the jubilee of the Huddersfield Choral Society. It seems strange then that neither press announcements nor printed programme of the concert makes any reference to the Society's Golden Jubilee. Certainly I find no other reference anywhere concerning the fiftieth anniversary celebrations of the Society, either appropriately, in 1886, or erroneously, in 1887.

The Queen's jubilee was celebrated musically in Huddersfield by the inclusion in the famous series of Huddersfield Subscription Concerts, begun about this time, of a special jubilee performance of Sullivan's *Golden Legend* in the November. The Choral Society declined to take part due to their taxing commitment to the production of *The Red Cross Knight*, but it was agreed that Choral Society members who chose to take part as individuals were to be paid seven shillings and sixpence each, should they so require, by John Watkinson, organizer of the Subscription Concerts and later to become the President of the Choral Society. Those members who did take part suffered

some shoddy treatment on the occasion of the Jubilee Festival and probably
wished they hadn't bothered.

Scholes tells us that the *Musical Times* took *The Red Cross Knight* very
seriously, devoting two pages of analytical review to it. This may explain why
a great deal of fuss was made by the *Huddersfield Examiner*, both before and
after the Huddersfield performance, the work, its composer, and the performance all coming in for considerable praise. One had heard too much and
for too long, it would appear, of all this foreign music, especially from
German composers, for all their genius! Scattered through the report of the
concert were expressions such as 'English of the English', 'Anglo-Saxon
spirit', 'national music', and 'puffed-up foreigners'. One could hardly fail to
understand the report's message. Prout, who conducted the work and was
loudly applauded at the end, was clearly delighted.

Following the Festival performance of *Faust* in 1881, Wood and Marshall
had promoted the production of the work again the following year using as
near as possible the same chorus and soloists. Only three of the original
soloists were available but the performance was reported as almost equalling
that of the Festival. In 1886 *Faust* was put on again despite the loss it was
anticipated it would incur. There was evidently enough money in the bank
and it was felt that at times art and culture must take precedence over bank
balance considerations. Thirty-six extra professionals were engaged in the
band and the soloists were Mary Davies, Watkin-Mills, and Edward Lloyd.
These singers were acquired through the services of the firm of Vert in Cork
Street, London, a concert agency which claimed to be the oldest one in the
world and which is first mentioned in the Society's minutes in connexion with
this performance. The Society performed *Faust* again in 1889, Charles Banks
replacing Edward Lloyd as tenor soloist. An augmented band and chorus of
450 performers was employed, over 350 of these being in the chorus.

The use of an augmented band and chorus was habitual during North's
period of conductorship but even after 1893, when the band and chorus was
announced as representing 'the full strength of the Society', the numbers were
little less than these, and remained so well into the twentieth century. One
wonders where they put them all! Recruitment to the choir certainly pro-
ceeded apace during this period and it must be remembered that these were
the great days of the Tonic Sol-Fa-ists, when sight-singers were turned out as
on a mass-production line, and the fashion was for large choirs. *The Musical
Herald* of 1 August 1896 carried an article about D. W. Evans who came to
Huddersfield in 1882 as Superintendent of Singing in the Board Schools. The
following year he joined the Choral Society as a bass singer. The account of

his work described in this article is sufficient to show how and why Huddersfield, which never had been short of up-and-coming young singers, was well able to feed the ranks of local choirs which were growing both in size and numbers.

This period of North's conductorship — during which he declined all offers of remuneration — saw the beginnings of some customs and practices familiar to us today. The first vocal sub-committee, so-named, dates from 1886, its purpose being primarily at that time to test the vocal abilities of would-be choir members. The Christmas Hymn began to be sung regularly before *Messiah* performances at Christmas-time although 1897 was an exception. In that year the concert fell on 17 December, which in those days was regarded as inappropriately remote from Christmas! *The Messiah* had regularly been given at the second concert of the season, just before Christmas, since 1872 — well before North's time — but in 1885 and 1886 there was an additional performance for the benefit of the general public. However, not until comparatively recently was this to become an established tradition. In 1889 and 1890 this public performance of *The Messiah* was given on Good Friday, although in 1891 and 1892 *Elijah* was performed at a public concert on Good Friday. A practice which was suggested in 1890 but never started, was that choir members be asked to retire at the age of sixty. It was flatly rejected!

On 7 June 1888 there was a special concert in Brighouse Town Hall to celebrate the Golden Wedding of Mrs Sunderland which that lady herself attended, with members of her family, and was presented with a testimonial in a solid gold casket. The secretary of the special committee set up to arrange this event and the presentation was John Eagleton. The choir, about 112 in all, was composed very largely of Huddersfield Choral Society members and the chief conductor was John North. The band, reported later as not always having played in tune at the concert, was lead by John Bowling of Heckmondwike who was later to become the Conductor of the Choral Society. The performance consisted of a selection from *The Messiah* and some miscellaneous items. Following upon this celebration a committee under the chairmanship of Ben Stocks was set up to inaugurate a prize fund which resulted in the institution of the Mrs Sunderland Musical Competition. This was to be administered by the governors of the Huddersfield Technical School, opened in Queen Street South in 1884. The School incorporated the functions of its forerunner, the Mechanics Institute, and the present Polytechnic and Technical College are its direct descendants. The first Competition took place at the School in April 1889, prizes being awarded in each of three classes, solo soprano vocalist, solo contralto vocalist, and solo pianoforte. The adjudicators were John North, James Sykes, Borough organist, and D. W. Evans, the bass soloist and singing superintendent mentioned above who was described on the programme as teacher of singing at the Technical School. J. E. Ibeson was the accompanist.

In the March concert of 1891 the Society performed Handel's *Theodora*, said to be Handel's favourite, but rarely performed since its first public hearing in London in 1750 when it was not well received. Anticipating a later performance in the same week, Handel is reported to have made a cynical but witty comment. When told of a City gentleman who intended booking all the boxes Handel replied 'he is a fool then, for the Jews will not come as they did to *Judas Maccabaeus* because it is a Christian story and the ladies will not come because it is a virtuous one'. The performance in Huddersfield a century and a half later was announced as the first in Yorkshire. Huddersfield Choral Society officials had attended a performance in Manchester during the previous season with a view to deciding its suitability for performance by the Society. They decided to cut certain items, a decision doubtless resulting, observed the *Huddersfield Examiner*, from the 'impatience of present-day concert goers'. 'Angels ever Bright and Fair' is at least one aria that survives in the common musical recollection from a largely neglected and forgotten work, and it was well sung on the occasion by Anna Williams. Vacant seats were conspicuous in the balcony where subscribers would have been sitting, no doubt, had it been a *Messiah* performance. *Plus ça change. . .*! The widow of Richard Mellor, organist of Ramsden Street Chapel before his death in 1874, whom we have mentioned earlier, donated £50 towards the cost of producing *Theodora*.

By the time of the first concert of the next season John North was dead. Despite efforts by his physician, Mr Hardy, and an eleventh-hour visit by Dr Scougal, both his friend and President of the Choral Society, he died of typhoid fever on Monday, 12 October 1891, aged 39. He left a widow and nine children. His funeral service was held at the Parish Church where he had been choirmaster, and was attended by representatives of most of the musical societies with which he was, or had been, associated, as well as of other bodies such as the Huddersfield Masonic Lodge of which he was a member. The Choral Society and Glee and Madrigal Society joined forces to sing 'Blest are the Departed' from Spohr's *Last Judgement* and Battye's setting of Psalm 90.

A man of immense vitality and talent, North had possessed a remarkable musical memory and sight-reading ability at the piano. He had composed dances, piano pieces, songs, a Te Deum and even, it seems, a piano concerto.

At quite an early age he had played the organ at the Baptist Chapel in Bath Buildings, Bath Street — formerly the Hall of Science of notorious memory — and afterwards also in New North Road when the new chapel was opened there in 1878. As a conductor and chorus master he was highly regarded. Under him, says the obituary in the *Huddersfield Examiner* of 17 October 1891, 'the Society attained a position and prestige . . . acknowledged by professional singers and instrumentalists from all parts of the country to be unsurpassed anywhere in the kingdom for all qualities which go to make artistic strength'. One great singer is quoted as saying of North's conducting of *Faust* that he 'only knew two men in the North of England who could conduct that work properly, and one was Sir Charles Hallé and the other Mr North'. It seems evident that the Society had sustained a great loss. The insanitary conditions of the Victorian urban environment carried off the vigorous and talented along with the weak and ignorant. It had even robbed the Queen and the country of her talented and beloved consort thirty years before and obviously having no more regard for the *respectable* than for the poor and destitute.

A memorial service was held on Sunday, 18 October at the Parish Church and at the Society's first concert of the season on the Friday (16 October) following the funeral, Rossini's *Stabat Mater* was performed along with selections from *The Messiah* and *Elijah* in place of Parry's *Ode on St Cecilia's Day* which was originally intended to have been given. The conductor was Mr John Bowling who, after being appointed on a temporary basis for the remainder of the season was elected Conductor at the Annual Meeting of 27 May 1892, two other candidates being outvoted. An earlier proposal to nominate Joshua Marshall as candidate, along with Bowling, received only the support of its proposer and seconder.

A native of Staincliffe, John Bowling lived in Heckmondwike where at one time he had a music warehouse managed by his brother Charles who died in 1882, aged 34. John mastered the violin in his teens having been trained by his uncle, John Bowling of Leeds. He joined Charles Hallé's band as a second violin and remained a member of that band for twenty years. As such he had been engaged by the Society for its performance of *The Red Cross Knight* of 1887 and for *Faust* in 1889. He had played the organ at various local churches and conducted a number of local choral societies including the one at Todmorden where North had been. He also examined for the Royal College of Music, taught the violin at the Yorkshire Training College in Leeds and was an adjudicator, after John North died, at the Mrs Sunderland Competitions. Unlike his predecessor, he received payment for conducting the Huddersfield Choral Society which in 1896 was recorded as one guinea per rehearsal and five guineas per concert.

Wilmshurst tells us no more of Bowling than that he was a competent musician, of a less magnetic personality than North, and that he maintained the Society's reputation for the ten-year period of his conductorship 'without perhaps enhancing it'. This seems to do him a little less than justice, though it may not be without a grain of truth. Although the circumstances of Bowling's departure in 1901 in favour of Henry Coward raise questions in one's mind regarding the support which he enjoyed within the Society, there seems to be little evidence of any strong movement to dislodge him after 1894. He won a clear majority over his fellow candidates, including Joshua Marshall, in 1893 but was returned uncontested in 1894 and thereafter, until 1901 when Dr Henry Coward was proposed and the members were urged to elect him by a unanimous vote. Bowling's work with the Society nevertheless seems invariably to have been appreciated both in official Committee statements and by Press critics.

To say the very least, Bowling seems to have maintained the Society's vocal and instrumental standards of performance. During his time an amateur permanent orchestra was established which was augmented as occasion demanded by professional players. Some of the most eminent vocal soloists of the day continued to be engaged and some, though not many, new musical trails were blazed. Handel's *Joshua*, given in March 1893, though not new music, was something of a rare offering. Comparison was made in the *Huddersfield Examiner* with its previous performance by the Society in 1867, when with an unbalanced chorus and 'the bald accompaniments of Handel being performed by a band inadequate to meet even the limited require-ments', the effect produced, it said, must have been very curious. A chorus of 344 singers, a band of 67 players and Prout's additional accompaniments to the work were, in the 1893 performance, evidently all more to the taste of both audience and local press critics of the time to whom the effect produced by an authentic performance, as of Handel's day, might have seemed even more curious.

Both in 1896 and in 1897 the view was expressed at the Society's Annual Meetings that it was undesirable to continue to perform works by the old masters simply in order to draw big houses. A big bank balance was not the Society's sole aim; enough to guarantee against emergencies was adequate. Both the Society and its public benefited from an extension of musical knowledge. Thus in 1893 Sullivan's *Golden Legend* was performed and in following seasons were heard Brahms's *Song of Destiny*, Macfarren's *St John the Baptist,* Dvořák's *The Spectre's Bride,* Cowen's *Ode to the Passions* and Stanford's *Revenge,* together in 1897, with a repeat of the *Golden Legend.* In Eagleton's view the Committee were all of one mind as to the giving of a new work each season but that this lost money because the public stayed away. The Brahms and MacFarren works were performed together at a concert in 1894 which drew the smallest ever of the Society's Town Hall audiences. The public was castigated by the *Huddersfield Examiner.* Many only had interest in concert-going because it was fashionable, it taunted. Music consisted of other than diatonic scales and was worth little if it was not progressive. Brahms and MacFarren shifted both choir, audience, and orchestra from out of their Handelian and Mendelssohnian grooves, it said, the effect of which on the choir, at least, was some loss 'of that unanimity of attack and true intonation for which they were famous'.

The term 'new work', of course, is used in a relative sense. The first British performance of *Song of Destiny* was in 1874, when the *Musical Times* reported it as 'recognized . . . as a work of genius of the highest order'. MacFarren's *St John the Baptist* was twenty years old, Stanford's *Revenge* had been written for the Leeds Festival of 1887 and *The Spectre's Bride* dated from the Birmingham Festival of 1885. Only Cowen's *Ode to the Passions,* said to be probably the best of all his choral works, was in any real sense new, having been performed first at the Leeds Festival in 1898, one year before its performance in Huddersfield. Although many of them may now have been forgotten, the introduction of works by contemporary composers was undoubtedly a healthy thing at that time. But Haydn, Handel, and Mendelssohn still predominated during the last decade of the century, and in addition to the works mentioned above, there were only occasional repetitions of *Hereward, The Red Cross Knight, Faust,* Costa's *Eli,* and a resurrection of Spohr's *God Thou Art Great.*

Nevertheless, costs had to be considered, and with subscription lists falling, efforts were repeatedly made to recruit new subscribers. The annual *Messiah* concert, though often the sole profit-maker, did not always provide an increased end-of-season bank balance. Despite a barrage of criticism of the public musical taste, the press offered, with few exceptions, nothing but superlatives to express the general satisfaction with the *Messiah* performances. Although, in commenting on the many empty seats at the performance of Cowen's *Ode to the Passions* in 1899, the *Examiner* observed that 'politically liberal, the [Huddersfield] people are musically Tory, and refuse to reform', its praise for the Society's efforts was invariably unstinting. *The Messiah* of 1895 had been the best ever, it reported, a view endorsed at the

Annual Meeting of 1896 by J. J. Grist, the Vice-President (who said that he hadn't missed a *Messiah* performance by the Society for forty years). Clara Butt had sung beautifully even though, suffering from an ulcerated sore throat, she had felt obliged to ask for the indulgence of the audience. The concert made a profit of £100, which helped to offset the loss of £48 from the Dvořák concert.

By 1899, superlatives exhausted, the *Examiner* report on the *Messiah* concert began

It cannot, in the nature of things, be said year after year that the performance of . . . *The Messiah* by the Huddersfield Choral Society is the best they ever gave, yet they maintain so wonderfully, year after year, their vocal expressive and artistic powers in such high degree that each successive performance almost invariably seems to be the best on record.

Such was the Choir's standing at this time that a dozen members were selected to take part in the Handel Festival at the Crystal Palace in June 1897, and fifty-two members sang in the Leeds Festival of October 1898.

Despite all this, by the turn of the century there were too many empty seats at the concerts, even when the classical works were being performed, and although the Society's musical merit was still applauded, its lack of discipline brought forth adverse comment. Poor attendance, and attention, at rehearsals was noted. For *Israel in Egypt* in March 1901, John Bowling's last concert, not only was it reported that there were many vacant seats but also that many choir members were late in arriving and the early choruses suffered in consequence! A state of demoralization was beginning to take hold which was affecting both the Society and its public. In March 1900 the very poor attendance at the Society's performance of *Judas Maccabaeus* had been a cause of some embarrassment, especially since it had been decided to donate the profits of this concert to the Mayor's fund for the wives and children of reservists engaged in the Boer War. Of the members' free gallery tickets sacrificed for public sale, only a hundred were sold. The work, which the Society had not performed for eighteen years, was thought to be an appropriate, popular choice for the occasion but, despite the musical success of the concert, it lost money and the Society had to offer the Mayor a donation from its own funds.

Concerning discipline, we may note that from this period dates the requirement for ladies to be uniform in matters of concert dress. They were all asked to wear white for concerts without exception and, to complement this, the men were asked all to appear in black. Interesting too is the fact that in 1897 it was decided that John Bowling should, in addition to being called

Conductor, also hold the office of Chorus Master. Edgar Ibeson, the organist, who received repeated praise in the press for his work at concerts, was also officially nominated as Accompanist.

The situation regarding the band at this time is also of interest. Local band members were sometimes, as for the *Faust* concert of 1898, required to give way to professional instrumentalists from outside. As a sop, they were allowed a free seat in the house. One wonders what the critical faction of Burton's day would have thought of this. Two members of the local band in 1900 who refused to play in future unless payed half a guinea per concert were notified that their services were to be dispensed with. This decision seemed to be the only alternative to one of giving payment to all members of the band, thereby revoking its amateur status, a step which was apparently not to be contemplated. A band sub-committee meeting of 12 January 1901 resolved to invite the most promising players of the Philharmonic Society to take part in a band rehearsal for *Israel in Egypt*. The malcontents in the permanent orchestra had best look to their laurels! The previous June, when a list of professional players to be engaged for the following season had been drawn up, it was decided to notify them of the adoption of the *diapason normal* at the Town Hall and to advise them to make arrangements accordingly. At that time the Town Hall organ was tuned to something like a semitone above normal pitch which caused much trouble to visiting instrumentalists and vocal soloists and must have taxed choir members at the top end of their register. However, it seems that no alteration of pitch was made at that time, since the need to reduce the organ's pitch was still an issue some sixteen years later. But this belongs to a new chapter and a new situation within the Choral Society, not to mention a new century with a new Monarch on the English Throne. The Edwardian age was about to begin and an exciting new musical breeze was blowing strong within the kingdom.

CHAPTER SEVEN

Maturity and Excellence

IN OCTOBER 1900 the Society resolved to introduce a new work each season, and for the following season the musical setting by S. Coleridge-Taylor of Longfellow's *Scenes from the Song of Hiawatha* was considered. Not long completed, this trilogy had recently been rapturously received at its first complete performance by the Royal Choral Society. At a Committee meeting in February 1901 a letter was read from Coleridge-Taylor accepting an invitation to conduct *Hiawatha* the following October and, not unrelated to this perhaps, it was resolved at the same meeting that the President and Secretary should 'wait upon Dr Coward of Sheffield . . . to invite him to allow his name to be put in nomination as conductor of this Society for the 1901–02 season'. Coward recalls in his *Reminiscences* that Ben Stocks and John Eagleton had, on 31 January 1901, attended a rehearsal of his in Sheffield in order 'to spy out the land'. He comments that they were evidently both satisfied because at the close they offered him the conductorship of the Huddersfield Choral Society. If this story is true and Coward's date is correct then evidently not only was pressure exerted to obtain a unanimous vote for Coward, as mentioned earlier, but also the Committee's approval of the approach to Coward was clearly pre-empted by these two gentlemen. Coward's further comments make fascinating reading. He says that before accepting, he asked why the previous conductor was leaving. They replied that whilst Bowling was highly regarded as a gentleman and a musician, he had one serious fault which made a change desirable. Thinking of various possible unfortunate habits which Bowling might have, Coward asked what the fault was. 'He can't conduct and the interest of the members is declining' is how Coward records the reply, and is the reason, he writes, that he accepted immediately.

It is difficult to decide what to make of all this. According to available reports, Bowling had been an efficient, careful, and competent, if not a very inspiring, conductor. He had served ten years as such, training and conducting a group of over three hundred musicians and playing host at concerts to many eminent soloists — surely no mean achievement for one unable to conduct. In reporting Bowling's death the *Huddersfield Examiner* of

21 February 1903 suggested that his extreme modesty and 'lack of a gift of speech' prevented him from getting the best from the band and chorus, despite their high regard and respect for him and his musical abilities. The mastering of new works of a more exacting nature than hitherto attempted by the Society, said the report, made it necessary for the Committee, 'with deep regret', to dispense with his services.

Whatever the exact nature of the case, it had evidently been decided that new leadership was required if the choir was to be rendered capable of tackling demanding new works and improved sufficiently in performance to maintain public support. In this event the choice of Henry Coward could hardly have been bettered. His influence immediately made itself apparent. Many things were done straight away to comply with his particular wishes. Members were not merely asked, but instructed to buy copies of new works, Coward believing in home study from personally-owned copies. At that time copies borrowed from the Society were only exceptionally allowed to be taken away from rehearsals. Attendance and conduct at the latter, as well as questions of band rehearsals and the like, came under Coward's scrutiny. The Committee resolved on 25 April 1903 to include in a circular to be sent to members 'an exhortation against inattention, insubordination and misbehaviour and an appeal to members to assist the Committee in carrying out law and order at the meetings, with an intimation that any members not being disposed to fall in with the proper rules and regulations of the Society will be individually and summarily dealt with by the Committee'. This was powerful stuff of which the Society's founder-members would doubtless have approved.

A tightening of choir discipline with Coward's advent was to have been expected, for his own remarkable career was largely consequent upon his own self-discipline. On page 75 of his *Reminiscences* we read his advice to all young people wishing to excel, and often given to his choralists: 'learn everything twice as well as you think necessary and then you will have done about half of what you should have done'. Just before his ninth birthday in 1858, Coward was apprenticed to a cutler. He educated himself, particularly in music which he studied via the Tonic Sol-fa method, of which he became a notable exponent, and eventually took the Oxford B.Mus. and D.Mus. degrees. He taught, wrote, composed, and conducted his way to a position of high repute, particularly in the field of choral training and conducting, finally gaining a knighthood in 1926. Blessed with a robust physical constitution which afforded him a lifespan of almost ninety-five years, he achieved what he did by the conscious exercise of self-will and determination.

A man of considerable moral rectitude, and converted early on in life to the cause of temperance, Henry Coward might seem to have had a character less colourful than were some aspects of his career. Already in his fifties when he came to Huddersfield, that career was yet to reach its highest peaks. Nevertheless, his achievements in Sheffield as founder of the Tonic Sol-fa Association (later to become the Sheffield Musical Union) and his position as chorus master, under August Manns, of the Sheffield Triennial Festivals, begun in 1896, had already established for him a considerable reputation. Coward had himself conducted at a Sheffield Musical Festival in 1895, but after the 1896 Festival under Manns, the special correspondent of the *Musical Times* remarked on the astonishing volume of 'full, rich tone' from the Sheffield chorus 'trained with extraordinary care and skill by Dr Henry Coward, a local professor'. He had heard no better sopranos and basses anywhere, he declared, and only rarely the equals of the tenors and contraltos. The *Musical Times* offered even higher praise after the 1899 Festival and, following this, Coward became a national musical celebrity.

Henry Coward

Similar praise was soon to be heaped upon the Huddersfield chorus. Coleridge-Taylor was delighted with the *Hiawatha* performance in 1901 and was reported as saying that he had never heard such singing anywhere. The first *Messiah* concert under Coward was said to have put that of the Leeds Festival into the shade, and there was not a vacant seat in the house. Forgetting past confessions of failure to discover new superlatives to praise the Society's *Messiah* performances, the *Huddersfield Examiner* declared it to have been not simply *its* best performance but *the* best-ever, anywhere. An overdue education in voice production had, it said, eradicated past vocal deficiencies, particularly of the basses, to the surprise even of some of the old hands who had thought they knew it all.

The Society and its public were introduced to Edward Elgar's music in 1902 when his *Scenes from the Saga of King Olaf* was given along with

Parry's *Blest Pair of Sirens* to a large audience. Parry was also a novelty, his *Ode on St Cecilia's Day* not having been given as planned back in 1891. In 1903 came Parry's *Judith* which the composer was invited to conduct. In a letter to Coward he wrote that he would 'give anything to hear the Huddersfield people do *Judith* but it is absolutely impossible as I am due in Gloucestershire the same night . . . I hope the performance will go to your satisfaction. The analysis you send me is remarkably good. The critic must be a good musician indeed and has got to the inside of it most searchingly'. The critic referred to was that of the *Huddersfield Examiner*, most probably a Mr Thomas Cole, whose death was reported in 1913. Long, erudite, analytical accounts of new or unfamiliar works used to appear regularly in the paper the week before their performance. If original, they indicate how fortunate was the newspaper in having so able a writer of musical matters to call upon. Parry did come up to conduct the Society's next performance of *Judith*, in 1905, and afterwards wrote an appreciative letter to the Society.

Hiawatha was given again in 1903 with the celebrated British baritone, Charles Tree, making his first appearance at the Society's concerts. In October 1905, five years after its somewhat disastrous performance at the Birmingham Festival, Elgar's *The Dream of Gerontius* was performed by the Society along with Stanford's *Revenge* at its first concert of the season. Since Birmingham, *Gerontius* had enjoyed deserved success and recognition wherever it was performed and Huddersfield proved no exception. The Society waited only until March 1907 before performing it again. On that occasion the *Huddersfield Examiner* reported that it was given with 'even greater éclat, intelligence, power and impressiveness than on the first occasion'. All credit was due, it said, to Dr Coward.

The Society's first-ever essay at Bach came in 1906 with his *B Minor Mass*, the first performance of this work in the district. The hall was full but some folk left at the interval, not to return. Others left early but not, evidently, due to a bad performance which, on the contrary, was highly praised. Perhaps some subscribers, being unused to Bach, found less than a full programme's worth quite enough. Coward tells us that the principal bassoon player of the London Symphony Orchestra was so impressed with the Huddersfield chorus in its 1907 *Gerontius* concert that, on his recommendation, the Society was invited to provide a choir to sing the *B Minor Mass* with the London Symphony Orchestra in the Queen's Hall on 16 December that year. Since the terms offered were good — £125 fee, and tea for a choir of 250 at the Queen's Hall — the Choral Society Committee made little hesitation in accepting. There was no shortage of candidates for selection of the chorus which travelled in a special train arranged to leave Huddersfield at 9.00 a.m. on Monday, 16 December and to return from King's Cross at midnight. John Watkinson (of the Huddersfield Subscription Concerts), President of the Society in 1907, quickly raised more than enough money by public appeal for a guarantee fund to pay for a hot luncheon for the choir on the outward journey and a hot supper on the return journey aboard the train, which arrived home at 4.30 a.m. on the Tuesday morning. The conductor at the concert was Hans Richter, who had come up especially to take a rehearsal in the High Street School Room beforehand. In a letter written to the choir after the concert he sent his kind regards and thanks for a 'clean and correct performance'.

The work had never been better heard in London, according to some newspaper reports, which mostly praised both choir and its chorus master, but *The Times*, whilst allowing that the choir sang 'accurately enough' observed that there was a 'higher ideal than this'. Richter's beat was blamed for some deficiencies, and indeed, Coward reports his own lack of regard for Richter's choral conducting. In response to complaints from correspondents, *The Times* admitted that its critic left shortly after the first chorus but added that he had left a substitute behind.

The Messiah that December was put on without a choir rehearsal as a result of all this exciting activity but evidently the performance suffered not at all. In the previous October Elgar's *The Kingdom* had been given, one week after its performance at the Leeds Festival. Completed in 1906, this work was the second of what was to prove an unfinished trilogy, the first being *The Apostles* which first appeared in 1903 but which was not performed by the Society until 1927. The Huddersfield choir was said to have at least equalled the Leeds chorus in the performance of *The Kingdom* in 1907 and in some respects bettered it. The Society did not perform this work again until 1948 and gave its third performance as recently as April 1984 in the year marking the fiftieth anniversary of Elgar's death. A memorable performance it was too.

Since the turn of the century not only had the nation lost its Queen but Yorkshire had lost its Queen of Song, for Mrs Sunderland died in 1905 at the ripe age of 86. The early years of the century also saw the passing, in 1902, of William Fitton, Edward Battye's successor as the choir Secretary, and, in 1903, of two long-serving members and former presidents, John J. Grist and William Harrop. In 1907 the President, John Shaw, died in office and was incorrectly described by John Watkinson, the President-elect, as the first president to do so. In fact, as noted earlier, the choir's first-ever president,

J. C. Fenton, died in office in 1858. For many years William Fitton used to select singers from Huddersfield to join the choir at the Crystal Palace Handel Festivals and, in 1903, a special sub-committee was set up to perform this task. That year, those selected joined either Coward's Sheffield contingent or one from Bradford. Of a total of fifty joining with Sheffield, only ten were listed as amateurs — the rest received a fee!

A consciousness, by some at least, of the Society's history and the desirability of preserving material records of its past, seems for the first time to be in evidence during the early years of the new century. At the General Meeting in 1907, John Watkinson, after referring to John Shaw's death, went on to relate his recollections of past days, recalling that he received piano lessons from Henry Horn and that he attended his funeral at St Paul's Church. Then, at the Annual Meeting in 1909 Mr E. Brearley of the Musical Committee suggested making a collection if possible of all past concert programmes since 1836 so that the Society's history might not be lost to posterity. The following year Brearley raised the matter again and John Eagleton said that he had a record of all past works performed by the Society but Brearley's suggestion that this should be published received no support at that time, it being considered too costly. Such an economic consideration seemed to upset Brearley who was told by Eagleton 'we are businessmen first'. What a boon it might have been to the task of compiling this history if immediate action had been taken following Brearley's suggestion.

The membership of the Society at this time comprised about twenty-six instrumentalists, more than one hundred soprano singers, about eighty contraltos and altos, sixty tenors and seventy basses. The Society was becoming more renowned but it could not boast of being Yorkshire's premier choral society. This distinction would undoubtedly have been reserved for Coward's Sheffield Musical Union, or at least, for a chorus composed largely of singers from that choir together with some from Leeds, Huddersfield, and elsewhere, which was *described* as Coward's Sheffield choir. It was such a choir which visited Germany in September 1906, singing with sensational success in Cologne and Frankfurt, and again in 1910, giving concerts at Aix-la-Chapelle, Düsseldorf, Essen, Leipzig, and Dresden. In October 1908 Coward took a choir to Canada, consisting of two hundred singers including seventeen from Huddersfield, where they gave concerts in Quebec and Montreal.

Before his departure for Canada, Coward wrote to Eagleton wishing all success for the first concert of the season and expressing great confidence in 'our greatly esteemed and loyal friend Mr Ibeson' who was to conduct

Rossini's *Stabat Mater* and Spohr's *Last Judgement* at the concert in Coward's absence. For its part, the *Huddersfield Examiner*, though in general appreciative of the concert, referred to these works as 'antediluvian'. For several years it had joined forces with a fairly widespread call for societies to perform a greater number of contemporary works. Only in the case of *The Messiah* did it not dare criticize on grounds of antiquity. Not that everybody shared such scruples, for at the 1909 Annual Meeting, the first, incidentally, to end with refreshments and a musical entertainment provided by the members, somebody suggested that *The Messiah* be given a rest for a season. Brearley, the history enthusiast, suggested Bach's *Christmas Oratorio* for a change but Coward, for one, opposed this, deploring any belittling of Handel. Eagleton said any change would prove disastrous — by which he meant financially disastrous, which cannot have gone down too well with Brearley. The proposition was turned down flat!

All the same, contemporary works did get a hearing. On 30 October 1909 Walford Davies came to conduct his own *Everyman*. This work was first performed in Leeds in 1904, and frequently thereafter for some years, often under the baton of the composer. He wrote to Ibeson after the Huddersfield performance saying that he 'thought the choir inspired' and thanking the choir for its kindness and its 'beautiful sostenuto on Friday'. At the October concert in 1910 Parry conducted his *King Saul* to a less than full house, and in March 1912 the Society performed Brahms's *Requiem* for the first time. Despite hopes expressed in the *Huddersfield Examiner* that this work would become part of the repertoire, the Society did not perform it again until 1969.

Sullivan's *Martyr of Antioch* was given in March 1911, and as a token of respect to Ben Stocks, whose death had just been announced, choir and audience (though not the band) stood during the singing of the unaccompanied chorus, 'Brother Thou Art Gone Before Us'. The second part of the concert consisted of Bach's eight-part motet *Sing Ye to the Lord* and other works which the choir was to sing the following June at the International Musical Congress in London. This, the fourth of its kind — previous ones having been held in Leipzig (1904), Basle (1906) and Vienna (1909) — was described by Scholes in his *Mirror of Music* as 'an amazing affair'. To be selected to represent English choral music was undoubtedly a great honour for the Society but, to be sure, the Sheffield choir could not have done it since the majority of that choir were off on a world tour with Coward who had to ask W. G. McNaught to conduct the Huddersfield choir in London in his stead. In the event, all the hard work of preparation of the unaccompanied pieces was well rewarded, for the Society's performance at the Queen's Hall on 1 June 1911 was a great success. There was some criticism in the press, however, that the concert included no pieces by a contemporary composer except for Sullivan's *O Gladsome Light* which was described in *The Times* as an 'insipid' piece.

Coward's world tour could also be described as an amazing affair. It included concerts in the U.S.A., Canada, Hawaii, Fiji, Australia, Tasmania, New Zealand, and South Africa given by a choir of two hundred Yorkshire singers on a trip which began in March 1911 and ended in the September of that year. Coward gives some account of it in his *Reminiscences* and, for sure, there can have been nothing quite like it either before or since. Some Huddersfield Society members went but essentially it was Sheffield's affair, the Musical Union's 'crowning achievement', as E. D. Mackerness calls it in his book *The History of Music in Sheffield*. Although the tour was organized and financially guaranteed by a Dr Charles Harris, originally from London but who had emigrated by that time to Canada and married to the wealthy widow of an iron magnate, it was no easy ride for the participants. They were required, Coward tells us, to learn one hundred and fifty pieces by heart, to attend one hundred sectional and combined rehearsals, practise at least thirty minutes each day and be *prepared to be away from England for twenty-six weeks*. We may note that when, in May 1914, Huddersfield Choral Society received an invitation to send a chorus of two hundred and twenty to London for a week to sing all the choral music at a Beethoven Festival proposed for April 1915, it was turned down partly due to the inadequacy of the amount offered in payment, but significantly because not enough members were able to spare the necessary time or to bear the sacrifice of wages.

Continuing the policy of performing new works, the Society performed Coleridge-Taylor's *Tale of Old Japan* in November 1912, the year following its first performance in its final form by the London Choral Society at the Queen's Hall, when it was hailed as the composer's greatest success since *Hiawatha*. Coleridge-Taylor himself was to have conducted his work in Huddersfield but due to his untimely death at the age of thirty-seven in September 1912, this was not to be. The following year, along with a second performance of Elgar's *King Olaf*, the Society gave Bantock's *Christ in the Wilderness*, a work first heard at the Gloucester Festival of 1907. Opinion regarding the Huddersfield performance was divided but the *Huddersfield Examiner* reported it as having been done 'quite splendidly'. The orchestra was criticized for faults attributed to lack of sufficient rehearsal, but the chorus 'one had never heard steadier', commented the report.

It would seem that in the period just preceding the outbreak of the Great War in 1914 the Society's performances were of better quality than had ever before been known. Coward's teaching methods may have been largely responsible for this, but it would be a mistake to imagine that all was sweet accord between chorus and chorus master. In 1913, the Committee, having had its attention drawn to the matter of attendance and behaviour at rehearsals, resolved to send a circular to members reminding them, among other things, of the numerous applicants for admission to the choir. The rule book of 1909 specifies a fifty per cent rehearsal attendance as necessary to qualify for a ticket to 'the orchestra' at concerts unless by consent of the conductor. It seems clear that there was a growing dissatisfaction with the amount of interruption on Coward's part to the actual singing at rehearsals. Presumably his zeal to impart knowledge and appreciation of the vocal art and of artistic interpretation, etc., annoyed those who traditionally came along on a Friday evening to enjoy a 'good sing'. In May 1914 senior officers of the choir sent Coward a letter pointing out to him the members' disaffection at having insufficient opportunity actually to sing during the one-and-a-half hours of rehearsal time (it had not yet been extended to two hours) and suggesting this as a reason for poor attendance, late arrival, and early departure at rehearsals. This may have influenced Coward's rehearsal technique for a while but it is unlikely that he would have let it disturb him very much. When the war began people fell into line a little more but in early 1919, with the war only just at an end, several members wrote to the Secretary complaining of the 'waste of time' at rehearsals and suggested that Major Walford Davies (who had conducted his own work *Everyman* for the second time in Huddersfield at the October concert in 1918) should be appointed conductor. Needless to say, the malcontents did not win the day and Coward stayed on for many a year to come.

Before the war the Society had sought not only to maintain an excellent standard but also a universal recognition of excellence. This meant singing at important concerts in London and elsewhere. Invitations could only come, it was argued, by learning and performing demanding works and by keeping abreast of the times musically. Not that the terms of such invitations were necessarily always likely to be acceptable and, unfortunately, their acceptance often turned out to be too expensive. This, of course, has a familiar ring to it but there were other problems. At the Annual Meeting in May 1914 the President, Mr E. J. Bruce, commented on a countrywide demand and fashion for lighter amusement than that which the Society was wont to offer. John Watkinson's Huddersfield Subscription Concerts had come to an end through lack of support, and the adverse balance shown on the Choral Society's financial statement was attributed by the President to a general decline in public interest, but any suggestion of raising subscriptions was ruled out as being too risky.

All this notwithstanding, it was decided that Verdi's *Requiem*, an expensive work to put on, should be given at the first concert of the following season in October 1914. It was hoped that this would provide a large influx of subscribers and relieve the ailing financial situation of the Society. The outbreak of war on 4 August 1914 delayed this performance for twelve months.

The immediate affect of the outbreak of hostilities on the musical world in Britain seems to have been that of a sharp, but short-lived, shock. Initially there was much gloom that financial restrictions, coupled with a feeling of the inappropriate, almost immoral, nature of musical entertainment in the circumstances, would inhibit further activity. Preparations for several of the great musical festivals were abandoned, despite some opposition to this course, and for its part, the Society cancelled the Verdi *Requiem* concert. Prospects were declared to be very bad, many subscribers having written requesting their names to be crossed off the list for the forthcoming season. It was decided to perform only *The Messiah* and Handel's *Israel in Egypt* during the 1914–15 season, the first time ever in the Society's history when it gave only two concerts in one season. A portion of the profits of these concerts went to various war relief funds, as did those from all the subsequent wartime concerts, but despite this, at the end of the season there was an increased balance at the bank due very largely to the fact that conductor, organist, accompanist, and solo artists had, to quote the press reports, 'voluntarily accepted reduced fees'.

The Verdi *Requiem*, all of forty years old, finally had its first performance in Huddersfield when the Society gave it, together with Sullivan's *In Memoriam*, at the concert held on 29 October 1915. The same soloists who had been booked for its proposed performance the previous year appeared, namely Carrie Tubb, Elsa Illingworth, Frank Mullings, and Robert Radford. Costa's setting of the National Anthem was sung, not for the first time, eliciting complaint, also not for the first time, from the *Huddersfield Examiner* critic who nevertheless praised the concert well enough. He would have preferred Elgar's setting of the National Anthem but was pleased that the *Requiem* had been sung in Latin rather than in the available, but 'unsuitable' English translation. He observed that one more foreign masterpiece had been added to the Society's performance achievements but — never to be satisfied apparently — that one might hope now that the Society would find time 'to reckon more fully with modern British composers'. The financial loss of the concert was £37, fortunately offset by a profit of £90 at the next *Messiah* concert and of £9 at the *Hiawatha* concert the following March.

The male section of the choir was somewhat depleted during the war period and lacking in youth but, it seems, managed to retain its tone largely unimpaired. Surprisingly, not many of the men seem to have been killed on active service, a fate which did, however, befall Coward's son. A vote of sympathy for the conductor was passed by the Committee in May 1917, only a few months after one of congratulations on the marriage of his daughter. But the Society sustained losses other than those due to the war. William Dawson, Assistant Secretary since 1878, died in April 1915, his place being taken by Percy Beaumont who was to serve the Society well for many years. Mr C. J. Binns, the Treasurer since 1891, died in the November, being replaced by T. H. Fitton, whilst in 1918 John Eagleton died only shortly after retiring as Secretary after forty-five years of service in that office. By this time John Watkinson had retired, as had also J. Edgar Ibeson, Organist and Deputy Conductor for thirty years and a local musician much admired and widely acclaimed for his musical abilities. One time conductor of the Glee and Madrigal Society, the Philharmonic Society, and the Holmfirth Choral Society, among many other musical activities, he died in 1920 aged fifty-eight. He was replaced in 1915 by Ernest Cooper, previously the Society's Accompanist.

Despite difficulties and adversities including a falling subscription list, a Government tax on entertainment and restricted train services and street lighting, the Society survived the war years largely unscarred. Indeed, by the end of the war the financial position had improved considerably due in part to the efforts of a special Ladies' Committee, set up to improve the subscription list situation, and to the successful 1917–18 concert season which included a performance of Elgar's *The Dream of Gerontius* conducted on this occasion by Sir Edward Elgar himself. At this concert, at which Elgar's *For the Fallen* and *To Women* were also sung, the soprano, Miss Olga Haley, granddaughter of Joshua Marshall, made her Huddersfield debut. Although just recovering from laryngitis, Gervase Elwes sang the part of Gerontius, and Robert Charlesworth sang the Priest and the Angel of Agony. Elgar wrote afterwards to say that the performance ranked among the best he had ever heard. He thanked the Society for its 'wonderful singing' and said he was glad to have had such a pleasant opportunity to become acquainted with the 'splendid society' of which he had 'always heard so much well-deserved praise'.

The Ladies' Committee, though a child of the economic circumstances of the time, also reflected the changing position of women in the community. It is well known that the war brought women to the forefront of the working life of the nation and indeed, before the war, the suffragette movement had made its mark. There had even been a lady member — the first ever — on the Society's Musical Committee since 1911, but *only* one. This was Madam England, who came up for re-election, according to the rules, every three years, and was re-elected on each occasion until 1929 by which time she had been joined, first by Mrs Irving Kay, in 1923, and then by Madam Lottie Beaumont in 1928. The last-named lady, at a few hours' notice, took on the contralto part in Sullivan's *Golden Legend* in October 1916 when the professional soloist, Dorothy Webster, was indisposed, and by all accounts acquitted herself well. Although there have always been, since that time, lady members serving on the Committee, only in very recent years have ladies held any higher position in the running of the Society.

The season which saw the signing of the Armistice began with the concert at which Walford Davies conducted his own work *Everyman*. Also at this concert Bach's *Sing Ye to the Lord* was sung, and, in memory of John Eagleton, Sullivan's *In Memoriam* was played. In the *Messiah* performance that season at which Lottie Beaumont was entrusted with the contralto part, some items were given added poignancy due to the prevailing mood of relief and thanksgiving that the war was over. The season ended with Rossini's *Stabat Mater* and Mendelssohn's *Hymn of Praise* at which concert Olga Haley again appeared as one of the soloists. These works met with some press criticisms, if not for being in the nature of 'confectionery', then simply just for being 'old'.

A Grand Victory Concert was held in July 1919 when the Philharmonic Society, and the Choral Society joined forces at the latter's invitation to give a concert of miscellaneous music. Coward conducted the choral works, the instrumental items being conducted by Frederick Dawson, conductor of the Philharmonic which, like the Glee and Madrigal Society, had managed to survive the Great War intact. Appropriate items by Elgar, Sullivan, Walford Davies and, that Englishman by adoption, Handel, were performed to everybody's satisfaction. The soprano soloist, Miss Madeline Collins, a north-country favourite of the time, received an ovation for each of her items.

Thursday, 26 November 1919 was Henry Coward's seventieth birthday. Born in Liverpool at the Shakespeare Hotel, Williamson Square, where his father was responsible for running the concert hall, Coward, in 1919, despite his years, was still extraordinarily active, serving as conductor, among other activities, of Hull, Derby, Leeds, and Sheffield Choral Societies in addition to that of Huddersfield. The latter sent him a congratulatory letter on his birthday but waited until the final concert of the season in February 1920 to give him a present. The choir was heard at its best at this concert, reported the *Yorkshire Post*, in a performance of Sullivan's *Martyr of Antioch* and Parry's *Blest Pair of Sirens*. After receiving a pair of bronzes, a water colour, and a cheque for £75, Coward spoke of his pride in the Society and expressed his determination not to stay to become 'a good old has-been'. He promised to go as soon as he ceased 'to inspire, to arouse, to stir, to go forward' although it was not clear who was to be the judge in this matter. When the time came to celebrate his eightieth birthday he was still with the choir, by this time having received his knighthood, which was celebrated by a party at High Street School on 27 August 1926.

The decade following the war and between these two birthdays was a time of rapid change in technological development, fashions, and behaviour. It was a time also of economic depression, but the Choral Society weathered the storms well, enjoying a buoyant financial situation which was without precedent. In 1923 the subscription list accounted for £1,065, the highest-ever to date, and not to be exceeded in the ensuing decade, whilst more people applied for tickets than ever before. The *Yorkshire Post* in 1926 referred to the Society as 'the only one of its kind which has the undivided support of the townspeople and so flourishes exceedingly'. In 1930 the President of the Halifax Choral Society referred to the Huddersfield Choral Society as the only really strong choral society outside London. Large profits for those days of up to £100 or more from *Messiah* concerts offset losses from many other concerts and despite the beginnings of a decline in choralism and the attractions of cinema, wireless, and gramophone, the Society continued to prosper both financially and musically. The Society was not itself involved in recording and broadcasting until the end of the decade, but the music it performed at its concerts reflects to some extent the changing musical mood of the times.

Granville Bantock's *Omar Khayyam* was performed in November 1920, with the composer himself conducting the Hallé Orchestra and with soloists Olga Haley and Frank Mullings. The concert lost £118 which was exactly the amount of the loss when it was performed again, also with the Hallé and with the same soloists, but under Coward's baton, in 1924. Wilmshurst, who had provided a translation of the *Stabat Mater* for inclusion in the concert programme in February 1919, gave a lecture on *Omar Khayyam* in September 1920 for the benefit and enlightenment of the members of the Society.

Although a very active committee member and ex-president of the Society, he was no performing musician, instrumental or vocal, but seems to have served the Society well as its scribe and scholar. In 1923 he wrote a note on Holst's *Hymn of Jesus* for the programme of the March concert that year when the work was performed together with Mendelssohn's *Hymn of Praise* making what the *Huddersfield Examiner* described as 'a pair of incompatible partners'. The *Hymn of Jesus* was sung twice at the concert, Coward saying a few words regarding the work to the audience prior to its first run-through. This, it must be said, was not his own idea for it had been done at its first production by the London Philharmonic Choir in June 1920. It was a 'difficult' work and there's nothing so good as a bit of audience enlightenment!

March 1921 saw the so-called three-hundredth celebration concert of the Society. It was a miscellaneous concert featuring Agnes Nicholls and John Coates as soloists, and made a profit of £44 but its reckoning as the three-hundredth concert resulted from blunders referred to earlier. Even the account given in an historical summary provided in the printed programme requires only elementary arithmetical investigation to discover the existence of error. Nevertheless the musical programme, designed to be representative of oratorio music performed by the Society in its eighty-five years of existence, was enjoyed well enough it seems, by performers and audience alike. Following this there was a run of what one might call 'opera seasons' with *Samson and Delilah* in 1921, *Aida* in 1922 and *Tannhäuser* in 1923; each being presented at the first concert of the season. They all lost money, but the *Messiah* concert came to the rescue each time. The Saint-Saëns performance was made economically possible by being put on, with Coward conducting, in the same week, with the same soloists, in both Sheffield and Hull, and certainly the Wagner had also recently been done in Hull. The choruses in *Tannhäuser* were reported by the *Huddersfield Examiner* to have 'never been better sung' but a general complaint concerned the paucity of chorus work in the operas for such a fine choir. Minor principal parts were taken by members of the Society who were paid two or three guineas each for their efforts. *Samson and Delilah* was repeated in 1930 and *Aida* in 1927. *Faust*, by Berlioz, was performed in 1926 and again in 1931, but of course this was not new ground in the field of opera for the Society.

In 1926 Ralph Vaughan-Williams came up to conduct his *Sea Symphony* in a concert which also included the first performance by the Society of Dvořák's *Stabat Mater*. The Hallé Orchestra was engaged and the soloists were Elsie Suddaby, Margaret Balfour, Walter Hyde, and Horace Stevens. Coward —

The Choir in Holland, 1928

now Sir Henry — conducted the Dvořák and at this concert he and his wife received presentations from the Society to mark both his knighthood and twenty-five years of service with the choir. Vaughan-Williams, who received ten guineas from the Society as an honorarium, was one of many eminent musicians whose opinion was solicited regarding the pitch of the Town Hall organ. Among these were Sir Edward Elgar, Sir Henry Wood, Dr Malcolm Sargent, Sir Walford Davies, and Sir Landon Ronald who were of one firm opinion; the pitch should be lowered. By 1929 we learn that the matter had been dealt with, for at the Annual Meeting that year tribute was paid to Samuel Firth, President from 1926 to 1928 who had recently died, for the part he had played in the business of getting the pitch of the organ lowered.

In 1927 the Society was for the first time involved in a gramophone recording which, oddly enough, was the occasion of some resentment rather than pleasure. Coward had evidently arranged with *Columbia Records* for a recording to take place without the sanction of the Committee but, amid declarations that the rehearsals for Elgar's *The Apostles* must not be allowed to suffer as a result, the Committee decided that despite 'insufficient time, the Society would do the best it could'. Evidently the performance of *The*

Apostles did not suffer unduly. Following the concert the *Huddersfield Examiner* critic wrote that it was a pity that the work was only heard once, since it could 'reveal but a portion of its riches at first hearing'. It was a long time before the Society offered the public a second hearing, for it was 1967 before they sang it again.

A somewhat more noteworthy event in 1927 was the invitation received in August from the Netherlands England Society in The Hague for the Huddersfield Society to take part in two concerts in Holland the following year. The decision to accept was made, finally, in January 1928 and on Easter Monday, 9 April 1928 a choir of two hundred singers left Harwich in the S.S. *St Denis* bound for the Hook of Holland. They returned on Friday, 13 April after an extremely successful visit during which they sang at the Concertgebouw in Amsterdam on the Tuesday and in The Hague on the Wednesday. The Thursday was spent in sightseeing. In Amsterdam they sang *Israel in Egypt* and gave the first performance in the city of *The Dream of Gerontius*. Coward conducted the Residentie Orchestra which had never before played Elgar's music. The concert proved to be an enormous success. This was significant because at that time many continental countries, including Holland, still regarded England as a musical backwater. The following day the press quoted the president of the Netherlands England Society, Dr Jansma, as saying that there was a superstition in Holland, as elsewhere on the continent, that whereas the English might excel in many branches of life and in all kinds of sports — 'we have all heard about "Huddersfield Town"', he said — in music they were very much behind. 'We now know' he added, 'that this is not so and that in choral singing you are behind no country in the world.'

The Hague concert did not go quite so well and there were empty seats in spite of the presence of the Dutch Queen Mother (Emma), Princess Juliana, and several high-ranking political figures. This did not lessen the praise for the performance which comprised Holst's *Hymn of Jesus*, a repetition of part of *The Dream of Gerontius* and a particularly well-appreciated Handel selection including the 'Hallelujah Chorus' from *The Messiah*. The *Hymn of Jesus* was also new to Holland, a fact which scarcely excuses the Dutch press from attributing the text of the work to W. L. Wilmshurst; scribe and scholar he may have been, but certainly not the author of an apocryphal text! As an encore at the concert in The Hague, and at every possible excuse during the trip thereafter, the choir sang Sullivan's 'O Gladsome Light' from *The Golden Legend*, a work which they had given at the March concert at home a month or so before leaving for Holland. Sydney Crowther — by this time (as *Playfellow*) writing the musical criticisms for the *Huddersfield Examiner* —

recalls memories of the trip to Holland in his updating of the Wilmshurst history brochure of the Society, produced in 1961, on the occasion of its 125th anniversary. 'I think it must have been on this tour' he wrote, 'that "O Gladsome Light" became the Society's special anthem'. Evidently it was sung on many occasions, impromptu or formally, either as a kind of extra-mural duty or simply when the choir wished to let its hair down.

The limit set on the number of voices in the choir which went to Holland was, not unnaturally, the cause of some embarrassment. Apparently nobody outside Committee circles, and perhaps not all within, understood upon what basis the selection of the members of this choir was made. The evidence was against any criterion based on attendance record at rehearsals and there seems to have been a little bitter feeling on the part of some members. Nevertheless, at the Annual Meeting in 1928 a resolution that no performance be considered unless it allowed for the possibility of the participation of the entire membership, was defeated by 204 votes to 28. Those who did go to Holland had to contribute £3 per head towards expenses (no trifling amount in 1928) but it seems that the whole thing made no call whatever on the Society's funds.

The 1929 season of concerts opened with Beethoven's *Mass in D*, the first but by no means the last performance by the Society of this most demanding work. Universally applauded by the critics, it suffered only from the fault of lack of orchestral rehearsal. Indeed, at one point there was a breakdown due to a misunderstanding. A contingent of the choir, some sixty-five singers, went to the new BBC Manchester studios in May the following year to broadcast this work with the Northern Wireless Orchestra. Coward conducted, and his eighty years proved no handicap. He was even talking about a possible trip to Vienna, with the choir joining forces with his Sheffield and Derby Societies, but this came to nothing, the Society apparently disapproving of the choice of music they would be expected to perform. The first of many broadcasts by the Society came later, in 1930, when it performed Handel's *Solomon* and the Berlioz *Te Deum* at its first concert of the season. Isobel Baillie was soloist at this concert as she had been at the performance of the Beethoven *Mass in D* both in Huddersfield and Manchester. Her first appearance with the Society had been in 1927 as 'Bella Baillie' in the *Messiah* concert. The choice of *Solomon*, arranged, incidentally, by Beecham, resulted no doubt from an interest in reviving Handel's lesser known works at about that time. Very many years had passed since the Society had sung *Solomon*. It gave a selection from the work back in 1847 and maybe, though by no means certainly, in 1861, but no evidence has come to light of a later performance until 1930.

Mention of Beecham gives occasion to note that he came to listen to the *Messiah* performance in 1928 and was reported as saying that he enjoyed the experience, describing the choir as a very fine example of the vocally rich Yorkshire choirs. This notwithstanding, he made no response whatever later to an invitation to conduct the Society at the final concert of the 1930–31 season. Hamilton Harty had also been invited and he did respond, saying that it would afford him 'much pleasure to collaborate with your chorus whose reputation is not unknown to me, and because they are so good'. After waiting more than two months with no reply from Beecham the Society engaged Harty to conduct in the Spring of 1931 when the Hallé Orchestra was again engaged for a concert of music by Bach, Delius, and Wagner. Evidently favourably impressed, Harty invited the choir to sing Bach's *B Minor Mass* at the Queen's Hall in December 1931 at a concert which was to be granted Royal patronage. This invitation was accepted and arrangements for the visit were made accordingly, but in September Hamilton Harty wrote to say that he was compelled to cancel the arrangement. Concert promotion was not sheltered from the effects of the economic depression.

By December 1930 it was known that Coward was intending to retire. That month he wrote a letter expressing his intention to go at the end of the 1931–32 season after serving for thirty years. He did not wish, he said, 'to linger superfluous on the stage' and had asked people to 'tell him about it if he is getting past it'. He requested to make his own choice of programme for his final season, and this could hardly have been denied him. It began with *Faust* on 6 November 1931 and ended in February 1932 with a concert including *Hiawatha's Wedding Feast*, *Blest Pair of Sirens*, and *Hymn of Praise* with Isobel Baillie and Heddle Nash as soloists. As early as March 1928 there had been a proposal to set up a sub-committee to consider the question of a new conductor but there is nothing to suggest that anyone had told him he was 'getting past it' and it seems that the decision to retire was his own. When his intention to retire became known, another sub-committee was set up to consider his successor, the final choice of which was undoubtedly influenced by reports from those members who had sung at the Leeds Festival in 1931 where the young Dr Malcolm Sargent had conducted Walton's *Belshazzar's Feast* and Bach's *Mass in B minor*.

Sargent was approached regarding taking the conductorship for the 1933–34 season and by February 1932 the matter was settled. He was to receive fifty guineas per concert, including a rehearsal in the afternoon of the concert, and five guineas for each of two rehearsals for every concert or for any extra rehearsal. Herbert Bardgett, accompanist of the Leeds Festival

Chorus and conductor of the New Leeds Choral Society, was to be appointed as Chorus Master and Ernest Cooper was to be Accompanist and Deputy Chorus Master.

Meanwhile, a testimonial fund was raised which, by February 1932, had reached nearly £200, to acquire a photographic portrait of Sir Henry, the balance to go to the founding of a Sir Henry Coward Musicians Fund to help rising young musicians in their studies.

The last of the Society's concerts conducted by Coward, part of which was broadcast by the Northern Region Station of the BBC, was memorable not only for the music but also for the presentation and speeches. Coward was presented with his portrait (which was to be hung in the Huddersfield Music Library) and with the testimonial concerning the Musicians Fund. His own assessment of the Society which he had served well for thirty years was made clear when he said 'this choir is second to none in England, second to none in the whole world. You have a thousand pounds in the hands of your treasurer, a subscription list that is the envy of all other societies in the land and above all you have your singers'.

To the extent that this was true, much of the credit was surely due to Coward himself. He was known for urging the choir to put aside what he called 'inertia' and had many well-tried methods for getting good diction from them and making them sing pianissimo so that 'you could hear the clock ticking'. Those who had been in the choir during the thirty years of his conductorship would have had many memories and tales to tell of him and of the Society. Some there are still today who can tell a few of those tales from personal recollection. In 1932, however, many of the older members had chosen the occasion of the coming of a new, young, conductor to retire themselves, but there was no shortage of equally new and young applicants for membership. In the *Daily Express* of 9 May 1932 a Committee member was reported as having said, 'Huddersfield is one of the few towns in the north where the coming of the talkies has not had an appreciable effect on the expression of enjoyment of beautiful music, and for every member of the Choral Society we can count on the loyalty of ten supporters'.

Some of this sentiment was expressed at the Annual General Meeting of the previous Friday evening when new rules were presented. These included the requirement of members to pay an annual subscription of seven shillings and sixpence to cover costs of the new appointments. One member, in supporting the increase, said he enjoyed coming to rehearsals more than going to the pictures. Looked at in that light, he remarked, seven-and-six a year was cheap.

CHAPTER EIGHT

Honour and Glory

JUST AS there could have been no better choice of conductor than Henry Coward in 1901, so there could have been none better than Malcolm Sargent in 1932. Sargent's biographer, Charles Reid, says Thomas Beecham was reported to have declared Sargent as 'the greatest chorus master we have ever produced'. Be that as it may, since the turn of the century the Huddersfield Choral Society enjoyed the privilege of association with two of the most eminent choral conductors of all time. Coward's pre-eminence as a chorus master had been universally acclaimed and there is no doubt that Sargent had a genius for handling choirs.

Though both were of firm Christian faith and staunchly patriotic, how different these two men were! Sargent, in addition to being an accomplished man of music and a masterful conductor, was something of a showman —and happy to admit to it. He enjoyed putting on the style. Possessed of great personal charm, he liked company, particularly that of women, who in great numbers, it may be said, adored him. He was meticulous regarding his appearance, loved going to parties and liked champagne. Above all, in 1932, he was, compared with Coward, relatively young, a mere thirty-seven.

He seemed to have boundless energy. That this was not limitless, however, was to become apparent soon after his appointment as the Society's conductor. For a period he had been consuming his energy in circumstances of serious physical affliction, the nature of which was discovered only just in time to save him. He was forced to stop early in 1933 when, in addition to many other plans, he was all set to go to Australia later that year to inaugurate a new symphony orchestra. It was more than three years before he finally made the trip. Like a stone dropped in a pool of water Sargent's illness sent a disturbance over a wide circle in the world of music, for his commitments were many and varied. Though still 'up and coming', he had already achieved enough to satisfy the ambitions of many a normal mortal. His career blossomed, as Reid says, 'at a pace and on levels which cannot be readily paralleled in his profession'.

Clearly such a busy man could not afford time to come up to Huddersfield for weekly rehearsals. He had reduced his rehearsal commitment to the

Bradford Festival Choral Society from three to one per concert shortly after becoming its conductor in 1925. With Huddersfield, as we have seen, the commitment was initially for more rehearsal time than this, but the majority of the preparation was to be the responsibility of Herbert Bardgett, organist and choirmaster at St Bartholomew's Church, Armley, Leeds. Previously choirmaster at St Mary's Cathedral, Glasgow, and lecturer on music for the Leeds Education Authority, Bardgett had also taken part in BBC schools' broadcasts on music. Both he and Sargent proved to be immensely popular with the members of the Society from the outset and their association with it was to prove a lasting one, though not in Bardgett's case, always an easy one.

As with the Bradford Society in 1925, the first work Sargent conducted in Huddersfield was Bach's *Mass in B minor* on 4 November 1932 and broadcast, like many which followed it, by the BBC. As has been mentioned previously, he had conducted this along with *Belshazzar's Feast* at the Leeds Festival the previous year. When the second of these two works was performed by the Society at the end of the 1932–33 season Sargent was already ill and Bardgett had to conduct it. Bardgett had also conducted the Christmas Hymn at the opening of the *Messiah* concert in December 1932, a practice which was to continue in future years. Sargent had refused to conduct 'that jingle', reports Hilda Wilmshurst in a letter she wrote in 1982 to Donald Haywood, the Society's President. It was, she reported 'firmly pointed out to him that this meant Christmas to Huddersfield [and] he was expected to do what Huddersfield wished'. Her father, she goes on, suggested that Bardgett should get some recognition for all his work, so why not let him conduct *Christians Awake*? 'So', she says, 'it was settled.' Sargent was not without his prejudices, and whatever the time-hallowed traditions might be in Huddersfield, he was having nothing to do with this one. I am told that he never did conduct the Christmas Hymn.

Sargent's first two concerts were received with considerable approval although his idiosyncracies in the matter of tempi did not pass without comment in the *Huddersfield Examiner*. His debut, the Bach concert, earned him virtually unqualified praise; the orchestra also won approving comment. Perhaps its members were just paying their respects, in the best way they knew, to one of their recently-deceased colleagues, the violinist, Harry Cotton. The choir sang 'Cast Thy Burden Upon the Lord' in his memory. Well-loved locally, he had been the Choral Society's Treasurer and Orchestral Secretary for some years, a member of its committee and one-time Vice-President of the Huddersfield Philharmonic Society.

The Society gave a second performance of *The Messiah* that year. This was in Manchester's Free Trade Hall on Christmas Eve, with Sargent conducting the Society's own orchestra. The principals were Lilian Stiles-Allen, Astra Desmond, Frank Mullings, and Thorpe Bates. The audience was small, but it was, after all, the fourth *Messiah* concert in Manchester in eight days and the third in three! Nevertheless the performance was a great success, as it was again the following year with Hamilton Harty conducting the Hallé Orchestra on that occasion.

In April 1933 Sargent underwent an operation for the treatment of abdominal tuberculosis. He was not expected to live. It was over eighteen months before he conducted again, returning to Huddersfield for the first concert of the 1934–35 season to conduct *Everyman* by Walford Davies and *Sea Symphony* by Vaughan-Williams. An enthusiastic welcome awaited him back to the Town Hall rostrum where the respective composers of these works had conducted them on the occasions of their previous performance by the Society.

Sargent's letter to the Society's President telling of his inability to conduct the concert on 24 February 1933 was received only a few days previous to that date. Since hurried enquiries showed that neither Sir Hamilton Harty nor Sir Adrian Boult were available, it was decided to ask Bardgett to conduct the concert. Thus Bargdett had what must have been the exciting, if not daunting prospect of conducting the Society's first performance of Walton's *Belshazzar's Feast* with an orchestra which included many Hallé players. Parts I and II of Haydn's *Creation* were also performed at this concert, which proved to be a triumph for Bardgett who was heartily cheered at the end of the performance. In November 1933 *Elijah* was conducted by Albert Coates who was substituting for Sargent at the Royal Albert Hall *Hiawatha* performances, and elsewhere. According to the *Huddersfield Examiner* of 4 November 1933, some hoped this would perhaps be the Society's last performance of *Elijah*, 'and if it is', said the report, 'the "Elijah" has had a glorious interment'. That it was by no means the last *Elijah*, and that the work will doubtless continue to be given, indicates how fashions in attitudes towards music change. Coates also conducted Verdi's *Requiem* in February 1934 together with *Songs of Farewell* by Delius, and some Sullivan items. Bardgett was, however, entrusted with the 1933 *Messiah* concert.

The Verdi concert, which was broadcast, began with Elgar's setting of the National Anthem following which the audience remained standing for a minute in silent tribute to the memory of Sir Edward who had died that very morning. The *Requiem* performance was a tremendous success. The contralto soloist, Mary Jarred, who was new to Huddersfield, made a deep impression and was to return on many a future occasion. Councillor Lunn, the Society's President, read messages during the interval from Henry Coward in Sheffield, Malcolm Sargent in Switzerland where he was con-valescing, and Frederick Delius, all of whom were 'listening-in' to the wireless transmission. Coward's was received during the transmission, for he sent 'heartiest congratulations on triumphal performance' and ended with 'Bravissimo! Full of tears, but rejoicing with you'. The Delius work, heard in the second half, was new to Huddersfield but was 'splendidly served by both chorus and orchestra', said the *Huddersfield Examiner* report. It had been Sargent who had conducted its first-ever performance at the Queen's Hall in 1932 with Kennedy Scott's Philharmonic Choir. On 10 June, less than four months after the Huddersfield performance, Delius died, only a week or two after the death of Gustav Holst. Thus in the space of six months we had lost Elgar, Delius, and Holst, three brilliant stars in a rising new galaxy of British composers. In a postscript to his message to the choir Delius had written 'I hear from all sides about the splendid work the Huddersfield Choral Society is doing'. He had, he said, written to several musical friends on the continent to get them to listen to the transmission of the performance. Sargent's message had been brief. It ran 'Listening tonight. Greetings, affec-tion and best wishes to all'.

Albert Coates was full of praise for the choir and was of the opinion that several famous conductors were anxious to make its acquaintance. They didn't get a chance however at that time, for Sargent was back at the Town Hall for the next two seasons without a break. His return in the autumn of 1934 to conduct *Everyman* and *Sea Symphony* was followed by concerts including works by Mozart and Wagner, as well as works by Elgar and Holst, two composers ever dear to Sargent's heart. These two seasons, which provided first-ever performances by the Society of Mozart's *Mass in C Minor* and Elgar's *The Music Makers*, established Sargent's reputation in Hudders-field in no uncertain manner.

Two centenary celebration concerts were planned for the autumn of 1936. At one of these a new and specially commissioned work by Ralph Vaughan-Williams was to be performed. By February 1936 it was known that Sargent would be in Australia, not to return until November. His suggestion that the concert dates be altered was rejected and he was asked to obtain either Coates or Hamilton Harty as substitute. When Vaughan-Williams heard that Sargent was not to conduct, he wrote saying that he would have to reconsider his decision to write a new work for the Society if anyone other than Sargent, however competent, was to conduct it. Sargent was alerted to the situation and evidently managed to talk Vaughan-Williams round, for the former wrote saying that he thought 'there would be no trouble in this matter'. All was well in the end and *Dona Nobis Pacem* was performed on Friday, 2 October 1936 with the Hallé Orchestra conducted by Albert Coates, and with Renée Flynn and Roy Henderson as soloists, in a programme which also included Walton's *Belshazzar's Feast* and Elgar's *Enigma Variations*. Vaughan-Williams was there and came on to the platform to acknowledge the applause for his composition. He said that he counted it an honour to have it performed for the first time by such a distinguished company. Sargent must have done some persuasive talking! Scholes wrote in *The Mirror of Music* that *Dona Nobis Pacem* attracted much attention at the time.

The second concert, given the following evening, included Parry's *Blest Pair of Sirens* and items from both *Hiawatha* and *The Mastersingers*. Henry Coward, now almost eighty-seven, was invited back to conduct the *Hiawatha* items which the *Huddersfield Examiner* reported that he did 'showing little diminution in his old eagerness of method'. Bardgett and Coates shared the conducting of the other items and during the interval a short account of the Society's history was broadcast by the BBC with W. L. Wilmshurst, Lawrence Crowther (President), and John L. Ramsden (Secretary) as speakers. A copy of Wilmshurst's brochure history was presented to each subscriber and choir member, copies being available to the public at sixpence each!

At the Annual General Meeting earlier that year the Vice-President, Geoffrey Jarmain, had prophesied that the Society would lose money in its centenary year. The centenary concerts did lose nearly £300 but the following year the new President, Irving Silverwood, was able to assert that the Society had never stood higher musically or financially. It was, he said, 'one of the oldest societies of this description and one of the wealthiest'. The introduction of an annual subscription in 1932 together with wise investment of the Society's funds, doubtless helped towards this condition. In 1933 the subscription had in fact been reduced to five shillings per annum due to the success of the previous season and orchestral members were exempted from payment in future, and even given a rebate, on the grounds that they received no tuition!

There were other indications of financial health. Despite Sargent's absence, due to illness, from the *Belshazzar* concert in February 1933, he was sent a cheque for his usual fee which, though he returned it, was sent back to him again even though the loss on the concert was £75. Reid tells us that, due largely to his own generosity and extravagance, Sargent was a relatively poor man in 1933 in spite of his successes. In his illness he was substantially supported by his friends and by money brought in from 'whip-rounds among choral singers and orchestral players' countrywide. Doubtless, this determination to pay him his normal fee was the Society's equivalent of a whip-round in Huddersfield. Poverty was clearly not an affliction suffered by the Society at this time and, as in the twenties, its subscribers and supporters seem not to have been affected by the economic depressions of the period. Unlike Sargent, the Society was careful with its money. His suggestion to engage Eva Turner for the Verdi *Requiem* in 1934 was rejected since she wanted sixty-five guineas. Walter Widdop's engagement for the Wagner concert in 1935 was cancelled when he asked for twenty-five per cent extra because the concert was to be broadcast.

Early in 1933 it was decided to discontinue paying an allowance to the Glee and Madrigal Society towards the hire of a rehearsal piano. This raised the whole matter of the ownership of the piano presented in 1887 after the success in London of John North's choir at the Welsh National Eisteddfod. The Choral Society had continued to use this instrument and had come to believe it to be their own. Reference to the suppliers, Messrs Archibald Ramsden of Leeds, seemed to confirm this but when Ernest Woodhead, president of the G. and M., actually produced a copy of a letter dated 1887, from Ramsden to Allen Haigh of the Choral Society, the matter of the joint ownership became clear. In the meantime the Choral Society had been presented with a Steinway piano as a centenary gift by Lawrence Crowther, its Vice-President. Friendly relations with the G. and M. were thereafter restored by approving a subscription to that society 'from year to year as the financial position warrants'. In 1934 came a suggestion that the old piano should be presented to the trustees of the High Street Schools as a joint gift from both societies. This seems not to have been followed up for the instrument apparently remained in the Society's service until 1960 when, unable to find a buyer for it, they had it taken away to be broken up.

The late nineteen-thirties which witnessed high drama in both Royal and political circles at home, and the gathering clouds of war, were years which saw the Society moving towards the pinnacle of its fame. Sir Henry Wood, who conducted the choir in the Bach *B Minor Mass* in November 1936 when Sargent was still in Australia, wrote afterwards to the Secretary saying 'what a wonderful and magnificent choir you have'. Reactions were similar following the Philharmonic Concert at the Queen's Hall in London in February 1937 when most of the choir was present to give a performance of *Belshazzar's Feast* and Mozart's *C Minor Mass* with Sargent conducting this time.

The *Daily Telegraph* commented that one might go round the world and not find the match of the choral singing heard on that occasion. Keeping abreast of things, the Society gave recently-composed works in 1937 and 1938 with *Deborah and Barak* by Armstrong Gibbs and *Five Tudor Portraits* by Vaughan-Williams in November 1937, and then George Dyson's *Canterbury Pilgrims* in November 1938. Albert Coates conducted the last of these since Sargent was again in Australia. Of these works only that of Vaughan-Williams survived in the Society's repertoire.

The Society accepted an invitation to send a contingent to sing with the Royal Choral Society and others at the London Music Festival Concert at the Albert Hall on 5 May 1939. A massive choir, also including members of the Bradford Festival Choral Society and the Croydon Philharmonic Society, gave a memorable performance of *The Dream of Gerontius* with the London Symphony Orchestra conducted by Malcolm Sargent. Heddle Nash sang *Gerontius* without a copy — as he had done in *The Messiah* in Huddersfield a few months previously. Gladys Ripley made her mark at this concert as a singer of Elgar's music, though not, it seems, too happily taking the optional high A, according to the *Daily Telegraph* critic, who thought that those who sing this part should leave this note entirely alone. What magic moments he would have denied us all! Toscanini was at the concert and Reid reports that he embraced Sargent after the performance, being 'overwhelmed by the beauty of the score and its performance'.

At about this time the Society was troubled by internal strife which was ended only after the heads of three of its chief officers had rolled. It is difficult to assess the true nature of the issues involved, but apparently it all centred around a dispute concerning the reduction in seating capacity of the Town Hall and the suggestion that members of the chorus should relinquish their right to complimentary gallery tickets. In a somewhat uncharacteristic fashion, the choir members took exception to the manner in which the proposals were laid before them. This seems to have constituted the core of the crisis which developed. The outcome was that in August 1938 the President, Mr Irving Silverwood, the Orchestral Secretary and Treasurer, Mr Albert Stocks, and the General Secretary, Mr John L. Ramsden all handed in their resignations. The first of these was 'accepted' but the latter two were 'accepted with regret' at a Committee meeting of 19 August. Hilda Wilmshurst remembers an emergency meeting in connexion with this matter being held at the Wilmshursts' home, where she was presumably by this time mistress, Mrs Wilmshurst having died in 1936. She recalls her father saying that without the meeting 'there would have been no more Choral Society', which sounds a trifle alarming.

Elected as the new President was Frank Firth, son of Samuel Firth, President from 1926 to 1928, and nephew of Ald. J. Firth, President from 1903 to 1905. Frank Netherwood became the new Treasurer and David Crawshaw the new General Secretary. Percy Beaumont who had been Choir Secretary (as distinct from General Secretary) had resigned in May 1938 despite petitions for him to stay. His place was taken by Mr Whitfield Senior. For some reason Percy Beaumont, back in 1930, had similarly resigned his position as Senior Vice-President. Though perhaps something of a reluctant administrator, he did sterling service for the Society as a minor soloist in more than one performance of *Aida* over the years.

The Munich crisis of 1938 no doubt eclipsed the crisis concerning the Choral Society's management, but by the beginning of 1939, encouraged by the false hope of Neville Chamberlain's promise of 'peace in our time', plans were being confidently made for the following season. It was planned that Sir Adrian Boult would conduct Beethoven's *Mass in D* at the November concert in 1939 since Sargent would be in Australia, and a specially-formed sub-committee was considering likely new works. In the event the concert was cancelled due to the outbreak of war on 3 September. It was decided nevertheless to hold the *Messiah* concert as usual at Christmas but in the afternoon instead of the evening. Profits were to go to War Relief Funds. The subscribers' ballot was dispensed with, the previous season's seats being offered to those who wished to use their tickets. Rehearsals, scheduled to take place on Saturday afternoons, were to be held in Queen Street Chapel, the Army having taken over the High Street School Room.

Although theatres and cinemas were reported as running more or less normally, there were doubts about the possibility of running anything like a normal concert season. By December, however, initial fears had been largely allayed and a splendid performance of *The Messiah* took place with Sargent conducting an orchestra which included several Northern Philharmonic players and some amateurs but led by Huddersfield's Reginald Stead, and at which Janet Hamilton-Smith, a soprano new to Huddersfield, made a great impression. During the singing of 'Since by Man Came Death' the audience stood in memory of Mr W. L. Wilmshurst who had died some months previously. A local solicitor by profession, he had played a great part in the Society's affairs, had been its president during the First World War and its first historian.

With promptings from Sargent, who regarded the works as inappropriate in the circumstances, the plan to perform Mendelssohn's *Hymn of Praise* and Handel's *Acis and Galatea* at the March concert in 1940, was set aside. Also, his suggestion of an alternative programme was postponed until the first concert of the following season. In contempt of the opinion of local music critics, *Elijah* was put on instead in the expectation of a capacity audience. In fact the Hall was not filled and, in addition to war-time problems, an influenza epidemic was raging which robbed the choir itself of eighty singers. This time the report in the *Huddersfield Examiner* expressed general approval of the concert and even the orchestra was said to have 'shown great improvement'.

As with other local musical societies, the outbreak of war had caused difficulties, and various disruptions arose in the Choral Society's plans. The Society faced a dilemma when it became clear that Sargent was unable to come to Huddersfield on those particular Saturday afternoons when the Town Hall was available during the 1940–41 season. At the risk of losing subscribers who did not wish to venture outdoors during black-out hours, it arranged for the concerts to start no later than 7.00 p.m. that season. For the remaining war-time seasons its concerts were held on Saturday afternoons commencing at 2.30 p.m. As it happened, Bach's *B Minor Mass*, performed at the last concert of the 1940–41 season, had to be conducted by Bardgett since Sargent was ill.

Subsequent to, if not consequent upon complaints of the paucity of choral music transmitted by the BBC at this time, the Society gave its first national broadcast of *The Messiah* in December 1940. This received good press reports, and letters of appreciation arrived from many parts of the country which no doubt pleased choir-member Mr C. W. Hinchcliffe whose fiftieth *Messiah* this was with the Society! Further publicity — and attendant income — came in 1941 when a Ministry of Information film, *Heart of Britain* featured the Society singing the 'Hallelujah' chorus. Filming had taken place during rehearsal in Queen Street in December 1940. A longer version of the film called *This is England* went out to America. In his presidential address at the Society's Annual General Meeting of 1941 Mr Waldo Briggs said that the fee of £100 received from the BBC for the *Messiah* broadcast was largely responsible for turning an £86 deficit in 1940 to a £48 profit that year. The first concert of the season had resulted in a loss of £22. The programme was that suggested by Sargent the previous season but postponed — a second performance of *Dona Nobis Pacem* by Vaughan-Williams together with Elgar's *The Music Makers*. Also performed were Elgar's *For the Fallen*, not sung by the Society since 1917, and Sargent's arrangement of Arne's original setting of *Rule Britannia*. Gladys Ripley, who had sung with the choir in the *Dream of Gerontius* concert at the Royal Albert Hall in 1939, made her debut with the Society in its own Town Hall on this occasion. Mr George Taylor, a choir member, sang the bass solo in *Dona Nobis Pacem*.

The male ranks of the chorus were thinning at this time due to the younger men being called up for war service but it seems that this did not have too adverse an affect on performances. There was a proposal in 1941 that the Bradford Festival Choral Society be approached to assist with tenors and basses, such was the shortage. Many people in uniform were to be seen in the audience at the Society's concerts. Some were there by special invitation, thus not only giving an opportunity to members of the armed forces to attend the concerts, but also filling what would otherwise have been unoccupied seats. At the 1940 *Messiah* concert twenty-seven soldiers from the Royal Corps of Signals occupied window seats costing five shillings each, generously paid for by Lawrence Crowther, the donor of the Steinway piano back in 1933. Much appreciated was the correspondence with Society members serving in H.M. forces: this was maintained during the war by the Choir Secretary, Mr Whitfield Senior.

In addition to broadcasts of the Society's usual concerts there were invitations to perform works at specially-arranged concerts for broadcasting. These were among many invitations which the Society was to receive from this time onwards from all manner of sources. In November 1943, under the auspices of the British Council, the Society joined forces with the Hallé Society in a broadcast performance of Walton's *Belshazzar's Feast* from the Huddersfield Town Hall with Clarence Raybould conducting. Denis Noble was the soloist and several distinguished guests, including William Walton, were in the audience. Quickly following was an invitation from the British Council to send a choir of one hundred voices to Liverpool in January 1943 to record this work in the Philharmonic Hall with Walton himself conducting the Royal Liverpool Philharmonic Orchestra. Walton wrote to the Society requesting its participation. 'I would like to feel', he wrote, 'that I had some friends to back me up. If the choir can see their way to help they will be doing a great service to me personally, and to British music in general in showing what a wonderful choir they are.'

In December 1942, at the invitation of the Hallé Society, a hundred and fifty members of the choir sang what was described as a thrilling performance of *The Messiah* at Belle Vue, Manchester to an audience of eight thousand. That year too, the Hallé Orchestra had played in Huddersfield for the Society's *Messiah* concert which, on their account, was given earlier than usual, on Saturday, 12 December in the afternoon. Early misgivings concerning Saturday afternoon concerts were short-lived. At the 1942 Annual

Sir Malcolm Sargent and Sir William Walton with Herbert Bardgett (*extreme left*)
and G. D. A. Haywood (*extreme right*) at the *Gloria* performance in 1961

General Meeting, Mr Frank Netherwood, the newly-elected President, said
he considered that both choir members and subscribers had derived great
satisfaction from the change from Friday evening to Saturday afternoon
rehearsals and concerts. But he said that he thought the choir's talent was not
being fully utilized and would like to see new works written for it of longer
than sixty minutes duration and, contrary to requirements by the BBC for
broadcasting purposes, for over a hundred and fifty voices. He advocated
inviting a dozen or so young composers to pay an early visit to one of the
Society's concerts. Following upon this suggestion, the Executive Committee
resolved later the same month to invite Arthur Bliss, George Dyson, and
Arnold Bax along, the youngest of whom, Arthur Bliss, was fifty-one! It was
in fact Sir George Dyson's *Canterbury Pilgrims* that a section of the choir
sang by BBC invitation in Manchester on 28 May 1943, the sixtieth birthday
of the composer who conducted the performance. The following month the
BBC broadcast a special performance by the Society from Huddersfield Town
Hall of Verdi's *Requiem*, again with the Hallé Orchestra, conducted by
Sargent and with soloists Eva Turner, Mary Jarred, Parry Jones, and Norman
Walker.

The Society invited William Walton to a social evening arranged to follow the afternoon performance of *Hiawatha* at the Society's final concert of the season in March 1943. The *Belshazzar's Feast* records were to be played by Walter Legge of HMV and Pamela Henn-Collins of the British Council was also to be there. In fact neither she nor Walton could come and even Walter Legge arrived only after the final record had been put on the turn-table. But Sargent was there and, in describing his work for the British Council, said how ignorant he had found the Swedes concerning English music. In 1942 he had flown to Sweden in the cramped bomb-rack of a *Mosquito* bomber to give concerts in Gothenburg and Stockholm. It would seem that in 1942 Sweden was in much the same state of ignorance regarding music in Britain as was Holland in 1928.

At the Society's Annual General Meeting in 1943, Mr Guy Crowther, then Vice-President, in commenting on what had been an outstanding year musically if not financially, said that it seemed a far cry from the doubts and hesitations of three years ago. 'Quite suddenly, it seems', he said, 'there had been aroused an interest in music.' Certainly the war years and the decade which followed, saw an immense increase in demand for music of every kind. Glenn Miller and Vera Lynn didn't get all the limelight! In name, if little else, Beethoven and Beecham became known to hundreds of thousands of people perhaps for the first time. Many people developed a genuine love for, and interest in, serious music as a result of all the musical activity of the time. For reasons not too difficult to imagine, war conditions, it would seem, make people turn to music. Certainly more people were acquainted with the name of the Huddersfield Choral Society under its conductor Sir Malcolm Sargent during the nineteen-forties and fifties than at any other time before or since.

Ralph Hill wrote in the *Sunday Times* in March 1944, following one of the Society's broadcasts, 'This choir is a national acquisition and its activities ought not to be confined to the North'. Broadcasts and recordings were very largely the reason for the Society's increasing fame, but the demand came from a hungry public and the choice of the Huddersfield choir to satisfy that hunger can only be attributed to the Society's musical excellence. With the ever-rising costs of orchestras and soloists the continued financial stability of the Society depended greatly on earnings from broadcasting and recording. Soloists of the highest calibre among British and Commonwealth singers were engaged, often at considerable expense.

The recording of *Belshazzar's Feast* in 1943 was followed in 1944 by a recording, again by HMV, of Holst's *Hymn of Jesus*. This took place during the Whitsuntide weekend, under the auspices of the British Council, with the

Royal Liverpool Philharmonic Orchestra conducted by Sargent. Then, in April 1945, in the Huddersfield Town Hall, *The Dream of Gerontius* was recorded with the same orchestra. In July 1946 came the *Messiah* recording, with Columbia Records, as the first of a two-year contract to record one major work each year. *Elijah* was recorded in 1947 instead of Bach's *B Minor Mass* as originally intended, the switch being made presumably with an eye on the American market by Columbia Records; the *Mass* had recently been recorded in the States. Reid tells us that, whilst abroad, Sargent 'crowed as disarmingly as a schoolboy over his *Messiah* recording with the Huddersfield Choral Society'. '83,000 sets sold in a few weeks!', Sargent would boast.

In December 1944 the Society performed *The Messiah* on four occasions. In addition to the usual Subscriber's concert there was a special, and highly acclaimed, broadcast of the work from the Town Hall on 27 December, and, for neither the first nor the last time, performances with the Liverpool Philharmonic in Blackpool and with the Hallé in Manchester.

By the date of the Annual General Meeting in 1945, when the retiring President, Frank Netherwood, was able to describe the financial situation of the Society as 'sound', the war in Europe was over. At an end too, was the long life of Sir Henry Coward who had died, aged ninety-five, during the previous season. Even with sound finances, however, the idea of giving a Victory Thanksgiving concert was, after due consideration, finally set aside when it was learned that the estimated loss from it might be as much as £150.

Problems arose regarding Bardgett's position as Chorus Master at the time. He asked for more money in 1945 and, through persistence, finally got what he wanted. In 1947 he asked to conduct one concert per year as a condition of his remaining as Chorus Master. This was not accepted but again by persisting he was finally offered a Christmas concert, and this seemed to satisfy him. As it happened, Sargent was ill the following December and Bardgett conducted the BBC Northern Orchestra for *The Messiah* in his place, and with great success. He also conducted the *Music for Christmas* concert given at the invitation of the BBC that year. For some reason which is not very clear, he was not offered a Christmas concert the following year but in 1949 he conducted a public *Messiah* concert, a practice which was continued each year thereafter. Although begun very largely in order to satisfy Bardgett's ambition to conduct the Society, the public *Messiah* concert has from the very beginning, always been immensely popular.

In 1948 Bardgett himself was ill and he apparently remarked on his return to the rehearsals that during his absence the choir had got slack. This led to an attempt by two choir members to challenge Bardgett's nomination as Chorus

Master for the following season. Oil must have been successfully poured on troubled waters, for his nomination went through unopposed, but there were further brushes in later years, and always regarding his status with the Society.

After a performance by the Society of Beethoven's *Mass in D* with the BBC Symphony Orchestra at the Royal Albert Hall on Sunday, 3 March 1946, Ralph Hill wrote in the *Daily Telegraph* that the choir was 'undoubtedly the finest choral instrument in Britain'. 'It has', he went on, 'the precision and elasticity of a great orchestra and its tone is as extraordinary in dynamic range as its quality is beautiful.' Other press comment was similarly enthusiastic. The occasion was the Henry Wood Birthday concert sponsored by the *Daily Telegraph* at which the soloists were Joan Hammond, Gladys Ripley, Parry Jones, and George Pizzey. The work had only recently been given a previous performance by the choir, for they sang it at the first concert of the 1945–46 season in Huddersfield.

An invitation to take part in the first Edinburgh International Festival of Music in 1947 was declined due to accommodation and transport costs, but in 1948 these difficulties were overcome and a choir of almost three hundred singers travelled overnight on Friday, 27 August and gave two broadcast concerts in Edinburgh which were widely acclaimed as a triumph. The choir was 'invincible', said *The Times* critic, and Arthur Schnabel, the pianist, declared that he had heard no finer choral singing anywhere in the world. The Princess Royal, present at the second concert with Lord Harewood, said she had been thrilled with the performance. According to the Lord Provost of Edinburgh, the City had expected great things but the performance had exceeded their highest hopes. On the Saturday evening at the Usher Hall with Sir Malcolm Sargent (he had received his knighthood the previous year) conducting the Royal Liverpool Philharmonic Orchestra, the choir had sung *Belshazzar's Feast* with Harold Williams as soloist, and Fauré's *Requiem* with Isobel Baillie joining Harold Williams. Ernest Cooper's playing of the important organ part in this work, according to Sidney Crowther, probably represented his finest hour with the Society. The following afternoon Bach's *B Minor Mass* was sung, again with the Liverpool orchestra, and soloists Kathleen Ferrier, Isobel Baillie, Eric Greene, and Owen Brannigan. Sargent's opinion of this performance was unequivocal. It was, he was reported as saying, the finest in which he had ever participated. There was some adverse criticism of the orchestra at both concerts but the occasion belonged to the choir, which was given a tumultuous reception.

The Society was riding on the crest of a wave. Retiring after ten years as Treasurer in May 1948, Frank Netherwood said he thought the name of the

Society should be 'The Huddersfield Royal Choral Society'. He said that earlier attempts to secure Royal patronage had gone well but had been turned down with a very poor excuse by the Home Secretary (later identified as Herbert Morrison). He had it 'on the highest authority', he claimed, that the choir could give three concerts a week for a year in the U.S.A. and secure an attendance of four thousand at each one.

Although the Society showed a profit in 1948, there were signs of difficulties and by 1949 the deficit was considerable. Costs were rising and action by the Musicians Union having prevented the broadcast of *The Kingdom* from the November concert in 1948, there was a consequent loss of revenue. The financial problems facing Yorkshire choirs, particularly that of Halifax, were the subject of a report in the *Yorkshire Post* in 1949 by Ernest Bradbury. 'Even the famous Huddersfield Choral Society cannot make a profit on their concerts' he wrote. Halifax, with its hundred and thirty-one years of almost continuous concert-giving had no remuneration from outside work, such as recording and broadcasting, as had Huddersfield. Perhaps only one Society at a time could he suggested, enjoy such fame as did Huddersfield. But rising costs, lack of male recruits and the lure of professionalism was, as Bradbury pointed out, a common concern. Regarding the last point, he tells the story of Roy Henderson's experience after singing with a West Riding choir when the conductor, instead of praising him, merely asked 'Well, what d'you think of t'choir?' Henderson replied that it was no doubt a good one. 'It is that, lad' replied the conductor, 'if tha'd broken down tonight there were half a dozen chaps behind thee ready to deputize — and maybe they'd have done better!'

There had been some relief from financial burden since the end of the war as the Society was able to register as a charitable institution and so avoid paying income tax. This had necessitated a change in the rules of the Society which were therefore revised in 1944. Despite financial difficulties there remained much confidence. At the Annual General Meeting in 1949 David Crawshaw, the newly-elected President said that it was not unlikely that the Society would be called upon to take some part in the Festival of Britain in 1951. And so it turned out. But before that event there were others worthy of our attention: for example the occasion when the present Queen, then Princess Elizabeth, and her husband, the Duke of Edinburgh, visited Huddersfield in July 1949. The Mayor of Huddersfield entertained the royal visitors to luncheon in the Town Hall where Bardgett conducted the choir in Parry's *Blest Pair of Sirens*. The Private Secretary to the Princess, John Colville, wrote later to the Mayor that the royal couple had greatly enjoyed their visit and he referred particularly to their enjoyment of the choir's singing. This was not allowed to go to the heads of the membership, however, for by the end of September, financial considerations caused the annual membership subscription to be increased to ten shillings. As an additional saving, complimentary tickets for members were no longer to be given for the first and third concerts of each season.

The Princess Royal, after hearing the choir at the Edinburgh Festival, expressed a desire to hear them in Huddersfield so in 1949 the Society invited her together with the Earl and Countess of Harewood to attend the *Messiah* concert. Also attending were the Earl and Countess of Scarborough as guests of the Mayor. The Earl of Scarborough was the Lord Lieutenant of the County. Marjorie Thomas made her debut at the Society's concerts on this occasion, singing in company with Peter Pears (who had sung at the Harewood's wedding), Ena Mitchell and William Parsons. The whole thing went off splendidly with Sargent conducting the Northern Philharmonic Orchestra.

The year 1948 which had seen the Society's first performance since 1907 of Elgar's *The Kingdom* also saw its first performance of *A Mass of Life* by Delius, which had never before been heard in Huddersfield, despite the fact that it was forty years old. Marking the beginning of several years' associa-tion of the Society with the Yorkshire Symphony Orchestra was the perform-ance the next year of Honneger's *King David* together with Fauré's *Requiem*. The following November came the singular event of the performance of Julius Harrison's *Mass in C* with the composer present to hear his work. In 1950 Sargent was appointed conductor of the BBC Symphony Orchestra and past-president Mr Frank Firth was able to inform the Society that this appointment would make no difference to Sargent's association with the Society. This was not the case with the Bradford Festival Choral Society, the conductorship of which he relinquished in 1951.

Mr Firth donated over one hundred pounds to the Society to help clear its deficit and to assist with the expenses to be incurred in the participation in the Festival of Britain concerts the following year. Choir members were later asked to subscribe thirty shillings per head towards these expenses. When, in May 1951, the Treasurer, Mr A. G. Crowther, in presenting the accounts despaired of any prospects of reducing costs of concerts, most members' thoughts would no doubt have been concerned more with the following month's Festival concerts in London and the York Festival concert in York Minster. The latter, which brought the Festival to its conclusion, was held on 16 June 1951. Verdi's *Requiem* was performed with Elizabeth Schwarzkopf, Eugenia Zareska, Heddle Nash, and Norman Walker and with Victor de

Sabata conducting the London Philharmonic Orchestra. Sidney Crowther described this performance as 'one of deep inspiration' and to be remembered by the most hardened of concert-goers 'as one of their finest evenings'. There was no applause, but outside after the concert, Crowther says 'was a crowd well over three thousand waiting to give them a tumultuous welcome' when the conductor and choir appeared at the South door of the Minster. Adrian Boult declared that it had been the finest performance of the work ever given in England, whilst de Sabata's comment on the whole affair, was 'I have never had an experience like it in my life'.

The London concerts consisted of one at the Royal Albert Hall on Saturday afternoon, 9 June and one on Sunday evening, 10 June at the Festival Hall. At the former the choir joined forces with the Royal Choral Society and Sargent conducting the London Symphony Orchestra in performing Vaughan-Williams's *Sea Symphony* and Walton's *Belshazzar's Feast* with Elsie Morison, Gordon Clinton, and Dennis Noble as soloists. Vaughan-Williams was there and was given a rousing reception when Sargent brought him to the rostrum. On the Sunday the Society, on its own this time, but singing with the same orchestra under Sargent, gave Beethoven's *Mass in D* with Elizabeth Schwarzkopf, Gladys Ripley, Heddle Nash, and Gordon Clinton as soloists. Present on this occasion, and having become, perhaps, something of a Huddersfield Choral Society fan, was the Princess Royal. *The Times* music critic wrote 'it would be hard to find any English choir better equipped to storm the high heaven on Beethoven's behalf than the Huddersfield Choral Society' and went on to describe the performance in glowing terms. Indeed, the choir was often referred to at the time as 'the world's best'. To complete its contribution to the Festival of Britain celebrations, the Society performed *A Sea Symphony* and *The Music Makers* in the Huddersfield Town Hall on Friday, 13 July 1951 with the Yorkshire Symphony Orchestra under Sargent.

In February 1952 King George VI died. The rehearsal on Friday, 15 February 1952 was ended with a short programme of music to mark the occasion of the King's funeral which had taken place that same day. Committee members and their wives were invited to occupy gallery seats in the rehearsal room in Queen Street for the occasion. A letter was sent to Clarence House from the President and Secretary telling the new Queen of this event and expressing sympathy, loyalty, and affection from the Society members. The Society still has a copy of this letter together with the appreciative reply from Clarence House, which was sent by return of post.

There was, during the period between the King's death and the Queen's coronation, a tremendous feeling everywhere of hope and expectation for the future. Here was the dawn of a new Elizabethan age. A never-to-be-forgotten experience was the television broadcast of the coronation ceremony in Westminster Abbey on that cold, wet, grey June day of 1953. Contentious though the decision may have been to allow the television cameras into the Abbey, the new medium of mass communication had proved its worth. It is not surprising that the Choral Society were very soon to receive invitations to make television appearances in addition to radio broadcasts. For a few years, at Christmas time, those parts of *The Messiah* which tell of the Nativity were televised live from the Town Hall at specially-arranged concerts before an invited audience when Sargent conducted the BBC Northern Orchestra. In 1955 the subscribers' *Messiah* performance was broadcast on sound radio but the following year it too, in part, was televised. These television productions were well received although television is not by any means the best medium for the presentation of choral works, especially if large choirs are used.

Sound broadcasts of the Society's performances continued, and among these was the performance of *A Mass of Life* by Delius in October 1953 from the Leeds Town Hall. This was the occasion of the Leeds Triennial Festival. The Yorkshire Symphony Orchestra under Sargent played, as it was to do again the following month when the same work was given at the subscribers' concert in Huddersfield. This latter occasion saw the presentation of a silver tea service to Sargent and a television set to Bardgett to mark the twenty-first year of their association with the Society. In the November of the following year there was another broadcast of *A Mass of Life* by the Society, this time from the Royal Festival Hall with Sargent conducting the BBC Symphony Orchestra. This was an exacting trip for the choir. Up early to catch the London train, they faced a rehearsal in the afternoon, the concert in the evening and a return journey by train starting from Euston at 11.35 and arriving in Huddersfield at 4.00 a.m.!

Amidst all this exciting activity the performance of new works was not neglected. In March 1952 there was Herbert Howell's *Hymnus Paradisi*, a work well understood and interpreted by Sargent. In November 1952 came Kodaly's *Missa Brevis* together with a second performance of Honneger's *King David*. There was a broadcast concert in 1955 which included *Morning Heroes* by Bliss (who was in the audience) with Richard Attenborough as orator. It was Herbert Howells again, with his *Missa Sabrinensis* in March 1956, when he had hoped to be present but was finally unable to attend. Though this was not its first performance, London did not hear it until a week later when the Royal Choral Society performed it. On both occasions

Marjorie Thomas sang in place of Gladys Ripley who had very recently died. The Huddersfield performance marked the last occasion on which Ernest Cooper played the organ at the Society's concerts. He was retiring after forty-one years as Organist although his association with the Society as Accompanist began in 1898. Only the previous year, in 1955, he had been awarded the M.B.E. for his services to music in Huddersfield. His place was taken by Eric Chadwick who ultimately succeeded Herbert Bardgett as Chorus Master when the latter died in 1962.

In 1952, to help cover costs of concerts estimated as more than double those in 1940, and to offset the effects of a reduction in seating capacity at the Town Hall that year, ticket prices were raised. Concerts continued to lose money and only income from investments, BBC radio and television broadcasts together with royalties from recordings, kept the Society going. New long-playing records were produced during the next few years. In 1954 *The Messiah* was recorded in January and *The Dream of Gerontius* in November. *Israel in Egypt* was recorded in June 1955, *Elijah* in May 1956 and *Belshazzar's Feast* in February 1958. In June 1959 a stereo recording of *The Messiah* was made. All this boosted both the bank balance and the reputation of the choir considerably.

Among notable concerts at this time was a performance of *The Dream of Gerontius* at the Philharmonic Hall in Liverpool on 16 March 1957, the centenary year of Elgar's birth, at the invitation of the Royal Liverpool Philharmonic Society. Marjorie Thomas, Richard Lewis, and John Cameron were the soloists and Sargent conducted the Royal Liverpool Philharmonic Orchestra which, since 1955, the Society had regularly engaged for its concerts in Huddersfield, and was to do so for a long time to come. Just a little of the comment appearing in *The Post* and *The Echo* in Liverpool following the concert is sufficient to indicate the quality of the performance. One read, for example, 'The nobility and devotion of the performance, even in retrospect, rose above criticism, and I question if Elgar himself ever heard its equal. The singing of this famous Yorkshire choir was beyond praise.'

There surely had been nothing to excel, however, the magnificent triumph of the concerts given in Vienna in June 1958. One hundred and fifty members of the choir travelled from a cold England to the Austrian capital where only the warmth of the weather might be said to have matched the warmth of the reception. In the famous Musikverein Concert Hall, and with the Vienna Symphony Orchestra conducted by Sir Malcolm Sargent they sang *The Messiah* on Sunday, 1 June with soloists Norma Proctor, Elsie Morison, William McAlpine, and James Milligan. The following Tuesday they sang

Belshazzar's Feast and the Fauré *Requiem* with Elsie Morison and James Milligan. Eric Chadwick was at the organ. The effects of these two perform-ances was sensational. Sargent later described it as 'a sight quite fantastic to behold'. For upwards of fifteen minutes there was cheering and applauding which continued after all the orchestral players had crept away. Sargent admitted that he was astounded at the ovation after the first concert, for all that he knew how good the performance had been. When it happened again on the Tuesday 'I almost cheered myself', he told reporters. The Austrian press was equally appreciative. Sargent thought that the Vienna press notices should be found a place of honour back home for 'future Huddersfield generations to see'. The agent who was responsible for arranging the trip, Lies Askonas, wrote to A. L. Taylor, the choir's Assistant Secretary, saying what 'a tremendous joy and privilege it had been to be present to witness the tremendous reception' which the choir had received. The message came, she said, from the President of the Austrian Republic and from many different quarters of the country as well as herself. The wonderful human warmth, tremendous discipline, and above all the unique artistry had done more for the prestige of their country, she wrote, than many a speech or exchange on the highest political level.

No greater honour could have been bestowed on the Society than the award of the Franz Schmidt Silver Medal by the *Gesellschaft der Musik-freunde*, Vienna. This followed the *Messiah* concert, the like of which had never before been witnessed in Vienna, so they said. The medal had never before been awarded to foreigners. The Society and Sir Malcolm Sargent each received a medal, a distinction they share with the Vienna Philharmonic Orchestra and the Vienna Boys' Choir.

The trip to Austria lasted a week. The choir left England on Friday, 30 May, travelled by cross-channel steamer and train, and returned similarly the following Friday. Some had stayed at hotels, some in private homes of the Viennese Choir, but all had had a tremendously warming and memorable sojourn. There had been wine, food, and song, civic and ambassadorial receptions, and a journey to the Vienna Woods. The *Neue Österreich*, reporting on *The Messiah*, said the guests were worthy 'to receive power and riches and wisdom and strength and honour and glory and blessing'.

Recalling all this today, many choir members who went to Vienna may feel that this was the choir's finest hour. Or was it the following year when again a contingent of a hundred and fifty members flew to West Berlin to give two performances of *The Messiah* at a festival commemorating the bicentenary of Handel's death? Fifteen minutes or so ovation were again afforded each of the performances on Saturday and Sunday, 26 and 27 September given in the concert hall of the College of Music with the Berlin Philharmonic Orchestra. Norma Proctor was with the choir again along with Jennifer Vyvyan, Walter Midgley, and Donald Bell, the young bass from Canada. Three specially-chartered aircraft took the party from Manchester on the Saturday morning and they arrived back in Huddersfield early on Monday morning having flown back home overnight. The Berliners were obviously very affected by what they heard. Press notices referred to the sincerity of the performance and its clear expression of the Christian faith. 'It almost gives the impression' one read in *Die Welt* 'that the state of creative trance in which Handel wrote this enormous work in just under three weeks has also descended upon the interpreters'. It was a personal triumph for Sargent, new to Berlin, who was presented with carnations at the end of the first performance. David Craw-shaw, General Secretary of the choir for the past twenty-one years, had 'known nothing like it before', he said. At the next Annual General Meeting, Mr F. R. Armitage, the President, said he wondered if in years to come 'our historians might well record our visit to Berlin as the best work we had ever done'. He called the performance 'our own efforts in international relation-ships'. Certainly the effect on the Berliners seems to have been almost as great as that of John F. Kennedy's famous 'Ich bin ein Berliner' declaration in 1963 in the *Platz* that they later named after him.

The choir's visit to the Brussels International Exhibition a little over a month after the Vienna visit (this time by as many members of the choir who were willing and able to go) had been in a different class. About two hundred and fifty of them flew to Brussels on Wednesday, 9 July to take part in two concerts in the Grand Auditorium at the Exhibition site. Like the Vienna trip, the British Council helped to finance it, Huddersfield having been chosen to represent British choral music in the Art Section of the Exhibition. On Thursday, 10 July they sang *Belshazzar's Feast* with Dennis Noble in a broadcast concert with the BBC Symphony Orchestra under Sargent. The next day they sang *The Dream of Gerontius* with Marjorie Thomas, William Herbert, and John Cameron. The first concert seemed, due to no fault of the choir, to be less than the best it could give, largely due to the placing of the chorus relative to the orchestra. After Sir Malcolm had been called back for a second time at the end of the concert, attention was taken away from the musicians to the departing royal guests, King Baudouin of Belgium and the Duke of Edinburgh, the latter finding opportunity to wave enthusiastically to the choir before disappearing. *The Dream of Gerontius*, the next day, went much better and was warmly applauded. The Belgian press reports were very appreciative but there was nothing to match the Viennese enthusiasm of the previous month, nor the response in Berlin the following year.

Talk at this time of a possible concert in Moscow, like an earlier prospect of visiting Italy in 1951 or 1952, came to nothing. The choir did not travel abroad again until 1963, by which time the Society had celebrated its one hundred and twenty-fifth anniversary in 1961 and the Borough of Hudders-field had honoured both the Society and its conductor. In October 1961, at a concert in the Town Hall which, appropriately, included a performance of Elgar's *The Music Makers* and some choruses from *The Messiah*, Sir Malcolm Sargent was made an Honorary Freeman of the Borough. The Society was honoured by receiving a *Complimentary Resolution* engrossed on vellum. The honour to Sir Malcolm was

in recognition and full appreciation of the illustrious service given to music in this country and the world . . . and particularly the contribution he has made to music making in this town as conductor of the Huddersfield Choral Society during the past twenty-nine years.

For the Society, the Borough Council declared the

desire to place on record their high appreciation of the glorious musical achieve-ments of the Huddersfield Choral Society since their formation in 1836 and to pay tribute to the illustrious contribution the Society have made to the art of music making, particularly in choral singing, during the past 125 years and the fame which they have thereby brought to the Borough of Huddersfield.[1]

In receiving the certificate of freedom Sir Malcolm said 'I am embarrassed as Sir Malcolm Sargent but proud if I can stand here in the name of music and of the choir which is second to none in the world'.

The following month the Society performed *Gloria* by Sir William Walton, a work specially commissioned by the Society to mark its hundred and twenty-fifth anniversary. The choir sang this very demanding twenty-minute-long piece well, and it was well received. It was followed by *The Dream of Gerontius* in which the same soloists, Marjorie Thomas, Richard Lewis, and John Cameron, participated. Sargent, whose thirtieth year as the choir's conductor was being celebrated, conducted the Royal Liverpool Philhar-monic Orchestra and the whole programme was broadcast on the BBC Third Programme. Sir William and Lady Walton were present and were guests at a dinner given by the President, Mr G. D. A. Haywood, after the concert in the College of Technology in Queensgate. A special celebration concert to mark the Society's anniversary, along with several other schemes, did not come to fruition but Sidney Crowther updated Wilmshurst's history of the Society

[1] The incorrect plurals occur in the original document.

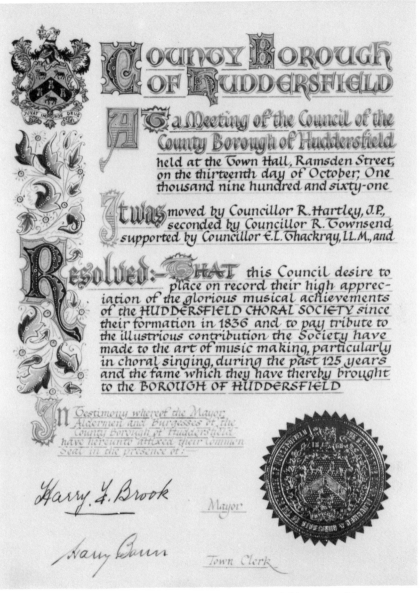

Testimonial from the County Borough of Huddersfield presented in 1961

and specially bound copies were presented to Sir Malcolm, the Mayor and Mayoress of Huddersfield and Crowther himself at a dinner following the Freedom of the Borough concert.

Gloria was performed again along with Dvořák's *Te Deum* at the Royal Festival Hall in November 1962 when the choir participated in the St Cecilia's Festival concert in aid of the Musicians' Benevolent Fund. The Royal Liverpool Philharmonic Orchestra was conducted by Sir Malcolm in the choral works and John Pritchard conducted the orchestral items. The Queen and Princess Alice were there, and the following day, at a dinner at the Savoy Hotel, Dr Allt of the Trinity College of Music reported that the Queen had confessed to a lump in her throat when the choir sang the *Gloria*. When Mr A. Guy Crowther, Acting-President at the time due to the sudden death of the President, Mr G. D. A. Haywood, had presented the Queen with a bound copy of Crowther's updated history, she told him that she had greatly enjoyed the singing.

June 1963 was a busy month for the choir. They sang Britten's *War Requiem* at the opening concert of the York Festival in the Minster on Saturday, 15 June with the BBC Symphony Orchestra under Meredith Davies, and over a hundred and twenty members of the choir were off to Europe again. The party flew to Munich on Tuesday, 4 June to sing *The Messiah* the following day at the Congress Hall of the Deutsche Museum with the Munich Philharmonic Orchestra. Sargent conducted the concert, which was part of a British Week in the City. From Munich they flew on to Oporto where they sang *The Messiah* again on the Friday. On the Saturday they went to Lisbon and sang it yet again. The cost of the trip, estimated at about £10,000, was funded by the British Council, the Munich Authorities and, in Portugal, by the Gulbenkian Foundation responsible for organizing the Festival in that country. In Munich the choir was given a ten-minute ovation and after the concert they were entertained in the Town Hall by the Lord Mayor. The Choir Secretary, Mr W. Drake, was presented with a gift by the choir for his work in arranging the trip. He reported that for the first time in his life he saw tears streaming down the faces of men listening to *The Messiah* in Portugal. 'At the end', he said, 'the applause seemed to go on for ever'. At the concerts in both Portuguese cities the audience stood not only, as is usual during the 'Hallelujah' chorus, but also during the singing of 'Since by Man Came Death' in tribute to the late Pope John XXIII who had died the previous Monday. This resulted in the cancellation of a garden party arranged for the Thursday but the choir was fêted well into the small hours following the Lisbon concert, before flying back to Manchester the next day.

There was little rest, for on the Wednesday came a rehearsal for the *War Requiem* with Meredith Davies, who had conducted its first performance in Coventry Cathedral the previous year. The choristers of York Minster and Leeds Parish Church provided the boys' voices in this work and the soloists were Heather Harper, Alexander Young, and Vladimir Ruzdjak. No applause was allowed then in the Minster, which must have made for frustration on the part of the audience after what was evidently a very fine performance. Meredith Davies wrote later thanking the choir for a 'memorable and inspiring experience'.

Later that year Sargent was in the U.S.A. and attempts having failed to obtain John Pritchard, Eric Chadwick conducted the Bach *B Minor Mass* at the Town Hall subscribers' concert on 22 November. He showed full confidence and ability in his control of the chorus and of the Royal Liverpool Philharmonic Orchestra. The latter was reduced to chamber size for the solos and, for the first time, a harpsichord was used at a Choral Society concert. During the interval at this concert the shocking news was announced of the assassination that day of John Kennedy, President of the United States of America, and the audience stood for a brief while in silent tribute. In San Francisco the following day Sargent's concert went ahead but in a modified form.

Unbelievable though it seemed, Sir Malcolm had reached his seventieth birthday in April 1965 and the Society was involved in two concerts that month to celebrate it. The music for both was the same; three settings of the *Te Deum*, by Verdi, by Walton, and by Dvořák, together with Elgar's *The Music Makers*. The first of these concerts was the final subscribers' concert of the season, on 2 April, after which there was a party with champagne and a birthday cake, and Sir Malcolm was presented with an antique wine-cooler by Mr S. W. Garsed, the President. For the other concert, on 29 April, Sir Malcolm's birthday, the choir travelled to London to join with the Royal Choral Society and the Leeds Philharmonic Society in a broadcast birthday concert at the Royal Albert Hall which was attended by the President of the Royal Choral Society, H.R.H. Princess Marina, Duchess of Kent, who entertained Sir Malcolm after the concert at a party in Kensington Palace.

The great event of 1965 was a visit to Boston, U.S.A., by a hundred and seventy members of the choir. They went to sing at the International Choral Festival held to celebrate the 150th anniversary of the Boston Handel and Haydn Society. Sargent was no stranger to Boston and neither was the reputation of the Huddersfield Choral Society. At the Boston Symphony Hall, and with the Handel and Haydn Symphony Orchestra, the choir sang

Handel's *Israel in Egypt* with Elizabeth Harwood, Marjorie Thomas, and Kenneth Bowen on Tuesday, 26 October. The following Friday, with Raimund Herincx and Marjorie Thomas they performed *Belshazzar's Feast*, *The Music Makers* and *Zadok the Priest*. These performances were hailed as triumphs by most of the Boston press but the praise was not entirely unqualified. Totally unqualified, however, was the warmth of the reception by the Bostonians during a visit which began when the choir arrived on Saturday, 23 October. They stayed at private homes during a week in which, in addition to performing at the two concerts, they rehearsed, went on sight-seeing trips and were entertained to a banquet. The Societies exchanged gifts before leaving, and many were the personal friendships established. There had been talk of going to Toronto, and later there seemed to be the possibility of a visit to Huddersfield's twin town, Besançon in France, but it was not to be so. The Boston visit was the last time the Society went on a trip across the seas and its golden memory lingers on. When will it go again?

The engagements at home continued to fill the diary. There was Beethoven's *Missa Solemnis* in York Minster as part of the York Festival in June 1966 with the London Symphony Orchestra conducted by Hans Schmidt-Isserstedt. This work was sung again the next month at a concert to mark the opening of the Tees-side Industrial Eisteddfod at Wilton with the Royal Liverpool Philharmonic Orchestra conducted by Stanford Robinson. Sargent, unable to be there, insisted on a first-class conductor as substitute.

Throughout all this, the Society was not without its problems. Ticket prices had been increased again in 1962 but costs of concerts were continuing to rise even higher. Numbers in the chorus were falling and new recruits of suitable quality, especially among the young, were not easy to come by. There was no youth choir in the town at that time and the Society did not follow up a suggestion in 1966 that a junior Choral Society be formed. This came from John Gulley of the Huddersfield School of Music, and George Stead's successor as conductor of the splendid Colne Valley Male Voice Choir. The Society's Organist, and by this date its Chorus Master, Eric Chadwick, whilst apparently satisfying the professional critics was not, as Chorus Master, without criticism from certain choir members. Problems arising from this seem to have been overcome with minimum fuss, though doubtless not to everyone's complete satisfaction. Chadwick also won approval from press critics as a conductor when he deputized for Sargent. The Society was 'fortunate in having a sorcerer's apprentice of such gifts', read the report in the *Huddersfield Examiner* in December 1966 when Sargent could not be there to conduct *The Messiah*.

This was because Sargent was ill. Who was there to guess that he would never again conduct a *Messiah* performance by the Society? Chadwick had had to conduct it the previous year for the subscribers' concert because Sargent was ill, but he was back again in March 1966 to conduct Holst's *Ode to Death* and Rossini's *Messe Solenelle*. Indeed, he came back again in March 1967 to conduct two memorable performances of Elgar's *The Apostles*, one in Huddersfield and the other in Liverpool. 'Good evening ladies and gentlemen' he said as he stepped on to the rostrum at the rehearsal for this work in the Town Hall, 'nice to be back again'. He did not look especially unwell. Even in May that year the President, Mr F. R. Armitage, explained how Sargent would not be available in the November because, due to his past illness having upset his schedule, he would be in America on the date of the concert.

For all his spirit, when he stepped up on to the conductor's rostrum in the Royal Albert Hall on the last night of the Proms in 1967, was it not suspected that he was being unduly hopeful when he talked of returning? Perhaps not, but, as we were soon to learn, we were not to see him again. As Charles Reid wrote in his biography of Sargent:

On Tuesday, 3 October 1967, not the narrow world of music alone but also an outer multitude were bereaved whose numbers and affection had never been truly plumbed before.

CHAPTER NINE

The Aftermath

FILLING THE VACUUM created by Sargent's death would prove to be a difficult task indeed. After the initial shock of his death came the eulogies, the memorial services and concerts, followed by the urgent business of making new arrangements for the immediate concert season. The obituaries described Sargent as elegant, brilliant, witty, a great conductor and choral trainer, and a champion of English music. He was remembered in Huddersfield at a special memorial service at the Parish Church where members of the Choral Society were conducted by Eric Chadwick in the singing of appropriate items. The congregation, consisting of local civic dignatories, friends, and music lovers, heard the Society's General Secretary, David Crawshaw, quote from a letter written by Sir Malcolm on 27 September but received only the day following his death. 'I hope all is well with you and the Choir will flourish in my absence' he had written at the end of the letter which began by explaining that he was not able to 'undertake any conducting until after next Easter'. He approved, he said, of the choice of conductors which the Committee had suggested for the following season. Whatever names had been submitted to him, they might well have included David Willcocks, who conducted the November concert in 1967, Charles Groves, who conducted the subscribers' *Messiah* performance in December 1967 and Edward Downes who conducted *The Damnation of Faust* by Berlioz in March 1968.

The November concert was a performance of *The Dream of Gerontius* with the Royal Liverpool Philharmonic Orchestra and the soloists Marjorie Thomas, Robert Tear, and John Cameron. This work had been requested by Sir Malcolm himself, as detailed in a letter from his personal secretary, Miss Sylvia Darley, written on 10 October 1967. Sir Malcolm wanted it to be followed by two minutes silence with everybody standing. Then, with the audience remaining standing, the 'Hallelujah' and 'Amen' choruses from *The Messiah* were to be sung so that everyone should 'go home happy'. All went as requested and at the end, as previously agreed, there was no applause.

An invitation to join with the Royal Choral Society in a memorial concert in October 1968, although initially accepted in principle, did not materialize. The Society did however join forces with the Royal Choral Society in its performance of *The Dream of Gerontius* on Ash Wednesday 1968 at the Royal Albert Hall.

Miss Darley came to the Town Hall, Huddersfield in September 1968 when the Choral Society took part in a concert forming part of the celebrations of the centenary of the Borough of Huddersfield. At that concert she presented the Mayor, Ald. T. P. Cliffe, with the Scroll of Freedom given to Sir Malcolm when he was made a Freeman of the Borough in 1961. She also gave a coloured portrait of Sir Malcolm and one of his batons to the Mayor, and these remain treasured possessions kept at the Town Hall since that time.

Obviously the matter of the appointment of a new conductor was occupying the attention of the officers and committee of the Society. No conductor had died in service since the nineteenth century and the three occasions on which it had occurred bore scarcely any comparison with the present situation. A sub-committee was set up to deal with the matter and letters were exchanged with the BBC, Miss Darley, and with the Royal Choral Society among others, to assist in arriving at a satisfactory outcome. By June 1968 it was made known that Wyn Morris was to be invited to conduct for the two seasons, 1969–70 and 1970–71, having been chosen from a short list of five. Morris had already been engaged to conduct Verdi's *Nabucco* at the final concert of the 1968–69 season in Huddersfield. He was also chosen by the Royal Choral Society to succeed Sir Malcom Sargent as its conductor.

The choice of Wyn Morris was perhaps an understandable one. He was interested in big orchestras and big choirs. He had become known as a highly promising orchestral conductor with a reputation of excellent interpretations of Mahler and Bruckner. In 1963 he had 'made a spectacular debut when he conducted Mahler's Ninth Symphony entirely from memory, and a great future was predicted for him' said the *Yorkshire Post* at the time of his appointment to Huddersfield. He was not new to the West Riding, having some sixteen or so years previously been apprentice conductor of the Yorkshire Symphony Orchestra. In 1957 he received the Koussevitzsky Memorial Award at Tanglewood in the U.S.A., being described then as one of the most outstanding talents for orchestral conducting in Tanglewood's history. He had toured both Britain and the continent with major orchestras and although not yet tried and tested as a choral conductor his apparent drive and determination to do some good in this field, especially with two of the major choirs in the land, seemed to make him a good choice. After his appointment he expressed the wish that the Royal Choral and the Huddersfield Choral Societies should be the best two choirs in the world. Certainly, in making the appointment, the Society did not act without good counsel and advice.

The obvious desire of Wyn Morris to act as chorus master as well as conductor, in Huddersfield as in London, was undoubtedly one factor leading to the resignation in 1969 of Eric Chadwick. He had retired as Organist in 1968 when his place was taken by the Society's Accompanist, Keith Rhodes, who was at the same time appointed Deputy Chorus Master. Chadwick had himself been Accompanist and Organist before his appointment as Chorus Master when Bardgett died, and in those days there had also been, since 1959, a Deputy Accompanist, in the person of that delightful pianist, Keith Swallow. When Keith Rhodes joined the Society in 1964 as its Accompanist, the post of Deputy Accompanist went out of existence and did not re-appear again until 1970 when Roger Dickinson was appointed to it. Nobody has been officially appointed to the post since 1976, but for many years Beth Sharp acted most excellently as unofficial deputy accompanist, and was officially appointed in 1985. Chadwick continued as Chorus Master and acted occasionally as Conductor until the advent of Wyn Morris, although feelings against him had in fact been gathering force for some time. As early as 1964 a representation by certain choir members had been made, severely criticizing the manner in which he performed his duties. Chadwick complained that the choir was not prepared to match up to his requirements for rehearsal discipline. The fact is that the rehearsals had come to lack much in the way of discipline anyway. When once a *command* of discipline — such as arises naturally from mutual concern with the business in hand — is lost, it is somewhat futile to begin to make gestures to *demand* it. Publicly the Society's case was put that a Chorus Master was originally engaged because Sargent was unable to perform the duty himself, which was true. Now that Wyn Morris was anxious to become closely acquainted with the choir and was wanting to take many more rehearsals himself, the post of Chorus Master was less of a necessity, although there had been no intention, it was said, to ask Mr Chadwick to leave. Whatever the Society's intention, Chadwick, appreciating the impossible nature of the situation, tendered his resignation. Judging by his public statements, at least, he had a high regard for the choir, was undoubtedly a very sound musician and had been of good service to the Society since first being appointed Organist following Ernest Cooper's retirement in 1956.

The effect on the Society of Wyn Morris's appointment was, perhaps, to endue it with guarded optimism. Electrifying effect in performance when the opportunity afforded was what Wyn Morris strove for and certainly very often attained. In Verdi's *Nabucco* in March 1969 with the Royal Liverpool Philharmonic Orchestra he 'got some fine climaxes with rich tone and the singing had variety of colour and always a splendid attack' one read in the *Huddersfield Examiner* report. His more fashionable treatment of the *Messiah* performance in 1969, with reduced orchestral forces, were not unkindly criticized in the press. On the contrary, one read of 'superb singing' by the choir. The March concert of 1970, when Dvořák's *St Ludmilla* was performed with, for the last time for several years, the Royal Liverpool Philharmonic Orchestra, ended an association between choir and orchestra 'in a blaze of glory' said one press report. The musical contribution of the Society to the lunch-time proceedings at the Town Hall in June the same year, when Princess Margaret came to open the new Welfare Centre in Huddersfield, was a marked success. Not only was the letter received later by the Mayor from her private secretary clear indication of the particular pleasure the Princess had received in hearing the choir sing, but correspondents to the local newspaper who had been present on the occasion also bore witness to the general pleasure which the choir's singing had afforded. One verse of the National Anthem with Wyn Morris conducting was 'joyful, magnificent, impressive', wrote Councillor Herbert Robinson, and had brought blinding tears to his eyes. A Mr Frank Stringer of Marsh wrote to congratulate the choir on its magnificent performance of both the first verse of the National Anthem and of *Zadok the Priest*.

Sir William and Lady Walton came to the first concert of the season in October 1970 when the choir sang his *Gloria* along with Bruckner's *Mass in F Minor* and Borodin's 'Dance No. 17' from *Prince Igor*. At this concert began a collaboration with the City of Birmingham Symphony Orchestra which was to last for several seasons. It was also the first time the ladies of the chorus were seen in their new pink dresses, which had been designed with colour television appearances in mind. This concert was well received, as also were the 1970 *Messiah* performances and the Verdi *Requiem* performance of March 1971. The Carol concerts, now regularly instituted, were generally enjoyed by all, but the 1971 *Messiah* performances and the Carol concert that year brought complaints of falling standards.

Despite apparent public approval, there were difficulties. The belief that standards had dropped severely since Sargent's death, and a general disenchantment regarding Wyn Morris began to gain ground. Certainly Wyn Morris, though a considerable musician, was in many respects not the easiest of men to deal with. He was held responsible for the severing of relations with the Liverpool orchestra and some loss of the BBC's goodwill towards the Society. He did not always answer letters. At the very beginning of his term of office he created embarrassment by asking to be released from his first official engagement as Conductor despite having previously given assurance of his availability. Charles Groves was brought in to conduct the *German Requiem* of Brahms and Walton's *Belshazzar's Feast* in his place and expressed concern about the unrehearsed state of the former work. He expressed surprise that the choir should be proposing to give a public performance of a work which, by its own admission, 'it didn't seem to know very well'. The press report following the concert commented on the 'tired' sound of the choir, its 'somewhat shaky intonation' and 'hardened tones' in the singing of the *Requiem*, attributing all these to the exacting nature of the work and not at all to inadequate preparation. The Walton piece went off well enough and perhaps Charles Groves left feeling that his reputation was still intact. It was in 1970 that the relationship with the Royal Liverpool Philharmonic Orchestra was severed. They declared that they would not play for the Choral Society beyond the end of the 1969–70 season so long as Wyn Morris remained as the Society's Conductor. In fact Wyn Morris stayed until 1972 but the choir did not sing again with the Liverpool orchestra until 1976.

Morris's departure was preceded by rumour and counter-rumour but when he did go he declared himself as not unhappy that his contract was not being renewed, that he was too busy anyway to continue as Conductor and that, whilst not prepared to discuss the matter further, he felt convinced that he was leaving the choir in a far better state than it was when he took over. Whatever the truth or otherwise of that conviction, the choir had certainly continued during his conductorship to receive more invitations to sing than it could either afford time or money to accept. Its finances remained healthy despite soaring costs, largely because incomes from royalties and investments more than offset losses from concerts. Grants from such bodies as the National Federation of Musical Societies also helped, although these were often reduced, the Federation giving as an excuse that the Society's concert programmes were insufficiently enterprising! A new recording of *Great Hymns* was made by the Delysé Record Co. (later taken over by Decca) sold well and brought in money, but it has not borne the test of time in any way comparable with the choir's earlier recordings under Sargent. Further proposed recordings of works by Strauss and Mahler never materialized.

The City of Birmingham Symphony Orchestra which replaced the Royal Liverpool Philharmonic at the Society's concerts had in fact played for the choir in 1968 under Alexander Gibson in a performance of Beethoven's *Mass in D*. The Liverpool orchestra was unavailable at the time but volunteered to bear the extra cost to the Society incurred by the replacement. Notable among the performances with the Birmingham orchestra were the Verdi *Requiem* in

March 1971 — reported in one newspaper as 'impressive and exciting' — Prokofiev's *Alexander Nevsky*, given together with the Mozart *Requiem* in October of the same year, and Mendelssohn's *Elijah* the following March. This was Wyn Morris's final appearance as conductor with the Society. Kiri Te Kanawa made the first of her several subsequent appearances with the choir in the Mozart *Requiem* and sang, reported the *Huddersfield Examiner* with 'a lovely voice, with clear, light intonation and in the quartets her melody line was never lost'.

Maybe Charles Groves was more pleased when he conducted the choir and the Royal Liverpool Philharmonic Orchestra in Beethoven's *Ninth Symphony* in May 1969 at a Huddersfield Corporation concert in the Town Hall. According to the Bradford *Telegraph and Argus* 'the choir gave a superb account that confirmed their place among the country's few really great choirs'. The next month saw the choir in York Minster for the Berlioz centenary on two busy consecutive weekends, where they sang the *Te Deum* and *Symphonie Funèbre et Triomphale* under George Hurst, and the *Grande Messe des Morts* under Antal Dorati, both with the BBC Symphony Orchestra. The following week the choir was off to Selby for a concert forming part of the Abbey's nine-hundredth anniversary celebrations where, in the Abbey with the Royal Liverpool Philharmonic Orchestra under Meredith Davies they sang Vaughan-Williams's *A Sea Symphony* and Walton's *Belshazzar's Feast* with soloists Elizabeth Simon and Raimund Herincx.

Broadcasting on radio and television engagements at this time included a special programme about the Society for the BBC *Omnibus* series (in which the Corporation had to be dissuaded by the Society from referring to it as 'the noisiest society') and a recording for the BBC series *Songs of Praise* in 1970. The former included excerpts from a concert of a miscellany of music selected from the choir's repertoire, conducted by Brian Priestman with the BBC Northern Symphony Orchestra and filmed in the Town Hall in May 1968. As she had done for the *Great Hymns* recording, Sandra Kelly, a member of the soprano section of the choir, sang solo parts in the *Songs of Praise* programme. The Society does not lack, and never has lacked, excellent soloists within its ranks.

In 1971 the choir joined forces with the Huddersfield Philharmonic Orchestra under its conductor Arthur Butterworth in a performance of Beethoven's *Choral Symphony (No. 9)*. The occasion was the second concert of the Philharmonic Society's so-called centenary season. In fact they were something like twenty years too soon! Sidney Crowther, the Philharmonic's historian for the occasion, wrote that the Philharmonic Society's founder, the

Wyn Morris

Sir John Pritchard

Owain Arwel Hughes

Revd John Thomas, died in 1864. Now, as we have noted earlier, he in fact survived until 1884 and if, as Crowther says, his Fitzwilliam Street Society (founded in 1875) became the Huddersfield Philharmonic Society seven years after his death, its centenary is due in 1991! Nevertheless, the concert, which included the choir singing *Zadok the Priest*, was a success and nobody noticed, or cared to take issue about, the chronological error.

With the departure of Wyn Morris the position of Chorus Master, vacant for nearly four seasons, was filled again in April 1972 by Douglas Robinson, chorus master at the Royal Opera, Covent Garden, since 1946 and a former pupil of Herbert Bardgett. A Leeds man by birth, he had at one time been organist and choirmaster there. He brought to Huddersfield a new spirit of enthusiasm and fresh inspiration to the business of rehearsing, especially with regard to musical and vocal interpretation. His appointment was soon followed by the announcement of the appointment of a permanent conductor in the person of John Pritchard (not then knighted) at the beginning of 1973. This appointment was as Principal Conductor and Musical Director for a period of not less than five years, beginning with the 1973–74 season. As he made clear at the time, his commitments were such that he might have to miss at least one concert per season but he expressed his desire to become involved in all the choir's musical affairs as Musical Director. He had known Douglas Robinson well as an associate for more than twenty years and had a high regard for his musicianship. It was Pritchard's suggestion that Robinson — or 'Robbie' as he came to be known — be made Associate Conductor as well as Chorus Master.

The choir had already sung under John Pritchard at a concert in Watford Town Hall in May 1972 with the New Philharmonia Orchestra, at the invitation of Ambassador College, Briket Wood. Handel's *Zadok the Priest* was performed along with Verdi's *Hymn of the Nations* (sung in Italian) with Alberto Remedios as soloist. In January 1973 John Pritchard, again with the New Philharmonia Orchestra, conducted a performance of *The Damnation of Faust* in which the Society participated (singing this time in commendable French) at the Theatre Royal, Drury Lane. The concert was part of a Festival, *Fanfare for Europe*, to mark Britain's entry into the European Economic Community. The Huddersfield Choral Society was the only provincial choir to be invited to take part in the festival. The concert was deemed a great success with choir, orchestra, and soloists, Kiri Te Kanawa, Stuart Burrows, and Don Gerrard all deserving of praise.

What was presumably Pritchard's own request to be Musical Director as well as Conductor may have arisen from a consciousness on his part that his appearances as Conductor would be minimal due to his many other commitments. In his first season he conducted only the final concert in April 1974, a performance of *The Dream of Gerontius* with the BBC Northern Symphony Orchestra. The following season he managed the subscribers' *Messiah* concert and the final concert when Verdi's *Requiem* was performed. He also conducted when the choir sang at the Royal Festival Hall in April 1975, with the Royal Philharmonic Orchestra for the Shakespeare Birthday Concert, in performances of Vaughan-Williams's *Serenade to Music* and *In Windsor Forest*. He conducted two subscribers' concerts in each of the next two seasons and the BBC Promenade Concert at the Royal Albert Hall in September 1976 when the Society was invited to participate, with a performance of *The Bells* by Rachmaninov; but between 1977 and 1979 he was mostly out of the country and conducted none of the Society's concerts anywhere. He did, however, appear again to conduct both *Messiah* performances in 1979 and his final engagement with the Society was as conductor in a performance of *Belshazzar's Feast* in York Minster with the Hallé Orchestra at the York Festival of 1980. During Pritchard's absence abroad the Society was served by such guest conductors as Raymond Leppard, Simon Rattle (of almost unseemly youth but with considerable command over the musical forces at his disposal), Robin Stapleton, Christopher Seaman, Owain Arwel Hughes, and Mark Elder.

When Pritchard resigned in 1980, his personal manager, Basil Horsfield, described the parting as amicable and said it was due to pressure of work. Already with an international reputation and experience as Musical Director of Glyndebourne Festival Opera as well as major British orchestras, Pritchard had, during the previous two seasons, been acting as chief conductor of the Cologne Opera and chief guest conductor of the BBC Symphony Orchestra. Thus the likelihood of his not being able to continue at Huddersfield had been on the cards for some time but the Society was evidently less ready to accept the notion of losing its highly regarded Musical Director than the latter was to be relieved of his commitment to the Society. Nevertheless the unsatisfactory nature of the arrangement was obvious to all and so the Society once again found itself in the market for a conductor.

Of all the past conductors and chorus masters of the Society, Pritchard was not the first to resign in mutually agreeable circumstances. If we disregard the case of Henry Coward who *retired* rather than *resigned* from his position, this distinction must go to Douglas Robinson who, in 1976, asked to be relieved of his contract at the end of the season since he had been made an irresistible offer of a post in Chicago. His place was taken temporarily by Peter Gellhorn, chorus master at Glyndebourne, who stepped in to prepare the choir for the November concert in 1976 when Dvořák's *Stabat Mater* and Vivaldi's *Kyrie* were performed. These rehearsals were a delight to all who attended them. Such was Peter Gellhorn's disarming personality, he even succeeded with impunity in giving what amounted to lessons in Latin grammar at rehearsals. His quiet, modest, but impish sense of humour and delightful wit were a splendid adornment to his evident musical talents and ability as a teacher and chorus master. Never short of an appropriate aphorism, he would say 'there is no difference between choral singing and singing', or 'difficult things are only difficult, they are not impossible'. Not quite satisfied with intonation on one occasion he remarked 'it should be an E sharp; it sounds like a sharp E' and when he wanted to hear more from the bass section at one point, he explained 'basses! its an A major there — because you say so!'

Douglas Robinson's place was taken on a more permanent basis at the beginning of the 1977–78 season by Graham Treacher of York University. He came as a teacher and conductor of some experience, which included conducting at BBC Promenade Concerts, a spell at Covent Garden as assistant chorus master and with the BBC Scottish Symphony Orchestra as associate conductor. His personality and rehearsal technique, though generally unexceptionable, did not find enough favour within the Society to prevail against mounting criticism, and he resigned during the 1980–81 season after approximately three years with the Society. Unlike his predecessor he conducted the choir only at a few concerts but, like him, he had the task of preparing it for performances with a number of different guest conductors in many and varied circumstances.

Though the period of popularity of great choral music, especially that within the repertoire of most choral societies, may have begun to wane a little, the Huddersfield Choral Society had not been short of invitations nor of engagements since Sargent's death, and continued to receive high praise for what it did. It performed *The Messiah* in Corby, Northants in 1972, paid a second visit to Ambassador College, Watford, in 1973, though without Pritchard this time. It also sang parts I and II of *The Creation*, with Douglas Robinson conducting, in the latter's native district of Armley, Leeds, in October 1974. This was with the Sinfonia of Leeds at St Bartholomew's Church and given in aid of the church's organ restoration fund. According to one newspaper report it was a brilliant performance. Not long beforehand some of the choir had also been to Armley to sing at H.M. Prison. Again with Douglas Robinson they gave a performance of *The Messiah*. This was not the first time Society members had been 'inside', for in 1972 some of the choir gave an abridged performance of *The Messiah* in Wakefield Gaol when they were joined in chorus by about twenty members of the prison's own choir.

There were television engagements too; *Masters of Melody* with *Yorkshire Television* in 1973, *Stars on Sunday* in 1974, televised concerts and also special television recordings such as the magnificent *Te Deum* of Berlioz made in May 1976 with Raymond Leppard and the BBC Northern Symphony Orchestra. This work, with the same orchestra and conductor was also performed at the Free Trade Hall in Manchester in September that year as one of the BBC Master Concerts. In both the performances the Society was joined by the Colne Valley Male Voice Choir and the choir of Cheetham Hospital School of Music in Manchester. In December that year the BBC televised a performance from Ripon Cathedral of *The Messiah* when the Society had Charles Mackerras as its conductor. Six months later came a live television broadcast of the Royal Jubilee Celebration Concert from the Royal Albert Hall when the Society joined other choirs from the U.K. in a concert with the BBC Concert Orchestra conducted by Owain Arwel Hughes. It consisted of music in not too heavy a vein including even Ivor Novello's *Rose of England*, sung by the choir. This piece was sung again when the Society took part in a Royal Jubilee Reception in Leeds Town Hall a few weeks later but with Keith Rhodes conducting this time. At this Reception the choir, together with the Black Dyke Mills Band, entertained the Queen and the Duke of Edinburgh during their Silver Jubilee trip to Yorkshire and South Humberside. The previous year too had seen a collaboration between the Society and the Black Dyke Band, in a recording by RCA for Chandos Productions Ltd, of a miscellany of Christmas music called *A Christmas Fantasy*. Huddersfield's own Silver Jubilee Celebration Concert, arranged by Kirklees, took place in September 1977. The Society's contribution to this was a performance of four Handel *Coronation Anthems* with Christopher Seaman conducting the Northern Sinfonia Orchestra. A few months earlier these anthems had been recorded by the Society for Enigma Records Ltd with John Pritchard conducting the same orchestra.

So it went on, with continuing enagements for concert and television appearances to York Minster for *The Messiah* in 1977, and again in 1978 for a programme of Christmas music; to Leeds Studios in 1979 for a contribution to the series of programmes called *Your Hundred Best Hymns*. Also televised in 1979 was a splendid performance of *The Dream of Gerontius* with Dame Janet Baker, John Mitchinson, and Rodney Macann and the Hallé Orchestra under James Loughran. This concert was organized by Kirklees and took place in the Huddersfield Town Hall. The *Yorkshire Post* reported it as one of the finest performances of Elgar by the Choir.

The subscribers' concerts during the 1979–80 season were given elsewhere than the Huddersfield Town Hall for the first time since its erection, and away from Huddersfield for the first time in the Society's history. During work to improve and redecorate the building early in the summer of 1979 dry rot was discovered in the fabric of the concert hall roof and extensive repair work was necessary requiring many months to complete. Plans were quickly made for the following season to hold the first two subscribers' concerts in St George's Hall, Bradford and the final one in Leeds Town Hall, there being no suitable alternative to the Town Hall in Huddersfield itself. Buses were to be provided to take subscribers requiring transport to these concerts but the extra capacity of the halls and the expected drop in subscribers' support meant that many more tickets would need to be sold to obtain capacity audiences. Extra publicity was arranged and there followed a successful season which included a performance of Dvořák's *Requiem Mass* under Brian Wright in Bradford and a performance of Rachmaninov's *The Bells*, together with Schubert's *Mass in E flat*, under Edward Downes. Both these concerts were recorded for later broadcasts by the BBC. St George's Hall was also used shortly after the Dvořák concert to record the choir singing a programme of music for the BBC Television series *The Much Loved Music Show* with Owain Arwel Hughes conducting.

To add to the difficulties of this period, new rehearsal accommodation had to be found. The Y.M.C.A. premises were no longer available to the Society which moved to more satisfactory accommodation at King Street Mission where it has rehearsed ever since. The faithful support of the subscribers during this difficult season helped considerably in maintaining the Society's finances on a sure footing despite the ever-increasing costs of running the concerts. In 1972 a financial sub-committee had been set up following the Treasurer's advice that the financial structure of the Society required re-examination. The following year the annual subscription for choir membership was raised from £1 to £3. It has been raised periodically since then and is now considerably more than that — more than many feel easy about paying. Yet it compares not unfavourably with what similar organizations (if such there be) demand, and there is no doubt that the joy and privilege which members experience in belonging to such a splendid Society prevails in the end.

Things have progressed a good deal from the days of cheese and ale after meetings in the Spring Street Infants School. Loyal and long-serving membership of the Society by people who belong to the area has nevertheless been one of its unchanging features from the beginning. In 1968 William Ellis,

Librarian from 1930 to 1948, celebrated sixty years with the Society. He was a member of the Methodist Church choir in High Street where the Society used to hold its rehearsals and sang in several other local choirs notably the Glee and Madrigal of which he had been a member for forty-four years. He died about ten years ago but his successor as Librarian (for a period of twenty-eight years), Herbert Whittaker, though now retired, continues to support the Society in all possible ways. Recently Arnold Harrop, a member of the bass section of the choir and one-time Committee member, retired after fifty-four years as a singing member. In 1969 Mr A. Guy Crowther retired from the Treasurership after twenty-one years in that office. A long stretch that! However, it was not a record for a Treasurer since Mr C. J. Binns served as Treasurer from 1891 until 1916. Then in 1971 David Crawshaw retired after thirty-two years as Hon. General Secretary — but again, not as long as John Eagleton.

For all the difficulties, uncertainties, and changing circumstances of the post-Sargent period the firmness of the core of the Society's structure was never in doubt. The Society continues to flourish and make good music. Indeed there are those who would say that it improved immensely in the latter respect as a result of the introduction of periodic vocal re-testing of choir members and the consequent reduction in the average age of the membership. It must be admitted that for all the virtues of long and loyal service to the Society, singing members at least must come to realize when it is time to retire.

The Society's strength has surely always depended on support by three firm pillars, whose substance is that of devotion. There is the love of, and devotion to music and singing by *all* the members, the devotion to the needs of sound organization and economic health by the officers and committee members, and the sense of devotion to the Society on the part of those who train and conduct it in its music making. Perhaps some flaws in the last of these three has been evident in the period under consideration in this chapter. All available evidence seems to indicate that the necessary repair work is well in progress.

CHAPTER TEN

A Renewal

'A POPULAR CHOICE FOR THE CHORAL' was the verdict of Malcolm Cruise, music critic of the *Huddersfield Examiner*, writing in March 1980 about the appointment of Owain Arwel Hughes as the Society's new conductor. He said that Hughes had been a favourite with Huddersfield audiences for some time and that the news of his appointment would have been received with great pleasure by many people. When he had appeared as guest conductor at the Society's concerts it had been 'most apparent', wrote Cruise, that the choir had 'reacted enthusiastically to his leadership'. True though this may have been, there were perhaps those who regretted the change of image in the conductorship from the grand to the popular that this appointment, in their view, represented. But in 1932, let us remember, Sargent projected what was essentially a popular, rather than a grand, image.

There can be no doubt about the popularity Mr Hughes enjoyed. The wide audiences which regularly watched the BBC television programmes which he presented at that time were sufficient to indicate this. His appearances in Huddersfield as guest conductor might then be thought to have been assured of a warm reception provided he performed only moderately well. But there was more to it than this. From the beginning he established a rapport with the choir which paid dividends, and continues to do so. His is certainly not the grand manner. Though he was Associate Conductor of the BBC Welsh Symphony Orchestra and had conducted most of the major British orchestras, he seemed not greatly changed from what one images he was like as a student — a typical young, ebullient, Welsh undergraduate at University College, Cardiff, where he took his degree in Music and Philosophy before going on to the Royal College of Music in London. Since those days his career had included the conducting of many highly acclaimed performances of some of the great choral works. The Society was fortunate to acquire the services of a man of such sympathetic qualities and musical abilities.

From his first official engagement with the choir as its Conductor, Owain Arwel Hughes has won the approval of both the chorus and its audiences for his interpretations and his handling of both choir and orchestra. That first engagement was a memorable one. It was the Society's first concert in the

The choir in the Town Hall with Owain Arwel Hughes for the *Messiah* concert, 1981

Town Hall since the latter's year-long closure for repair and redecoration. The need was felt to appear somewhat less formally dressed during the second half of the concert when taking part (to use what seems an appropriate phrase) in David Fanshawe's *African Sanctus*. Multicoloured shirts, a variety of neckwear, and absence of jackets in the men's chorus was complimented by dresses of all colours and cuts in the ladies' section of the choir, in an attempt to provide an appropriate visual accompaniment to the performance of this most extraordinary musical work. David Fanshawe, a student colleague of Hughes, came himself to operate the tape-recorded sequences in the work which came, in striking contrast, after two pieces by Mozart and one by J. S. Bach. Totally ignoring the performance of the latter classical pieces, the music critic in the following day's *Yorkshire Post*, with reference it seemed, to Fanshawe's work alone, wrote 'One cannot recall a more physically exciting, exhilarating or stimulating concert — and even the more traditionalist subscribers appeared to be affected by its vitality and sheer exuberance!' Equally enthusiastically received were the *Messiah* performances and the Verdi *Requiem* that season. Indeed, everything the Society did was given high praise.

An important factor in this new situation was the influence of the dynamic new Chorus Master (Chorus Mistress?) in the person of Nina Walker from Covent Garden, appointed to succeed Graham Treacher. She was like a breath of fresh air at rehearsals, although *breath* is perhaps too mild a word to convey her often whirlwind effect on proceedings. Women have not usually taken a leading part in the affairs of the Choral Society and it was not without some apprehension, particularly among the male members of the chorus, that her appearance was awaited. Sexual discrimination, though essential in matters of voice, is indefensible, one would think, in appointment of officers, committee members, conductors, and chorus masters of choral societies. Without necessarily suggesting that such discrimination has been employed in the past, one may note that within two years of Nina's appointment the Society elevated a woman to the position of Publicity Officer when Mrs Sue Green took over from Mr Michael Robinson. How long before the Society has a woman secretary or president?

Originally brought in as a temporary measure to fill the gap left by Treacher's resignation Nina was, on the conductor's recommendation, very soon appointed on a permanent basis. Chorus master of the Royal Choral Society from 1971 to 1976 and a member of the music staff of Covent Garden since 1974, her roots nevertheless lay north of the Wash. As slight nuances of speech sometimes betrayed, she was Cheshire-born. She had studied piano and composition at the Royal Northern College of Music in Manchester and an account of her experience in the field of vocal training makes quite impressive reading. She recalls coming to Huddersfield with her grandparents when she was eight years old to hear the Choral Society sing *The Messiah*. Her understanding of the dramatic interpretations of music required from opera choruses was of great value to the choir. Particularly was this the case in rehearsing the Verdi *Requiem* during her first season, and for the *Alexander Nevsky* music of Prokofiev given in October 1982, not to mention the unforgettable concert performance of Puccini's *Turandot* at the Barbican Centre in London in 1982.

The *Turandot* performance was the first to include Alfano's authentic ending to the work, much of the research work concerning which had been carried out by Owain Arwel Hughes, who conducted the London Symphony Orchestra in the performance at the Barbican Hall. That night was one to remember. Superb soloists including Sylvia Sass as Turandot, whose performance was magnificent, and Barbara Hendricks, whose Liu was delightful, added to the excitement of the occasion. The ageing, but vocally virile, Hugues Cuenod as the Emperor, provided an extra touch of magic to an altogether enchanting evening. The choir, in particular, received a most heartening ovation at the end of the performance when they were brought to their feet by the conductor. One press critic reported that the choir had not, as may have been hoped, taken London by storm. Possibly not by storm, but the enthusiasm of the audience specifically for the choir's contribution was undeniable.

Nina Walker was particularly effective in producing good Italian diction for the *Turandot* performance and also for providing an appropriate Italianate accent in the Latin for Verdi's *Requiem*. Her not totally successful attempts to eradicate the English-sounding 'ay', as in *day*, at the end of such Latin words as *Domine* — a very common fault with all English choirs and many English-speaking soloists — reminded one of Peter Gellhorn's similar atttempts. He used repeatedly to remind the choir that it was a matter of sounding only one vowel, not two, and on one occasion he good-humouredly complained that he had heard some people in the choir using three!

Nina's understanding of drama was also beneficial when it came to preparing for the performance of Mendelssohn's *Elijah* in October 1981 with the Hallé Orchestra under Hughes. Heather Harper, Helen Watts, Stuart Burrows, and Michael Rippon were the soloists at this concert, which was promoted by Kirklees to celebrate the centenary of the opening of the Town Hall in 1881. At the original opening also, it will be remembered, *Elijah* was sung with the Festival Chorus under Joshua Marshall. The centenary concert given on the same day of the year, 20 October, as the first of the original Festival concerts a century before, replaced the first subscribers' concert of the 1981–82 season and was to have been recorded for television. However, due to what is euphemistically called 'industrial action' the film crew withdrew at the last minute and a splendid performance was lost to the television-viewing public and to posterity. All who attended the concert were able, therefore, to regard themselves as particularly privileged for it was a singular success.

Also to mark the Town Hall centenary the Yorkshire composer, Anthony Hedges was commissioned to write the work which was given its first performance by the Society in April 1982 at its final concert of the season. Appropriately it concerned the erection of a building, as its title, *The Temple of Solomon*, indicates. It was performed along with two other works, Walton's *Gloria*, also commissioned twenty years previously for the Society's 125th anniversary, and Elgar's *The Music Makers*. Hedges's work was very well received by audience and critics alike but the performance of *Gloria*, less so. It was no less appropriate an item, however, since Walton had his eightieth birthday that week. Elgar, of course, especially *The Music Makers*, is almost always appropriate singing for the Society. One remembers, for example, the magnificent performance given, in the most trying of temperatures, of *The Dream of Gerontius* in July 1983, at the final concert of the International Musical Eisteddfod at Llangollen. *The Kingdom* was performed in April 1984 and was surely much over-due, the Society having previously sung it in 1948 and for the first time in 1907.

Not quite one year following the Society's performance of his *Gloria*, Sir William Walton died suddenly in March 1983. He had already been asked by Owain Arwel Hughes to write a work for the forthcoming hundred-and-fiftieth anniversary of the Society in 1986 and had readily agreed to write a setting of the *Stabat Mater*, confirming this only two days prior to his death. The Society may still have its *Stabat Mater*, if all goes well, because the commission has been accepted by Paul Patterson.

Elgar's *The Dream of Gerontius* had also been the work chosen for a concert which marked the promotion, for the first time ever by the Society itself, of a concert in London. In January 1982 this work was given with the Royal Philharmonic Orchestra at the Royal Festival Hall to a two-thirds capacity audience which, considering the bad weather and the fact that it was Thursday evening, was deemed remarkably good. Musically successful, the venture proved somewhat crippling financially and it is clear that the Society needs considerable sponsorship for such enterprises as this. But, as the President, Donald Haywood, wrote in the Annual Report that season, 'critics from the national press were able to justify with conviction the enviable reputation which our Society has held and still holds'.

Workshop weekends, begun with such spectacular success in February 1981 at the Grand Hotel, Scarborough, had a short life. Another one at home in Huddersfield and a third in Blackpool, though totally worthwhile and enjoyed by all who took part in them, were not subsequently repeated. Insufficient support was forthcoming for a fourth one in 1984, again to be held in Blackpool. The expense to members was too much of a burden especially if they wished to bring their wives and members of their family. These weekends had not been without their benefit and, in particular, the extra time needed to come to grips with the pronunciation of the Welsh language was provided at Blackpool in 1983 when the choir was due in Cardiff on St David's day. To begin a concert of miscellaneous items in St David's Hall, they were to lead the singing of *Land of My Fathers* in the native tongue! Since there was no adverse comment one supposes the choir pulled it off! The whole audience joined in, of course, and perhaps it was regarded as in no way remarkable that the choir knew the words — doesn't everybody? Anyway, the choir must have made a favourable impression because it was invited to perform *The Messiah* the following December at the final concert of the Cardiff Festival with the BBC Welsh Symphony Orchestra. Sheila Armstrong, Doreen O'Neill, Martyn Hill, and Michael Rippon were the soloists at what proved to be a triumphant occasion for the choir and, indeed, for Owain Arwel Hughes, whose faith in the Society was seen to have some justification. The choir was afforded what it so often deserves but has seldom, if ever, received at home in Huddersfield, a standing ovation.

By this time the Society had lost its first lady Chorus Master. Pressure of work at Covent Garden following the loss there of the Chorus Master, meant that Nina Walker could not get up to Huddersfield. Keith Rhodes, as usual in such circumstances, helped out at rehearsals. He will be missed now that he is resigning after twenty-one years with the Society. Guest chorus master, Richard Steinitz of the Polytechnic Music Department, and conductor of the Glee and Madrigal Society acted as guest chorus master for a short period. In September 1983, however, the temporary services of Brian Kay were obtained to prepare the choir for a performance of Britten's *War Requiem* the following month with the Hallé Orchestra. This performance was highly praised in the press. After the resignation of Nina Walker in January 1984, he was invited to become Chorus Master in her place. To everyone's delight and

Brian Kay

satisfaction he accepted the appointment, describing it later as the most
thrilling he had ever taken, anywhere. The performance of Elgar's
The Kingdom in April 1984, was
described in the *Huddersfield
Examiner* as a triumph for the
new Chorus Master. The improved
quality of the choral tone and
balance are commented upon both in
the *Examiner* and the *Yorkshire Post*
reports. A founder-member of the
King's Singers, with whom he
remained for fifteen years, Brian
Kay aims at the same precision of
ensemble singing by a chorus of over
two hundred as has been achieved,
altogether exceptionally, by that
famous group of six. He too, along
with Peter Gellhorn, it would seem,
sees no difference between choral singing and singing. He is quietly making
his point and brings to rehearsals not only dedication, demand for hard work,
and sound musical understanding, but a refreshing and intelligent wit such as
might only be expected from a one-time member of the Cambridge Footlights
Club.

A new spirit now seems to have entered the body of the Society and this
augurs well for the future. Much of what Wilmshurst had to say in concluding
his centenary history of the Society in 1936 regarding the future, and again
Sidney Crowther's endorsements and additions to those sentiments in his
updated publication of 1961, seem scarcely less apt now at the time of the
Society's one-hundred-and-fiftieth anniversary celebrations. The Society
came into being at a time when there was a great wave of enthusiasm for
oratorio and other choral music. This carried a multitude of independent-
minded, non-conformist, tonic solfa-ists along with it through nineteenth-
century Victorian Britain, and into a twentieth century which saw a
renaissance of English music. Great amateur provincial choral societies may
sometimes be dismissed as belonging to an age which is past; as anchronisms
that find no significant place in the modern world. The Huddersfield Choral
Society, one hundred and fifty years old, and still very much a power in the

land, is either evidence that such a view is mistaken or is itself a notable exception to a general rule. What is not of the past is the sublime quality of the great choral works which the Society continues to perform. So long as there remain men and women capable of being inspired by listening to or performing such music, choralism will only die through neglect. The Choral Society in Huddersfield does not have to die because a fashion for oratorio passes, or has passed. Rather will a tradition of performing great choral music be perpetuated while the Huddersfield Choral Society lives, and because it lives. It will be perpetuated, moreover, not only in Huddersfield but wherever there are people who want to listen. For the Choral Society has broken its parochial bonds asunder long since, and has something of inestimable worth to offer the world at large. No serious signs of neglect are evident in the Society, nor have there been these past hundred and fifty years. It is a Society with a glorious past, a by no means inglorious present, and with good reason to expect a glorious future.

Past Performances of the Huddersfield Choral Society

ITEMS in rounded brackets (), are unsubstantiated. Most of them are reproduced from previous lists of this kind. Though many must be correct, some are suspected of being errors. Obvious cases of error have, needless to say, not been included here. There are bracketed items which occur in no previous lists, some of these being performances that were planned but for which evidence is lacking that they actually took place.

The location of those concerts which took place outside Huddersfield is indicated in square brackets [].

The years are printed in bold type for performances conducted by the composer of the work.

An asterisk against a work indicates that it was written for the Society, or specially commissioned.

BACH, Johann Sebastian, 1685–1750
Cantata 80 — A Stronghold Sure   (1942).
Mass in B Minor   1906, 1907 [London], 1919, 1932, 1936, 1941, 1946, 1948 [Edinburgh], 1956, 1963, 1985.
Sanctus from B Minor Mass   1931.
Motet — Singet dem Herrn   1911, 1911 [London], 1918, 1980.

BANTOCK, Granville, 1868–1946
Omar Khayyam   1920, 1924.
Christ in the Wilderness   1913.

BARNBY, Joseph, 1838–1896
Rebekah — A sacred Idyll   1870.

BEETHOVEN, Ludwig Van, 1770–1827
Mass in D — Missa Solemnis   1929, 1945, 1946 [London], 1951, 1951 [London], 1960, 1966 [York], 1966 [Middlesborough], 1968, 1983.
Mass in C   1978.
The Mount of Olives   1843, (1849), 1850, 1853, 1860, 1862, 1864 — twice, 1867; (1871).

Symphony No. 9 — The Choral Symphony   1953, 1969, 1971, 1978.
Choral Fantasia   1982.

BENNETT, W. Sterndale, 1816–1875
The May Queen   1862, 1876.
Ode   1862.
Woman of Samaria   1870, 1872.

BERLIOZ, Hector, 1803–1869
The Childhood of Christ   1959.
Damnation of Faust   1881, 1886, 1889, 1898, 1906, 1913, 1926, 1931, 1939, 1949, 1957, 1968, 1973 [London].
Grand Messe des Morts   1969 [York].
Symphonie Funèbre et Triomphale   1969 [York].
Te Deum   1930, (1943), 1945, 1969 [York], 1976 [Manchester].

BIEREY, Gottlob Benedikt, 1772–1840
Faith and Adoration   1847, 1853.

BLISS, Arthur, 1891–1975
Golden Cantata   (1963 — BBC Recording).
Morning Heroes   1945, 1955.

BORODIN, Alexander, 1833–1887
Polovtsian Dances — Prince Igor   1937, 1970.

BRAHMS, Johannes, 1833–1897
Requiem   1912, 1969, 1978, 1978 [Manchester], 1979 — part 6.
Song of Destiny   1894, 1925, 1977.
Four Serious Songs   1966.
Academic Festival Overture   1968.

BRITTEN, Benjamin, 1913–1976
Spring Symphony   1962.
War Requiem   1963 [York], 1983.

BRUCKNER, Anton, 1824–1896
Mass in F Minor   1970.
Mass in E Minor   1982.

CLIFFE, Frederick, 1857–1931
Ode to the North Wind   1929.

COLERIDGE-TAYLOR, Samuel, 1875–1912
Hiawatha   1901, 1903, 1910, 1916, 1924, 1943.
Hiawatha's Wedding Feast   1932, 1936.
A Tale of Old Japan   1912.

COSTA, Michael, 1808–1884
Eli   1874, 1883, 1899.

COWEN, Frederick, 1852–1935
Ode to the Passions   1899.

DAVIES, H. Walford, 1869–1941.
Everyman   1909, 1918, 1934.

DELIUS, Frederick, 1862–1934
Mass of Life   1948, 1953, 1953 [Leeds], 1954 [London], 1961.
Sea Drift   1931, 1977.
Songs of Farewell   1934, 1942.
Song of the High Hills   1958.

DURUFLE, Maurice, 1902–
Requiem   1966.

DVOŘÁK, Antonin, 1841–1904
Requiem   1979 [Bradford].
The Spectre's Bride   1895.
St Ludmilla   1970.
Stabat Mater   1926, 1976.
Te Deum   1957, 1962, 1962 [London], 1965 [London], 1965, 1976.

DYSON, George, 1883–1964
Canterbury Pilgrims   1938, **1943** [Manchester].

ELGAR, Edward, 1857–1934
The Apostles   1927, 1967, 1967 [Liverpool].
The Spirit of England
  — For the Fallen   **1917**, 1940.
  — To Women   **1917**.
The Dream of Gerontius   1905, 1907, **1917**, 1928, 1928 [Holland], 1936, 1939 [London], 1941, 1945 (recording), 1947, 1951, 1954, 1957 [Liverpool], 1958 [Brussels], 1961, 1967, 1968 [London], 1974, 1979, 1982 [London], 1983 [Llangollen].
The Kingdom   1907, 1948, 1984.

King Olaf   1902, 1913.
The Music Makers   1935, 1940, 1947, 1951, (1954), 1955, 1961, 1965
[London], 1965, 1965 [Boston, U.S.A.], 1973, 1982.

ELVEY, George J., 1816–1893
Resurrection   (1844).

FANSHAWE, David, 1942–
African Sanctus   1980 — with the composer participating.

FAURE, Gabriel, 1845–1924.
Pavane   1973 [Watford], 1977.
Requiem   1948 [Edinburgh], 1949, 1958 [Vienna], 1958, 1977.

GARDINER, William, 1770–1853
Judah   1837 — a selection, 1847.

GIBBS, Armstrong, 1889–1960
Deborah and Barak   1937.

GUILMANT, Alexandre, 1837–1911
Grand Mass no. 3   1883

HANDEL, George Frederick, 1685–1759
Joshua   (1846), 1867, 1893.
Acis and Galatea   1845, 1848, 1853, 1855, 1859, (1861), 1862, 1870, 1875,
1889, 1896, 1944.
Alexander's Feast   1847, 1854, (1861).
Dettingen Te Deum   1842, 1860, 1947.
Israel in Egypt   1837, 1839, (1847), 1849, (1850), 1854, 1855, 1857, 1861, 1865,
1870, 1882, 1888, 1901, 1909, 1915, 1928 [Amsterdam], 1929, 1938, 1944,
1950, 1953 [Leeds], 1954, 1955 (recording), 1965, 1965 [Boston, U.S.A.].
Jephtha   (1844), (1847), 1850, (1854), (1863), 1866, (1879).
Judas Maccabaeus   1836, 1838, 1842, 1845, (1847), (1848), 1849, 1850, 1854,
1857, 1858, 1863, 1868, 1872, 1882, 1900.
Let Thy Hand Be Strengthened   1977.
The Messiah   1836, 1838, 1840, 1841, 1844, 1847, 1848, 1849, 1855, 1856,
1858, 1859, 1861, 1862, 1863, 1866 and thereafter at least once annually.
The dates given here are those of authenticated performances of The Messiah,
whether of a selection or of a virtually complete performance. Regular annual
performances may have taken place prior to 1866 but we cannot be sure,
though almost certainly choruses or solo items from the work would have been

given at some time during each of these early years. There have been occasional performances outside Huddersfield (notably in Cardiff in 1983) as well as abroad, e.g. Vienna 1958, Berlin 1959, Munich 1963, Oporto and Lisbon 1963.

My Heart is Inditing   1977.
Samson   1843, 1845, 1846, (1847), 1850, 1851, 1853, 1854, 1855, 1857, 1859, 1861, 1864, 1874, 1879, 1897, 1917.
Solomon   1837, 1847, (1861), 1930.
The King Shall Rejoice   1975, 1977.
Theodora   1891.
Zadok the Priest   1840, 1965, [Boston, U.S.A.], 1970, 1971, 1972 [Watford], 1977 [London], 1977, 1982.

HARRISON, Julius, 1885–1963
Mass in C   1950.

HARTY, Hamilton, 1879–1941
The Mystic Trumpeter   1928.

HAYDN, Joseph, 1732–1809
The Creation   1836, 1838, 1843, 1844, 1845, 1847, 1850, 1852, 1853, 1855, 1857, 1858, 1859, 1860, 1861, 1864, 1865, 1866, 1867, 1968, 1869, 1874, 1877, 1881, 1885, 1895, 1908, 1933, 1942, 1954, 1974, 1974 [Leeds], 1975.

The 1836 performance was given at the Society's very first meeting on 15 July of that year at the Infant School Room in Spring Street.

The Seasons
— Spring   1842, 1843, 1844, 1850, 1852, 1854, 1862, 1873, (1874), 1876, 1890.
— Summer   1843, 1853, 1862, 1873, (1874), 1876, 1890.
— Autumn   1853, (1874), 1876, 1890.
— Winter   1876, 1890.
Mass in B Flat (Theresien Messe)   1973.

HEDGES, Anthony, 1931–
Temple of Solomon*   1982.

HOLST, Gustav, 1874–1934
The Hymn of Jesus   1923, 1928 [The Hague], 1936, 1944 (recording), 1947, 1950, 1959, 1964.
Ode to Death   1966.

HONEGGER, Arthur, 1892–1955
King David   1949, 1952, 1964.

HOWELLS, Herbert, 1892–1983
Hymnus Paradisi   1952.
Missa Sabrinensis   1956.

IRELAND, John, 1879–1962
These Things Shall Be   1960.

JACKSON, William, 1815–1866
The Deliverance of Israel from Babylon   1845, 1848, 1853.
Psalm 103*   (1841) — Reported to have been written especially for the Society at
     this date. A later setting was evidently published in London in 1856.

KODALY, Zoltán, 1882–1967
Missa Brevis   1952, 1964.
Psalmus Hungaricus   1975.

LISZT, Franz, 1811–1886
Psalm 13   1978.

MACFARREN, George, 1813–1887
Joseph   1878, 1880.
St John the Baptist   1875, 1880, 1894.

MASCAGNI, Pietro, 1863–1945
Easter Hymn   1974.

MAHLER, Gustav, 1860–1911
Symphony No. 2 in C. Minor   1982 [London].

MENDELSSOHN, Felix, 1809–1847
Athalie   1868, 1872, 1876, 1902.
Elijah   1859, 1863, 1869, 1871, 1872, 1876, 1878, 1881, 1884, 1885, 1888,
     1891, 1892, 1894, 1896, 1904, 1911, 1918, 1925, 1933, 1940, 1947 and
     1956 (recordings), 1960, 1972, 1981.
     The 1881 performance of Elijah was part of the Musical Festival to mark the
     occasion of the opening of the Town Hall. Society members sang as part of the
     Festival chorus. Charles Hallé conducted.

Hymn of Praise   1862, 1864 — twice, (1865), 1868, 1869, 1871, 1873, 1880,
     1889, 1896, 1902, 1912, 1919, 1923, 1932.

A Midsummer Night's Dream   (1864), 1869, 1871, 1873.
St Paul   1854, 1855, 1857, 1860, 1863, 1865, 1866, 1871, (1872), (1873), 1875,
    1879, 1883, 1886, 1892, 1900, 1914.
Walpurgisnacht   1867, 1877, 1912.
When Israel Came out of Egypt   1893, 1907, 1928.
Woman of Samaria   1872.

MOZART, Wolfgang Amadeus, 1756–1791
Ave Verum Corpus   1979 [Bradford, BBC TV], 1980.
Exultate Jubilate   1980.
Isis and Osiris   1974.
Mass 12   (1861), 1862.
Mass in C Minor   1935, (1937, [London]), 1957, 1973.
Requiem   1944, 1971.

NOVELLO, Ivor, 1893–1951
Rose of England   1977 [London], 1977 [Leeds].

ORFF, Carl, 1895–
Carmina Burana   1978, 1984, 1984 [Liverpool].

PARRY, Hubert, 1848–1918
Blest Pair of Sirens   1902, 1907, 1920, 1921, 1932, 1936, 1949, 1956, 1968,
    1982.
King Saul   1910.
I was Glad   1973 [Watford].
Judith   1903, 1905, 1922.
Jerusalem   1926.
Ode to St Cecilia's Day   1909.

POULENC, Francis, 1899–1963
Gloria   1966, 1978.

PROKOFIEV, Sergie, 1891–1953
Alexander Nevsky   1971, 1982.

PROUT, Ebenezer, 1835–1909
Hereward   1885, 1887, 1898.
Red Cross Knight*   1887, 1892.

PUCCINI, Giacomo, 1858–1924
Turandot   1982 [London].

RACHMANINOV, Serge, 1873–1943
The Bells   1949, 1975 [London], 1980 [Leeds].

RIMSKY-KORSAKOV, Nikolai, 1844–1908
Slava   1973 [Watford].

ROMBERG, Andreas, 1767–1821
Lay of the Bell   1841, 1842, (1844), (1846), 1849, 1852, 1875.
The Transient and Eternal   1839, 1843, 1848, 1852.

ROSSINI, Gioacchino, 1792–1868
La Petite Messe Solonelle   1958, 1966, 1975.
Stabat Mater   (1862), 1865, 1873, 1877, 1881, 1891, 1908, 1919.

> The 1881 performance of Stabat Mater was given at the Musical Festival to mark the occasion of the opening of the Town Hall when Society members formed part of the Festival chorus.

SAINT-SAËNS, Camille, 1835–1921
Psalm 150   1973 [Watford].
Samson and Delilah   1921, 1930.

SCHUBERT, Franz, 1797–1828
Mass in E Flat   1980 [Leeds].

SPOHR Louis, 1784–1859
The Last Judgement   1849, 1852, 1859, (1861), 1862, 1865, 1870, 1881, 1908.

> The 1881 performance was at the Musical Festival for the opening of the Town Hall.

God Thou Art Great   1875, 1895.

STANFORD, Charles Villiers, 1852–1924
The Revenge   1897, 1905, 1916.

STRAVINSKY, Igor, 1882–1971
Choral Variations on Von Himmel Hoch   1977.
Symphony of Psalms   1977.

SULLIVAN, Arthur, 1842–1900
The Golden Legend   1893, 1897, 1904, 1916, 1928, 1934 — excerpt.
Martyr of Antioch   1882, 1884, 1890, 1899, 1911, 1920.

TIPPETT, Michael, 1905–
Child of Our Time   1976.

VAUGHAN-WILLIAMS, Ralph, 1872–1958
A Sea Symphony   **1926**, 1934, 1943, 1947, 1951, 1951 [London], (1956), 1959,
    1964, 1969 [Selby], 1972.
Dona Nobis Pacem*   1936, 1940, 1943, (1954), 1959.
Fantasia on Christmas Carols   1978.
Five Tudor Portraits   1937, 1938, 1949, 1957.
In Windsor Forest   1975 [London].
Serenade to Music   1968, 1975 [London], 1976.
Towards the Unknown Region   1964.

VERDI, Giuseppe, 1813–1901
Aida   1922, 1927, 1937, 1946, 1953, 1962.
Four Sacred Pieces   1973, 1979, 1984.
Hymn to the Nations   1972 [Watford].
Nabucco   1969, 1974 — Slaves' Chorus.
Requiem   1915, 1925, 1934, 1942, 1943, 1951, 1951 [York], 1955, 1963, 1971,
    1975, 1981.
Te Deum   1938, 1941, 1965 [London], 1965.

VIVALDI, Antonio, 1678–1741
Kyrie   1976.

WAGNER, Richard, 1813–1883
The Mastersingers
    — Overture and chorale, Act I, Act III Homage to Sachs   1931, 1935, 1936.
Hail Bright Abode   (1890), 1912, (1935), 1936.
Parsifal — Act I Prelude   1935.
Tannhäusser — selection   1890, 1923 (Act II, Sc. III), 1935 (Intro. & Act II, Sc. I).
Lohengrin — selection   1890, 1935.

WALTON, William, 1902–1983
Belshazzar's Feast   1933, 1936, 1937 [London], 1942, **1943** [Liverpool,
    Recording], 1948 [Edinburgh], (1950), 1951 [London], 1952, 1958, 1958
    [Brussels], 1958 [Vienna], 1965 [Boston, U.S.A.], 1969, 1969 [Selby], 1972,
    1977, 1980 [York].
Coronation Te Deum   1954, 1965 [London], 1965.
Gloria*   1961, 1962, 1962 [London], 1970, 1982.

WESLEY, Samuel, 1766–1837
In Exitu Israel   1904, 1911.

APPENDIX II

Society Officials since 1836

Conductors, Chorus Masters, Organists and Accompanists

Permanent Conductors

Henry Horn (styled 'Leader') 1836–52
James Battye (styled 'Conductor' from 1854) 1852–58
Robert Senior Burton 1858–74
Joshua Marshall 1874–85
John North 1885–91
John Bowling 1891–1901

(Sir) Henry Coward 1901–32
(Sir) Malcolm Sargent 1932–67
Wyn Morris 1969–72
(Sir) John Pritchard 1973–80 (styled 'Musical Director')
Owain Arwel Hughes 1980–

Assistant (or Deputy) Conductors

Rev. John Thomas 1869–71
Arthur Burnley 1915–22

Ernest Cooper 1922–32
Douglas Robinson 1973–76 (styled 'Associate Conductor')

Permanent Chorus Masters

Herbert Bardgett 1932–62
Eric Chadwick 1962–69
Douglas Robinson 1972–77

Graham Treacher 1977–81
Nina Walker 1981–84
Brian Kay 1984–

Deputy Chorus Masters and Accompanists

Ernest Cooper 1932–56

Keith V. Rhodes 1967–85

Organists

Henry Lister Parratt 1881–85
J. Edgar Ibeson 1885–1915
Ernest Cooper 1915–56

Eric Chadwick 1956–68
Keith V. Rhodes 1968–85

Accompanists

Eric Chadwick 1956–62

Keith V. Rhodes 1964–85

Deputy Accompanists

Keith Swallow 1959–64
Roger Dickinson 1970–74

Elaine M. Riches 1974–77
Mrs Beth Sharp 1985–

Officers of the Society

Presidents (styled 'Foremen' or 'Chairmen' from 1836 to 1856)
Foremen or Chairmen

George Armitage 1836–37
Joseph Howard 1837–38
John Crosland 1838–42, 1844–45, 1855–56

Henry Horn 1842–44, 1847–48
James Peace 1845–47
Edward Battye 1848–49 (–1852?)
William Hirst 1852–55

Presidents

John Crosland Fenton 1856–58
John Brooke 1858–62
J. C. Laycock 1862–63, 1864–72
Samuel Howell 1863–64, 1872–74
John A. Brooke 1874–76
John J. Grist 1876–79, 1897–99
William Harrop 1879–82, 1893–95
Stanhope Smart 1882–84
(Ald.) Ben Stocks 1884–85, 1899–1902
Allen Haigh 1885–87
J. A. Wrigley 1887–89, 1895–97
William Day 1889–91
Dr E. F. Scougal 1891–93
J. R. Mellor 1902–03
J. Firth 1903–05
John Shaw 1905–07
J. Watkinson 1907–09
J. E. Webb 1909–11
F. A. Reed 1911–13
E. J. Bruce 1913–15
W. L. Wilmshurst 1915–17
G. T. Rhodes 1917–19
Col Liddell 1919–21
William Johnson 1921–23
Dr H. Pullon 1923–24
C. F. Arnold 1924–26
Samuel Firth 1926–28

J. W. Hepworth 1928–32
Clr J. E. Lunn 1932–35
Lawrence Crowther 1935–37
Irving Silverwood 1937–38
Frank Firth 1938–40
Waldo Briggs 1940–42
Frank Netherwood 1942–45
A. Guy Crowther 1945–47
F. W. Gadsby 1947–49
David Crawshaw 1949–51
Ald. J. Cartwright 1951–53
Clr H. Armitage 1953–55
Albert Mosley 1955–57, 1963–64
Percy Barber 1957–59
F. R. Armitage 1959–61, 1966–68
G. D. A. Haywood 1961–62
S. W. Garsed 1964–66
J. F. C. Cole 1968–70
Clr J. H. Wilkin 1970–72
Ald. T. P. Cliffe 1972–74
Horace Shaw 1974–76
George S. Firth 1976–78
William Drake 1978–80
J. Donald Haywood 1980–82
George H. Slater 1982–84
Paul L. Michelson 1984–

Hon. Secretaries

John Crosland 1836–38, 1845–46
Edward Battye 1838–45, 1846–48,
 1853–60
George Calvert 1848–49
James Battye 1849–53
William Fitton 1858–60 (joint),
 1860–70
H. B. Kaye 1869–70 (joint)
R. H. Armitage 1870–73
John Eagleton 1873–1918
William Dawson 1878–1915 (joint)
G. T. Rhodes 1918–23
Percy Beaumont 1915–23 (Assistant)
 1923–38 (joint)
P. L. Rhodes 1923–30 (joint)
H. Cotton 1923–27 (joint), 1929–33
J. L. Ramsden 1930–39 (joint)
F. W. Sykes 1933–35 (Orchestral)
Albert Stocks 1935–38 (Orchestral)
Ernest Cooper 1939–40 (Orchestral)
David Crawshaw (General) 1938–69
Whitfield Senior (Choir) 1938–41

Percy Barber (Choir) 1941–61
 (Orchestral) 1961–67
A. Lionel Taylor (Assistant) 1946–61
 (Choir) 1961–62
Albert Mosley (Orchestral) 1948–51
Hubert Garlick (Assistant) 1961–64
 (Ticket) 1964–80
Peter Lockwood (Ticket) 1974–80
 (joint)
 ('Ticket Officer') 1980–82
William Drake (Choir) 1962–70
 (General and Choir) 1970–73
 (General) 1973–75
 (Subscribers) 1980–
Richard Barraclough (Choir) 1973–75
 (General) 1975–84
J. Graham Fearnley (Choir) 1975–83
J. Stafford (Choir) 1983–
Dr J. Hughes (General) 1984–
J. Donald Haywood (Sponsorship)
 1984–

Hon. Treasurers

Thomas Hartley 1836–44, 1845–48
Henry Horn 1844–45
John Crosland 1848–55
William Hirst 1855–59
George Longley 1859–70
H. B. Kaye 1870–74
Stanhope Smart 1874–78
T. G. Sharpe 1878–84
A. C. Sharpe 1884–86
Robert H. Armitage 1886–90

George Wimpenny 1890–91
C. J. Binns 1891–1916
T. H. Fitton 1916–27
H. Cotton 1927–33
Albert Stocks 1933–38
Frank Netherwood 1939–48
A. Guy Crowther 1948–69
J. Donald Haywood 1969–80
Charles A. Brook 1980–

Hon. Librarians

James Battye 1842–49 (1836–49?)
George Longley 1849–59 (?), 1859–74
Robert H. Armitage 1874–86
T. S. Crowther 1886–98
Jonathan Lee 1898–1936
Newton Dawson 1911–15 (joint)
J. B. Farrard 1915–26 (joint)

J. L. Ramsden 1926–30 (joint)
William Ellis 1930–36 (joint), 1936–48
Joe Broadbent 1944–48 (joint)
Herbert Whittaker 1948–61 (joint),
 1961–63, 1963–76 (joint)
Hubert Garlick 1956–61 (joint)
E. Malcolm Schofield 1963–65

Richard Barraclough 1965–71
Gareth Beaumont 1971–77 (joint),
  1977–80, 1980–82 (joint)

Edwin Smith 1976–77
M. Rawnsley 1980– (joint)
Stephen Brook 1982– (joint)

Publicity Officers
Richard Barraclough 1971–73
Michael J. Robinson 1981–82
Mrs Sue Green 1983–85

Programme Officers/Editors
Ernest Bradley 1973–80
Michael J. Robinson 1980–81
Mrs Sue Green 1982–83

Registrar
J. Timothy Lewis 1971–

Hon. Auditors

Robert H. Armitage 1866–67
G. Barlow and G. Calvert 1867–68
W. Todd and A. Sykes 1868–69
A. Sykes and Monroe 1869–72
G. Bradley and W. Todd 1872–74
G. Bradley and J. Hartley 1874–75
W. B. Dayson and J. B. Hirst 1875–77
W. B. Dayson and J. Hartley 1877–78
J. A. Stocks and A. Gardiner 1878–79
A. Gardiner and C. J. Binns 1879–80
T. H. Beaumont and T. Bray 1880–81
  (–82?)
R. Bower and W. A. Beevers 1882–83
W. Johnson and T. Bray 1883–85
W. A. Beevers and H. T. Parks 1885–86
W. Radcliffe and F. Lodge 1886–87
W. Radcliffe and T. Bray 1887–90
N. Dawson and R. Weavil 1890–91
D. Swindells 1891–?

J. Sykes and J. Lee 1894–96 (–97?)
J. Lee and H. Parker 1897–98
T. Cartwright and F. W. Brooke
  1898–99
Messrs Whiteley & Brown 1899–1900
  (–1903?)
J. H. Wrightman and P. B. L. Lawton
  1903–04
J. H. Wrightman and A. Brown 1904–08
A. Brown and N. Dawson 1908–11
A. Brown and R. Barraclough 1911–16
  (–1918?)
H. Wheawill and F. Kershaw 1918–39
F. Kershaw and F. E. Revell 1939–48
F. E. Revell and E. N. Revell 1948–49
E. N. Revell and E. S. Etchells 1949–57
E. N. Revell and F. Crosland 1957–75
E. N. Revell and J. Black 1975–84
J. Black and B. Wilkinson 1984–

Society Members – Anniversary Season, 1985–86

President: PAUL L. MICHELSON

Vice-President: RICHARD BARRACLOUGH *Past President*: G. SLATER

Conductor: OWAIN ARWEL HUGHES *Chorus Master*: BRIAN C. KAY
Accompanist: To be appointed *Deputy Accompanist*: MRS BETH SHARP
General Secretary: DR JOHN HUGHES *Choir Secretary*: J. STAFFORD
Subscribers' Secretary: W. DRAKE *Sponsorship Secretary*: J. DONALD
 HAYWOOD
Treasurer: CHARLES A. BROOK *Programme Officer*: T. MOSCOVITCH
Librarians: MELVYN RAWNSLEY and *Registrar*: J. T. LEWIS
 STEPHEN BROOK

Auditors: J. BLACK and B. WILKINSON

Executive Committee

P. L. Michelson, R. A. Barraclough, Miss B. R. Beever, C. A. Brook, S. Brook, A. G. Crowther, D. Crowther, W. A. R. Crowther, C. A. Davies, W. Drake, J. C. England, H. Garlick, K. Garsed, T. Moscovitch, Miss J. M. Hardcastle, J. D. Haywood, J. S. Hughes, Miss S. M. Kelly, J. T. Lewis, M. Rawnsley, K. Rothery, J. Self, Mrs P. M. Simpson, Dr A. L. G. Smith, G. Slater, J. Stafford, J. S. Taylor, Mrs M. Walker, H. Whittaker, Mrs R. M. Williams, R. H. Wilman, G. Smith

Choir Members

FIRST SOPRANOS

Mrs H. Barker	Mrs J. V. Quarmby	Mrs M. Henry
Miss J. M. Newman	Miss E. C. Smith	Mrs P. Broadbent
Miss J. Parker	Mrs S. C. Garside	Miss A. V. Cotton
Mrs P. A. Bromley	Mrs J. Foster	Mrs N. Tompkins
Mrs D. K. H. Phillips	Mrs J. P. Walters	Mrs P. C. Allsopp
Mrs N. Haigh	Mrs V. Elsey	Mrs J. Exley
Mrs M. Woodhead	Mrs C. Randerson	Mrs P. M. Croft
Miss S. M. Kelly	Mrs J. Smith	Mrs B. K. Foster
Mrs D. E. Sharp	Miss J. Lindsay	Mrs C. M. Beaumont
Miss M. Stead	Mrs S. Pioli	Mrs J. Smith

Mrs E. C. Merlin
Mrs S. A. Baker
Mrs M. Cox
Mrs V. Hey
Miss P. Jennings

Mrs D. Lingard
Miss M. Sanderson
Mrs R. E. Stones
Mr J. Mair

Mrs J. M. Williams
Mrs M. Bond
Mrs J. S. Longbottom
Miss P. J. McMorris

SECOND SOPRANOS

Miss A. Crawshaw
Mrs S. S. Bostock
Mrs J. Pearson
Mrs M. Newman
Mrs B. Hollings
Mrs B. N. Roebuck
Mrs J. M. Reeve
Mrs V. M. Spencer
Mrs S. Garside
Miss J. E. Fozzard
Mrs S. C. Green
Mrs. S. M. Spreckley
Mrs M. Dyson
Miss M. E. Atkinson
Miss B. R. Beever
Mrs H. Brooks

Mrs J. C. Rankin
Miss J. H. Sargent
Mrs M. Collins
Mrs J. E. Burhouse
Mrs P. Medley
Mrs S. M. Wilson
Dr D. M. Wetherill
Mrs E. A. Hoyle
Mrs M. Halmshaw
Mrs M. Webb
Mrs J. Mirfin
Mrs A. Shaw
Mrs R. Chambers
Miss C. E. Thompson
Mrs D. Smith
Mrs J. Brownsword

Miss C. R. B. Griffiths
Mrs M. Bywater
Mrs M. Jackson
Mrs M. Walker
Miss T. J. Holt
Mrs W. D. Coppell
Mrs M. Mallinson
Mrs B. M. Tippen
Mrs M. P. Wilson
Mrs F. L. Stafford
Miss M. L. Scott
Miss J. A. Harvey
Miss Y. Gibson
Mrs F. Steinitz
Mrs A. Jenkinson

FIRST CONTRALTOS

Mrs S. E. Wilman
Mrs D. Boardman
Mrs M. Norton
Mrs M. J. Townsend
Mrs J. Preston
Miss R. Mortimer
Mrs M. Swift
Mrs C. M. Daniel
Mrs C. M. Learoyd
Mrs J. Cartwright
Mrs K. M. Northern

Mrs J. Brook
Mrs S. Burrow
Mrs J. E. Hobson
Miss J. M. Hardcastle
Mrs R. Walsh
Mrs M. R. Donaldson
Mrs M. Fairless
Miss F. C. Storer
Mrs N. M. Talbot
Miss W. M. Ellis
Mrs A. Wade

Mrs B. S. Brook
Mrs C. M. Donaldson
Miss S. Boyer
Mrs S. H. Cole
Mrs J. L. Sims
Mrs P. Smith
Mrs J. Milne
Mrs F. Hiley
Mrs P. J. Hird
Miss M. E. Hoyle
Mrs D. Earnshaw

SECOND CONTRALTOS

Mrs J. Wheeldon
Mdm M. E. Beatson
Mrs N. Shaw
Mrs P. V. E. McNeil
Mrs P. M. Simpson
Mrs R. Beaumont
Mrs M. W. Walker
Mrs A. M. Lindley

Mrs S. Beattie
Mrs B. Eaton
Mrs E. Williams
Mrs S. M. Walshaw
Mrs S. R. Ellis
Mrs J. Kilburn
Mrs B. Brook

Mrs A. Walker
Mrs M. Upson
Mrs L. W. Thomson
Miss M. F. Shaw
Mrs T. J. Sanderson
Mrs S. M. Christie
Mrs R. Lofthouse

FIRST TENORS

C. H. Eastwood
D. M. Messenger
R. Barraclough

R. A. Edwards
G. H. Gledhill
C. Brooke

D. Croft
J. S. Manning
A. Graham

M. Fairless
H. L. E. Newman
J. Andrews

M. Lindley
A. Quarmby
J. T. Morgan

M. W. Houston
E. Watterson
E. Bradley

SECOND TENORS

J. G. Fearnley
J. T. Lewis
S. Brook
G. T. Lumby
D. Osborne

H. W. Clough
R. Firth
M. J. Robinson
P. Wilby
J. W. Sawyer

J. Avison
J. Newcombe
R. B. Drummond
M. Benn
T. H. Earnshaw

FIRST BASSES

R. H. Wilman
T. J. Moscovitch
G. Dransfield
J. F. W. Brown
I. Daniel
T. W. Walshaw
D. Hartley
P. Lockwood
N. Dearnley
G. Sutton
G. M. Beaumont
C. V. Winterburn
M. Rawnsley

W. Halstead
M. C. Crossley
C. H. Bailey
K. Rothery
A. Pogson
M. Fearnley
D. Hirst
R. Williams
J. M. Peaker
M. Hinchliffe
C. P. Stobart
J. B. Hirst
J. Curran

G. H. Slater
L. Wilkinson
P. R. Foster
A. C. Ray
E. Lofthouse
C. M. K. Spencer
D. Haigh
M. Shill
J. P. Sims
C. E. Schofield
E. M. Schofield
P. A. Beerwerth

SECOND BASSES

F. L. Appleyard
D. Crowther
H. H. Broadbent

P. Helliwell
C. Gardner
J. Stafford

R. Sharp
C. S. Arnold

Associate Members

Abbs, Mrs E.
Akroyd, Mrs C.
Atkinson, Mrs B.
Baines, Mrs L.
Bamforth, Mrs A.
Bardon, L.
Baxter, Mdm A.
Baxter, Mrs E.
Beaumont, Mrs A.
Beaumont, Mrs E. E.
Beaumont, F.
Beaumont, Miss G. M.
Beaumont, Mrs M
Beaumont, Mrs O.
Bellringer, Mdm M.
Berry, Mrs M.
Bevers, Mrs J. M.
Black, Mrs. E. M.

Briggs, Mrs M. E.
Burkinshaw, L.
Cameron, Mrs E.
Craven, Mrs J. M.
Clarke, Mrs M.
Crossley-Brook, Miss B.
de Mello, D. C.
Draper, Mrs S.
Ellis, Mrs M. T.
England, Mrs N. S.
Fairclough, Mrs W.
Fielding, Mrs M. J.
Firth, Mrs J. H.
Galvin, Miss A.
Garner, Mrs R.
Gearing, Mrs E.
Graham, Mrs M. J.
Haigh, J. W.

Harrop, A.
Hellawell, Miss J. D.
Hinchliffe, Mrs D.
Hirst, Mdm L.
Holroyd, Mrs J.
Iredale, Mdm H.
Jamieson, Mrs M.
Kaye, Mrs M.
Kelly, Mrs M.
Law, Miss A.
Law, Mrs E. L.
Lawton, Miss M.
Littlewood, Miss J.
Mager, Mrs M. E.
Marsden, H.
Marshall, Mrs A.
Mettrick, Mrs B.
Morgan, Mrs J. M.

Mosley, A.
Moxon, Mrs D.
Murphy, Mrs S. A.
Oddy, Mrs M. G.
Pickering, E.
Pogson, Mrs M.
Riches, Mrs E. M.
Rider, Mrs S. M.
Roberts, Mrs M. B.
Roebuck, Miss J. I.
Schofield, Mrs A.
Schofield, M. W. E.

Searby, Miss H.
Shaw, Mrs A. M.
Shaw, Miss C. M. D.
Shaw, Mrs E.
Shaw, H.
Shaw, Miss M.
Smith, Mrs W.
Smithson, Mrs B.
Stocks, Mrs S.
Stott, Mrs M.
Sykes, H.
Sykes, Miss M.

Sykes, Mrs J. M.
Taylor, Mrs E. M.
Taylor, G.
Thornton, Mdm A.
Thorpe, Mrs J. M.
Watson, C.
Wildman, Mrs B.
Wilson, Mrs M.
Wood, Miss D.
Woodhead, Mrs D.
Young, Mrs F. M.

Subscribers

BALCONY

Abbey, F. W.
Andrews, P. L.
Armitage, Mrs I.
Armytage, Lady
Arnold, J.
Ashton, Mr & Mrs R. E.
Backhouse, Miss S.
Barlow, Dr A. M.
Barraclough, R.
Beaumont, Miss J.
Benster, Mr B.
Bentham, Mr & Mrs R.
Berry, D. G.
Blackburn, V. M.
Blakeborough, D.
Booth M.
Bower, Mrs R. B.
Brigg, F. S.
Broadbent, E. T.
Broadbent, H. P.
Broadbent, Mrs P. E.
Brook, Miss B. C.
Brook, C. A.
Brook, Mrs D. B.
Brook, Mr & Mrs K.
Brook, P. A.
Brook, Mrs S. R.
Brooke, Mr & Mrs E.
Butterworth, Mrs M.
Cheeseman, Mrs J. C.
Cliffe, T. P.
Clifford, Mrs K.
Clyne, O.
Cole, Mrs B.
Cole, Mr & Mrs A. E.
Cooke, D. J.

Cran, J. D.
Cran, T. H.
Croft, D.
Crosland, F.
Crowther, A. G.
Crowther, G. B.
Crowther, Mrs H. I.
Crowther, H. R.
Crowther, W. A. R.
Davidson, Mrs N.
Davies, C. J.
Dawson, J.
Drake, J. N.
Drake, W.
Dugdale, D.
Dyson, J. A.
Dyson, W. R.
Eastwood, R. R.
England, J. C.
England, Mrs N. S.
Fearnley, J. G.
Field, Mrs I.
Firth, G. S.
Firth, J. M.
Flack, J. G.
Fox, R. C.
Francis, L. R.
Galvin, Dr J.
Galvin, Dr T. J.
Garsed, Mrs C.
Garsed, K.
Gledhill, Mrs E. M.
Glithro, P.
Gray, Mrs N.
Green, Miss G. M.
Greenhalgh, W. K.

Griffiths, Mrs C.
Haigh, Mrs C.
Hall, D. M.
Hallitt, Mrs A. J.
Halmshaw, Dr F. R.
Halstead, Miss M. L.
Hardcastle, Miss M. L.
Hare, M.
Harrison, W. H.
Hawkyard, P. G.
Haywood, J. D.
Haywood, Mrs M.
Heppenstall, Mrs A. D. B.
Hey, R. G.
Hickling, Mrs M.
Hinchliffe, Mrs E.
Hirst, Mrs E.
Hodgson, J. A.
Hole, P. J.
Hughes, Dr & Mrs J. S.
Iredale, R.
Jackson, Miss C. E.
Jackson, P.
Jarvis, G. H.
Jessop, Mrs S. M.
Johnson, P. T.
Johnson, Mrs R.
Johnson, Mrs S. W.
Kaye, Mrs E. A.
Kaye, Mrs M.
Kelly, Miss S. M.
Lacy, Mr & Mrs B. B.
Lawton, P. G.
Lewis, J. D.
Lightowler, R. B.
Lindley, Mrs M. E.

Lockwood, Mrs B. A.
Lockwood, F. R.
Lockwood, Miss I. M.
Lockwood, Mrs O. M.
Lockwood, P. S.
Michelson, P. L.
Midgley, J. C.
Mortimer, Miss R.
Morton, Mrs A.
Naylor, Mr & Mrs J. I. M.
Netherwood, Mrs J. M.
Newman, Dr J. F. M.
Northern, G. R.
Oates, J.
Ogden, R. A.
Parker, Miss J. K.
Pearson, Mrs J.
Petty, Dr B. W.
Platt, Mrs A.
Pogson, Mrs M. C.
Pogson, Mrs P.
Powner, G.
Pullon, Dr H. R.
Ripley, Mrs B.
Robinson, Dr B.
Robinson, Mrs M. E.
Ross, Dr G.

Rothery, S.
Rothery, Mrs U. M.
Scott, Mrs M. J.
Self, J.
Sharp, Mrs A. H.
Shaw, Mr & Mrs G.
Shaw, H.
Sheard, R. I.
Sheard, Miss J.
Sheard, Mr & Mrs R. A.
Sherratt, Miss J. M.
Simpson, Mrs P. M.
Singleton, G. P.
Sisson, D.
Slater, G. H.
Smith, A. E.
Smith, Dr A. L. G.
Smith, G. H.
Staveacre, Mrs A. M.
Stringer, G.
Sugden, Mrs H. B.
Sykes, Mrs G. B.
Sykes, Mrs J. N.
Tanner, R. J. R.
Tattersall, G.
Taylor, J. S.
Thomas, Mrs M.

Thompson, W. E.
Thornton, Mr & Mrs J. R.
Tinker, C. D. H.
Tippen, Mr & Mrs D.
Tovey, Mrs M.
Twiss, C.
Walker, Mrs M. W.
Watkins, C.
Watkins, P. V.
Wetherill, Dr J.
Whiteley, F.
Whiteley, H. G.
Whiteley, Mrs R. H.
Whittaker, H.
Whittaker, Mr & Mrs W. E.
Whitwam, Miss A. M.
Wilkinson, Mrs N. I.
Wilkinson, Dr N. V.
Williams, Mr & Mrs H. M.
Wilson, F.
Wood, Miss C.
Wood, C. G.
Wood, F. T.
Wood, Dr K. M. & Miss
  E. F.
Yates, Mr & Mrs W. B. H.

FIRST AREA

Akroyd, Mrs C.
Andrews, Mrs J. M.
Andrews, N. I.
Arkley, Miss E.
Armitage, Miss B. E.
Armitage, D. G.
Armitage, Mrs H.
Atkinson, Mrs B.
Baines, Mrs L.
Bairstow, Dr T. E.
Bamforth, J. H.
Ball, Mrs M. H.
Barron, Mrs M.
Batley, L.
Battye, R.
Battye, Mr W. & Mrs O. M.
Beaumont, Mrs A.
Beaumont, Miss F. E.
Beaumont, Miss M.
Beaumont, Mrs P.
Beaumont, P. R.
Beaumont, S.

Black, Mrs E. M.
Bond, Mrs M. E.
Booth, F. A.
Booth, Mrs M.
Bostock, Mrs S.
Bradley, Mrs E.
Bradley, Mrs S.
Brierley, R.
Broadbent, Mrs R.
Brooke, Mrs N.
Brook, S.
Brook, Mrs S.
Buckley, M.
Bunch, G. A.
Burhouse, K.
Bywater, Mrs M.
Cawthra, Mrs. S. W.
Chappell, D. A.
Dean, C.
Dearnley, D. N.
Dixon, Misses M. H. & M. E.
Draper, M.

Drinkwater, Mrs D.
Durrell, Rev. J.
Ellis, J. R.
Fordham, Miss J. M.
Frankland, C. C.
Gardner, C.
Garlick, H.
Garside, Mrs D.
Garside, R.
Gee, E. A. H.
Gibson, Mrs B.
Gill, Miss B.
Gledhill, A. R.
Grady, Mrs M. P.
Grange, Mrs E.
Green, C. S.
Green, M.
Greenhalgh, Mrs M. E.
Griffiths, Mrs R. H.
Haigh, Mrs H.
Haigh, Mrs M. M.
Hamilton-Meikle, Mrs

Harris, W. G.
Harrop, A.
Hartley, P.
Harwood, Mrs J.
Hellawell, Miss J. D.
Higgins, D.
Hiley, M. A.
Hirst, Mrs H.
Hobson, E. W.
Hodge, S.
Hodgson, B.
Holroyd, Miss S.
Hopkinson, Mrs N.
Horsfall, Mrs P. M.
Houldsworth, Sir Basil
Howard, A. G.
Howley, Mrs D. E. E.
Hunt, Mrs M.
Hynes, E.
Ingham, Mrs K. J.
Iredale, Miss A.
Ives, D. S.
Jagger, M. S.
Jarman, Miss P. M.
Johnson, Mrs F.
Jones, Mr & Mrs R.
Jordinson, Dr H.
Kay, R. I.
Kaye, Miss H.
Kendall, Miss M.
Kennedy, G.
Kilburn, Mrs J.
Lawton, Miss M.
Lee, G. M.
Lee, M. T.
Lightbody, Dr J.
Littlewood, Miss J.

Lockwood, D. I.
Lockwood, Mrs J.
Lockwood, R.
Lodge, B.
Lumby, G. T.
Madden, Mrs J.
Mallinson, J. E.
Marsden, Mrs M. E.
Marshall, Mrs L.
Mear, Mrs D.
Mellor, Miss M. D.
Mitton, Mrs B.
Mitton, G.
Morton, C. R.
McAllister, R.
McDonald, Mrs J.
Osborne, D.
Parkin, J. M.
Payne, Mrs J.
Phillips, Mrs D. K. H.
Pickering, A. & A.
Pritchard, I. C.
Rawnsley, S.
Rayner, V.
Revell, E. N.
Robinson, Miss M.
Roebuck, D. W.
Sandland, J.
Sayles, Miss E. M.
Schofield, Miss M. D.
Sharp, Mrs B.
Shaw, Miss C. M. D.
Shaw, Mrs E.
Shaw, Mrs G. W.
Shaw, Miss M.
Shaw, P. M.
Smith, Miss E. C.

Smith, Mrs H.
Smith, Mr H. B. & Mrs M. I.
Smithson, Miss B.
Stead, Miss M.
Stott, Mrs R.
Sunderland, Miss E. M.
Sutton, Mrs M.
Swann, D. P.
Sykes, Mrs D.
Sykes, K.
Taylor, J.
Taylor, Rev. W. J.
Thomas, Mrs P.
Thomson, J. A.
Thornton, R.
Thorpe, Mrs J. M.
Tomkins, D. B.
Townsend, D. N.
Turner, G. K.
Turner, Mrs M.
Turner, R.
Wainwright, J.
Walker, Mrs N.
Welham, Mrs L.
Wise, Mrs N. M.
Whitehead, B. D.
Whittell, Mrs M. E.
Wittrick, Mrs G. M.
Wilkinson, Mrs B. M.
Wilkinson, F. G.
Wilson, D. A.
Wintersgill, Dr P.
Wood, Miss D.
Wood, Mrs N.
Yates, Mrs E.

SECOND AREA

Abbs, Mrs E.
Addy, W.
Appleyard, Mrs C.
Armer, Mr & Mrs D.
Armitage, G. L.
Aspinall, Mrs E.
Atkinson, Mrs J. M.
Aylward, W. R.
Baxter, Mrs E.
Beaumont, Miss E.
Bedford, Mrs J. M.
Bentley, Mrs M. E.
Booth, Mrs M.

Boothroyd, Mr & Mrs G.
Boothroyd, J.
Boothroyd, Miss K.
Breare, Mr & Mrs K.
Brigg, M. J.
Brooke, Miss B. J.
Brooke, G.
Brooksbank, G. E.
Clarke, A.
Daniel, I.
Daubney, N. J. S.
Donkersley, Miss M.
Downs, Mrs C.

Dyson, P. S.
Eccles, Mrs B.
Ellis, B. M.
Ellis, Miss H.
Emberson, I. M.
Faulkner, Mr & Mrs J. A.
Firth, T. H.
Fishwick, G.
Fones, Mrs A. C.
Forshaw, Mr & Mrs J. T.
Gardner, M.
Gibson, Mrs H.
Gledhill, Mrs B.

Graham, Mrs M.
Gregory, S. J.
Haigh, M. D. F.
Hall, Miss P. M.
Hargreaves, Miss A.
Harris, J. K.
Hay, Miss B.
Heaton, G.
Hepworth, S.
Hey, Mrs W.
Hill, Dr & Mrs M. A.
Horton, G. H.
Hoyle, F.
Hynes, D. M.
Isbil, Mrs R.
Jackson, Mrs J. M.
Jamieson, Mrs M.
Jessop, Mrs T.
Jones, Mrs E. M.
Kinder, A.
Knox, Dr G. W.
Law, Miss A.
Lindley, Mr & Mrs M.
Lister, A. S.
Lockwood, Mrs J.
Lockwood, Mrs M. R.
Mager, Miss E.
Marshall, I.
Masson, Miss H. C.

Moorhouse, Mrs E.
Moss, B. W.
Myers, P. W.
McGrath, Miss K.
McKerchar, G.
Newman, H. L. E.
Noden, Miss K.
North, Mrs W.
Parker, Miss M.
Parkin, A.
Pollard, E.
Pratt, Mr & Mrs E. J. N.
Preen, Mrs E. G.
Radcliffe, B.
Reeder, Mrs C.
Rex, D. C.
Rhodes, D.
Ripley, Mrs G.
Roberts, S.
Roberts, Miss W.
Robson, Mr & Mrs G. H.
Roebuck, Miss J. I.
Rothera, Mrs H.
Sanderson, Mrs R.
Schofield, N.
Shah, J.
Shaw, J. A.
Shaw, Miss M. F.
Shaw, Mrs R.

Sheard, J. K.
Smith, Mr & Mrs C. H.
Smith, Mrs D. M.
Smithies, R.
Stanley, Mrs B.
Stead, M.
Steel, Miss P. M.
Storey, Mrs J.
Sunderland, Mr & Mrs P.
Sykes, E.
Sykes, G. N.
Sykes, Mrs G. M.
Sykes, Mr & Mrs J. G.
Tasker, D.
Taylor, Miss K.
Taylor, Miss E. R.
Thomson, F. R.
Thornton, A.
Walker, Mrs L.
Wardle, F.
Whitehead, A.
Whittaker, Mrs J. M.
Williams, B.
Willington, J. A.
Wood, Mrs M.
Wright, Mrs M.
Wyllie, Mrs L.

Bibliography and Source Material

Ahier, Philip	*The Story of the Three Parish Churches of St Peter the Apostle, Huddersfield* — in three parts (Huddersfield, 1948–50).
Balmforth, Owen	*Jubilee History of the Corporation of Huddersfield* (Huddersfield, 1918).
Brook, Roy	*The Story of Huddersfield* (London, 1968).
Bryant, Arthur	*English Saga 1840–1940* (London, 1940).
Chadwick, Stanley	*Theatre Royal* (Huddersfield, 1941).
Churchill, Winston S.	*A History of the English-Speaking Peoples*, Book 10, *Recovery and Reform (1815–1868)* (London, 1966).
Coward, Henry	*Reminiscences* (London, 1919).
Crowther, Sidney H.	*The Huddersfield Choral Society, 1936–1961* 'Sir Henry Coward to Sir Malcolm Sargent' — forming the second part of the book (Huddersfield, 1961).
	An Orchestral Centenary — Huddersfield Philharmonic Orchestra (Huddersfield, 1971).
	Huddersfield Glee and Madrigal Society 1875–1975 (Huddersfield, 1974).
Crump, W. B.	*Huddersfield Highways Down the Ages* (Huddersfield, 1949).
Cudworth, William	*Musical Reminiscences of Bradford* (Bradford, 1885).
Dyson, Taylor	*History of Huddersfield and District* (Huddersfield, 1932).
Elkin, Robert	*Queen's Hall 1893–1941* (London, 1944).
Grove, Charles	*The New Grove Dictionary of Music and Musicians*, ed. by Stanley Sadie (London, 1980).
Hobkirk, Charles P.	*Huddersfield: Its History and Natural History* (London, 1859 and 1868).
Hustwick, Wade	*Bradford Musical Union Souvenir Centenary Brochure 1865–1965* (Bradford, 1965).
Jacobs, Arthur, ed.	*Choral Music* (Harmondsworth, Middlesex, 1963).
Kennedy, Michael, ed.	*The Autobiography of Charles Hallé, with correspondence and diaries* (London, 1972).
Mackerness, E. D.	*A Social History of English Music* (London, 1964).
	Somewhere Further North — A History of Music in Sheffield (Sheffield, 1974).
Reid, Charles	*Malcolm Sargent* (London 1968 and 1978).

Rodgers, J. A.   *Dr Henry Coward — The Pioneer Chorus Master* (London, 1911).

Scholes, Percy A.   *The Oxford Companion to Music,* revised sixth edition (London, 1945).
      The Listener's History of Music, 3 vols (London, 1956).
      The Mirror of Music 1844–1944, 2 vols (London, 1947).

Sewell, G. F.   *History of the Bradford Festival Choral Society 1856–1906* (Bradford, 1907).

Sterndale-Bennett, J. R.   *The Life of Sterndale Bennett* (Cambridge, 1907).

Sutcliffe-Smith, J.   *A Musical Pilgrimage in Yorkshire* (Leeds, 1928).
      The Life of William Jackson of Masham — The Miller Musician (Leeds, 1926).

Sykes, D. F. E.   *The History of Huddersfield and its Vicinity* (Huddersfield, 1898).

Wilmshurst, W. L.   *Huddersfield Choral Society Centenary 1836–1936* (Huddersfield, 1936).
      The Huddersfield Choral Society, 1836–1961 'The First Hundred Years' — forming the first part of the book (Huddersfield, 1961).

Wroot, Herbert E.   *Bradford Old Choral Society Souvenir 1821–1921* (Bradford, 1921).

Young, Percy M.   *A Concise History of Music* (London, 1974).

GENERAL REFERENCE VOLUMES AND JOURNALS

Magazine of Music, June, July 1889 — Article by J. G. Schofield.
Musical Herald, August 1896 — Article concerning D. W. Evans.
The Musical Times, February 1845, p. 71; May 1866, pp. 288–89; and April 1902, pp. 239–41.
Brighouse Echo, 12 May 1905 — Article on Mrs Sunderland.
Heckmondwike Herald and Liversedge and Spen Valley Courier, 19 February 1903 — obituary of John Bowling of Heckmondwike.

FROM THE LOCAL COLLECTION AT THE HUDDERSFIELD PUBLIC LIBRARY

Bound volumes of a selection of programmes of *Huddersfield Choral Society Concerts, 1861–1950.*
A bound collection of *Reports of Local Societies.*
A bound volume of *The Yorkshire Musician* for the years 1887, 1888, and 1889.
Official Handbook of Her Majesty's Jubilee Celebrations, June 22 1897 (Huddersfield, 1897).

A selection of White's *W. Riding Directories*, 1837 to 1881.
Slater's *Yorkshire Directory* of 1848.
Baines's *Directory and Gazetteer of the County of York, W. Riding, 1822.*
A selection of Kelly's *W. Riding Directories*, 1901 *et seq.*
Post Office Directory for Yorkshire, 1857.

MICROFILM

Halifax and Huddersfield Express from 1831 to 1841.
Halifax Guardian from 1832 to 1843.
Huddersfield Chronicle from 1850 to 1916.
Huddersfield Weekly News from 1874 to 1897.
Huddersfield Examiner from 1851 to the present day.
Leeds Mercury from 1738 to 1850.

Other important material was made available to me from the archives of the Huddersfield Choral Society and some other very useful items were kindly either given or loaned by various individuals.

Index

Abbey, John, 60
Aix-la-Chapelle, 85
Albani, Marie, 62
Albert, Prince (consort), 40, 48, 51, 75
Albion Mills, 7
Alfano, Franco, 142
Alice, Princess, 122
Allt, Dr, 122
Almondbury, 1
Amateur Vocal Union, The, 42
Ambassador College (Watford), 133, 135
Amsterdam, 95
Ancient Mariner, The (Barnett), 51
'Angels Ever Bright and Fair' (Handel), 74
Armitage Bridge, 39
Armitage, F. R., 119, 125
Armitage, George, 11, 12, 16, 19
Armley (Leeds), 100, 135
Armoury, The, 53, 57, 60, 61
Armstrong, Sheila, 144
Arne, Thomas, 107
Askonis, Lies, 118
Attenborough, Richard, 116
Australia, 87, 99, 102, 104, 105, 106

Bach, J. S., 83, 97, 100, 141
  WORKS: *Christmas Oratorio*, 86
  Mass in B Minor, 83, 97, 100, 104, 107,
    111, 112, 123
  Singet dem Herrn, 86, 91
Baillie, Isobel, 96, 97, 112
Baker, Janet (Dame), 136
Balfour, Margaret, 93
Banks, Charles, 72
Bantock, Granville
  WORKS: *Christ in the Wilderness*, 87
  Omar Khayyam, 92
Barbican Centre (London), 142
Bardgett, Herbert, 97, 100–03, 107, 111, 113,
    116, 117, 128, 133
Barnby, Joseph (*Rebekah*), 53
Barnett (*The Ancient Mariner*), 51
Barnsley, 46
Barraclough, Richard, 18

Barras, Mrs, 57
Basle (Switzerland), 86
Bates, Joah, 7
Bates, Thorpe, 101
Bath Buildings, 75
Bath St Baptist Chapel, 75
Battye, Edward, 2, 8, 11–13, 16, 22, 27, 36,
    37, 39, 49, 53, 84
Battye, James, 2, 4, 8, 11–13, 16, 17, 20, 22,
    29, 30, 32–37, 39, 41, 43–45, 47, 53
  WORKS: *Hail, Memory, Hail*, 4, 53
  My Soul Truly Waiteth upon the Lord, 30,
    44
  Psalm XC, 44, 74
Baudouin, King, 119
Bax, Arnold, 109
BBC, 96, 98, 100, 103, 107, 109, 111, 120,
    127, 129, 131, 134–37, 139
—Concert Orchestra, 136
—Northern Orchestra, 111, 116
—Northern Symphony Orchestra, 131, 134,
    136
—Symphony Orchestra, 112, 114, 116, 119,
    122, 131, 134
—Scottish Symphony Orchestra, 135
—Welsh Symphony Orchestra, 139, 144
Beaumont, Percy, 90, 106
Beaumont, Lottie, 91
Beecham, Thomas, 96, 97, 99, 110
Beethoven, 3, 9, 20, 29, 110, 115
  WORKS: *Choral Symphony (No. 9)*, 9, 131
  Mass in D (Missa Solemnis), 96, 106, 112,
    115, 124, 130
  Mount of Olives, 29
Beethoven Festival (London), 87
Belgium, 119
Bell, Donald, 119
Bennett, William Sterndale, 43, 49, 51
  WORKS: *The May Queen*, 51
  The Woman of Samaria, 51
Berlin, 118–20
Berlin Philharmonic Orchestra, The, 119
Berlioz, Hector, 63, 131
  WORKS: *Damnation of Faust, The*, 62, 63,
    71, 72, 75, 77, 79, 93, 97, 126, 133
  Grande Messe Des Morts, 131

Symphonie Funèbre et Triomphale, 131
 Te Deum, 96, 131, 136
Besançon, 124
Binns, C. J., 90, 138
Birmingham, 43, 51, 77, 83
—Symphony Orchestra, City of, 129, 130
Blackburn, William, 1
Black Dyke Mills Band, 136
Blackpool, 68, 144
Bliss, Arthur, 109
 WORK: *Morning Heroes*, 116
Boer War, 78
Borodin, Alexander,
 WORK: *Prince Igor* (Dance No. 17), 129
Boston (USA), 123, 124
 Handel and Haydn Society, 123
Boult, Adrian, 101, 106, 115
Bowen, Kenneth, 124
Bowling, Charles, 75
Bowling, John, 73, 75, 76, 78, 80
Bowling, John (of Leeds), 75
Bradbury, Ernest, 113
Bradford, 1, 30, 31, 40–43, 50, 56, 58, 63, 85,
 137
—Choral Society, 4
—Festival (1853), 40 (1856), 41, 42
—Festival Chorus, 47
—Festival Choral Society, 4, 37, 40, 41, 42,
 48, 58, 100, 105, 108, 114
—*Telegraph and Argus*, 131
Brahms, Johannes, 76, 77
 WORKS: *Requiem*, 86, 130
 Song of Destiny, 76, 77
Brannigan, Owen, 112
Brearley, E., 85, 86
Briggs, Waldo, 107
Brighouse, 5
—Bridge End Chapel, 5
—*Echo*, 6
—Parish Church, 5, 6
—Town Hall, 73
British Council, The, 108, 110, 119, 122
Britten, Benjamin,
 WORK: *War Requiem*, 122, 123, 144
Broadcasts (Radio and TV), 96, 100, 103,
 116, 117, 120, 131, 136, 137, 139
Broadley, John, 11, 12, 19–21, 30
Brook, Mr, 6
Brooke, John, 39, 49
Broughton, James, 47, 58
Bruce, E. J., 88

Bruckner, Anton, 127
 WORKS: *Ninth Symphony*, 127
 Mass in F Minor, 129
Brussels, 119
Buckingham Palace, 48
Burrows, Stuart, 133, 142
Burton, Robert Senior, 43, 44–49, 51, 54,
 55–59, 79
Butt, Clara, 78
Butterworth, Arthur, 131
Byram Buildings, 57, 66

Calvert, George, 22
Cambridge, 145
Cameron, John, 117, 119, 120, 126
Canada, 85, 87, 119
Carol Concert, 129
Cardiff, 139, 144
Castellan, Jeanne, 40
Chadwick, Eric, 117, 118, 123–26, 128
Chamberlain, Neville, 106
Chandos Productions, 136
Chapel Royal, Windsor, 6
Charlesworth, Robert, 90
Chartists, The, 9, 26
Cheetham Hospital School of Music, 136
Cherry Tree Inn, The, 22, 26, 29
Cherubini, Luigi, 30
Chicago, 134
'Christmas Fantasy' (Recording), 136
Christmas Hymn, The, 32, 73, 100
Cliffe, Ald. T. P., 127
Clinton, Gordon, 115
Clough Head, 2
Coates, Albert, 101–03, 105
Coates, John, 93
Coates, William, 57
Cole, Thomas, 83
Coleridge-Taylor, Samuel, 80, 82, 87
 WORKS: *Hiawatha*, 80, 82, 83, 87, 90, 97,
 101, 103, 110
 A tale of Old Japan, 87
Collins, Madeline, 91
Colne Valley Male Voice Choir, 124, 136
Cologne (Opera), 85, 134
Columbia Records, 94, 111
Commercial Inn, The, 11
Committee, Ladies', 90, 91
Conacher, James and Sons, 63
Concertgebouw, 95
Cooper, Ernest, 90, 98, 112, 117, 128

Corby, Northants, 135
Costa, Michael, 40, 42, 59, 89
  WORKS: *Eli*, 59, 68, 77
  National Anthem, 89
Cotton, Harry, 100
Court House, Queen St, 2
Covent Garden Opera, 40, 53, 133, 135, 141, 144
Coventry Cathedral, 123
Coward, Henry, 46, 69, 76, 80–88, 90–99, 102, 103, 111, 134
Cowen — 'Ode to the Passions', 77
Crawshaw, David, 106, 113, 119, 126, 138
Crimean War, The, 44
Crosland, John, 11, 12, 16, 22, 27, 32, 43, 48
Crosland, Joshua, 38
Crosland, Miss, 34, 35, 48
Cross Church Street, 5
Crossland, W. H., 57
Crowther, A. Guy, 110, 114, 122, 138
Crowther, Lawrence, 103, 104, 108
Crowther, Sidney, 4, 70, 95, 112, 115, 120, 122, 131, 133, 145
Croydon Philharmonic Society, 105
Crystal Palace, The, 49, 51, 78, 85
Cruise, Malcolm, 139
Cudworth, William, 1, 4, 5, 7, 29, 30
Cuenod, Hugues, 142
Cumberworth, 33
Curwen, John, 9, 43

Daily Express, 98
Daily Telegraph, 105, 112
Darley, Miss Sylvia, 126, 127
Davies, Mary, 62, 63, 72
Davies, Meredith, 122, 123, 131
Davies, Walford, 86, 88, 91, 94
  WORKS: *Everyman*, 86, 88, 91, 101, 102
Dawson, Frederick, 91
Dawson, William, 69, 90
Deighton, 1, 6, 12
Delius, Frederick, 97, 102
  WORKS: *Mass of Life*, 114, 116
  Songs of Farewell, 101
Delyse Record Co., 130
Denham, John, 5
Derby Choral Society, 92, 96
Desmond, Astra, 101
Dewsbury, 1, 46, 58
Diapason Normal, 79

Dibdin, Charles, 7
Dickinson, Roger, 128
Donizetti, Gaetano, 40
Dorati, Antal, 131
Downes, Edward, 126, 137
Drake, William, 122
Dresden, 85
Dress, Concert, 78, 129
Drury Lane Opera Company, 43
Düsseldorf, 85
Dvořák, 78, 94, 137
  WORKS: *Requiem Mass*, 137
  The Spectre's Bride, 77
  St Ludmilla, 129
  Stabat Mater, 93, 135
  Te Deum, 122, 123
Dyson, George, 109
  WORK: *Canterbury Pilgrims*, 105, 109
Dyson, John, 11, 12
Dyson, Mr, 6, 12

Eagleton, John, 58, 67, 69, 73, 77, 80, 85, 86, 90, 91, 138
Edinburgh, Duke of, 113, 119, 136
Edinburgh, International Festival, 112, 114
Eisteddfod, International (Llangollen), 143
—Teesside Industrial, 124
—Welsh National, 70, 104
Elder, Mark, 134
Elgar, Edward, 82, 84, 90, 91, 94, 95, 102, 105, 117, 136
  WORKS: *Apostles, The*, 84, 94, 95, 125
  Dream of Gerontius, The, 85, 90, 95, 105, 107, 111, 117, 119, 120, 126, 127, 134, 136, 143
  Enigma Variations, 103
  For the Fallen, 90, 107
  Kingdom, The, 84, 113, 114, 143, 145
  Music Makers, The, 102, 107, 115, 120, 123, 124, 143
  National Anthem, The, 89, 101
  Scenes from the Saga of King Olaf, 82, 87
  To Women, 90
Elizabeth II, Queen, 113, 115, 122, 136
Elkin, Robert, 62
Elland, 13
Ellis, William, 137, 138
Elwes, Gervase, 90
Ely, 12, 40
England, Madam, 91

Essen, 80
Evans, D. W., 72, 74
Exeter Hall, London, 42

Fanfare for Europe, 133
Fanshawe, David, 141
  WORK: *African Sanctus*, 141
Fauré, Gabriel,
  WORK: *Requiem*, 112, 114, 118
Fenton, Captain Lewis, 38
Fenton, Colonel, 38
Fenton, Edgar, 37–39, 41, 49
Fenton, John C., 37–39, 41, 43, 44, 85
Fenton, Jones & Rayner, 38
Ferrier, Kathleen, 112
Festival of Britain, 113–15
Fiji, 87
First World War (see Great War, The)
Firth, Frank, 106, 114
Firth, Ald. J., 106
Firth, Samuel, 94, 106
Fitton, T. H., 90
Fitton, William, 39, 49, 50, 84, 85
Fitzwilliam St, 56
—Philharmonic Society, 56, 131
Flynn, Renée, 103
Formes, Karl, 40
Frankfurt, 85
Franks, Revd J. C., 18
Franz Schmidt Silver Medal, 118
Free Trade Hall, The, 101, 136
Freeman, John, 4
Freemasons, 44
Frobisher, Mr, 5, 6

Gardiner's *Judah*, 3, 18
Gardoni, Sgr, 40
Garner, Mr, 48
Garsed, S. W., 123
Gellhorn, Peter, 134, 135, 142, 145
George Hotel (or Inn), 4, 22, 41
George VI, King, 115
Gerrard, Don, 133
Gibbs, Armstrong — *Deborah and Barak*, 105
Gibson, Alexander, 130
Gills, John, 11
Glasgow Cathedral (St Mary's), 16, 100
Gledhill, Joe, 2
Glee and Madrigal Union, The, 43

Globe Inn, The, 22
Gloucester Festival, The, 87
Glyndebourne Festival, 134, 135
Golcar, 2
Goss, Mr, 30
Great Hymns (Recording), 130, 131
Great War, The, 88–92, 106
Green, Mrs Sue, 141
Greene, Eric, 112
Greenwood, George, 27
Gresham Prize, 30
Grist, J. J., 59, 78, 84
Groves, Charles, 126, 130, 131
Guilmant, Alexandre, 63, 66
Gulbenkian Foundation, 122
Gulley, John, 124
Gymnasium Hall, 54, 55

Hague, The, 95
Haigh, Allen, 63, 66, 104
Haley, Mrs E., 58
Haley, Olga, 58, 90–92
Halifax, 1, 5, 7, 15, 31, 113
—(and Huddersfield) *Express*, 16–20
—*Guardian*, 20, 32
—(Quarterly) Choral Society, 1, 5, 6, 32, 48, 92
Hall of Science, 23, 26, 75
Hallé, Charles, 43, 59, 62, 63, 75
Hallé Orchestra, The, 92, 93, 97, 101, 103, 108, 109, 111, 134, 136, 142, 144
Hallé Society, The, 108
Hamilton-Smith, Janet, 106
Hammond, Joan, 112
Handel, George F., 3, 7, 9, 28–30, 39, 40, 47, 59, 74, 76, 77, 86, 91, 96, 118, 119
  WORKS: *Acis and Galatea*, 29, 47, 106
  Coronation Anthems, 136
  Esther, 29
  Israel in Egypt, 18, 20, 29, 40, 43, 51, 78, 79, 89, 95, 117, 124
  Jephtha, 3, 29
  Joshua, 58, 76
  Judas Maccabaeus, 6, 17, 20, 29, 43, 74, 78
  Messiah, 7, 17, 20, 21, 28, 29, 32, 34, 36, 40, 41, 42, 44, 50, 51, 53, 55, 57, 59, 67, 71, 73–75, 77, 78, 82, 84, 86, 89–93, 95–97, 100, 101, 105–08, 111, 114, 116–18, 120, 122, 124–26, 129, 134–36, 141, 142, 144

Saul, 39
Samson, 6, 29, 33, 43, 54, 58
Solomon, 18, 29, 96
Theodora, 74
Zadok The Priest, 124, 129, 133
Handel Festival, 59, 69, 78, 85, 96
Hanson, John — *Winter*, 54
Harewood, Earl and Countess of, 114
Harewood, Lord, 112
Harper, Heather, 123, 142
Harris, Dr Charles, 87
Harrison, Julius — *Mass in C*, 114
Harrogate, 58
Harrop, Arnold, 138
Harrop, Sarah, 7
Harrop, William, 60, 84
Hartley, Henry, 39
Hartley, Thomas, 3, 11–13, 16, 39, 40
Harty, Hamilton, 97, 101, 102
Harwood, Elizabeth, 124
Hawaii, 87
Haydn, Joseph, 3, 7, 9, 12, 28, 30, 35, 36, 40, 43, 59, 77
    WORKS: *The Creation*, 16, 20, 29, 36, 40, 43, 51, 61, 67, 101, 135
    The Seasons, 29, 35, 51
Haywood, D. G. A., 120, 122
Haywood, Donald, 100, 144
Heckmondwike, 73, 75
Hedges, Anthony, 143
    WORK: *The Temple of Solomon*, 143
Henderson, Roy, 103, 113
Hendricks, Barbara, 142
Herbert, William, 119
Herincx, Raimund, 124, 131
High Street, 58, 70
—Methodist Chapel, 67, 138
—School, 58, 66, 84, 92, 104, 106
Hill, Martyn, 144
Hill, Ralph, 110, 112
Himmel, Friedrich, 12, 28
Hinchcliffe, C. W., 107
Hirst, Miss, 44
Hirst, Mr, 34, 35
History of Music in Sheffield (Mackerness), 87
History of Bradford Festival Choral Society (G. F. Sewell), 4, 37, 40
History of Huddersfield and its Vicinity (D. F. E. Sykes), 38
HMV, 110
Holland, 95, 96, 110

Holmfirth Choral Society, 70, 90
Holst, Gustav, 102
    WORKS: *Hymn of Jesus*, 93, 95, 110
    Ode to Death, 125
Holy Trinity Church, 16
Honley, 12, 69
Honneger — *King David*, 114, 116
Horn, Henry, 3, 6, 11–16, 19, 20, 22, 29, 30, 32–35, 38, 39, 44, 47, 67, 85
Horn, Mary, 3, 13, 33
Horsfield, Basil, 134
Horsley, Mr, 30
Howard, Joseph, 11, 12, 16
Howell, Samuel, 49
    WORK: *Hymn of Praise*, 51
Howells, Herbert, 116
    WORKS: *Hymnus Paradisi*, 116
    Missa Sabrinensis, 116
Huddersfield, Borough of, 57, 63, 120, 127
—Freedom of, 120, 122, 127
Huddersfield Chronicle, 3–5, 13, 33, 35–37, 39, 40, 42–44, 48–51, 53–57, 59, 61, 66
Huddersfield College of Technology, 120
Huddersfield Examiner, 2, 49, 67, 71, 72, 74–78, 80, 82, 83, 86, 87, 89, 93, 95, 100–03, 107, 124, 129, 131, 139, 145
Huddersfield Friendly Musical Society, 1, 3
Huddersfield Glee Club, 1, 4, 6, 33
Huddersfield Glee and Madrigal Society, 4, 58, 60, 61, 66, 68, 70, 74, 90, 91, 104, 138, 144
Huddersfield Masonic Lodge, 74
Huddersfield Musical Festival, 1856, 41–43
Huddersfield Musical Festival, 1881, 61–63, 66, 71, 72, 143
Huddersfield Parish Church (See Parish Church, Huddersfield)
Huddersfield Philharmonic Society (Original), 12
Huddersfield Philharmonic Society — and Orchestra (current), 56, 69, 70, 79, 90, 91, 100, 131
Huddersfield Polytechnic — (and School of Music), 33, 73, 124, 144
Huddersfield Public Library — (and Music Library), 17, 49, 98
Huddersfield Subscription Concerts, 71, 84, 88
Huddersfield Technical School, 73, 74
Huddersfield Town Hall, 49, 60, 62, 63, 66, 67, 77, 79, 94, 101, 102, 105, 107–09,

111, 113, 115–17, 120, 123, 125, 127, 129, 131, 136, 137, 141–43
Huddersfield Welfare Centre, 129
Hughes, Owain Arwel, 134, 136, 137, 139, 142–44
Hull, 31, 92, 93
  Choral Society, 92
Hullah, John Pyke, 9
Hummel, 28
Hurst, George, 131
Hyde, Walter, 93

Ibeson, J. Edgar, 63, 66, 68, 74, 79, 85, 90
'I Hear You Calling Me' (Marshall), 58
Illingworth, Elsa, 89
Illustrated London News, The, 42
Industrial Revolution, The, 7–9
Inkersall, Mr, 48
International Choral Festival (Boston, USA), 123
International Musical Congress, 86
Italy, 120

Jackman, Jabez, 11, 12, 40
Jackson, William (of Masham), 4, 29–31, 40
  WORKS: The Deliverance of Israel from Babylon, 4, 29–31
  Psalm CIII, 4, 29
  The Sisters of the Sea, 4
Jarmain, Geoffrey, 103
Jarred, Mary, 101, 109
John XXIII, Pope, 122
Johnson, James, 28
Jones, Parry, 109, 112
Jubilee — Queen Victoria's Golden, 71, 72
—Huddersfield Choral Society's Golden, 71
—Royal Celebration Concert, 1977, 136
—Silver, Celebration Concert, Kirklees, 136
Judah (Gardiner), 3, 18

Kay, Brian, 144, 145
Kay, Mrs Irving, 91
Kaye, Mr, 6
Kelly, Sandra, 131
Kemp, T., 27
Kennedy, John F., 119, 123
Kensington Palace, 125
King All Glorious (Barnby), 53

King, Frederick, 62, 69
King Street Mission, 137
King's Singers, 145
Kirkheaton, 1
Kirklees, 136, 142
Knowles, Timothy, 6
Kodaly — Missa Brevis, 116
Koussevitzsky (Memorial Award), 127

Lambert, James, 11, 12
Lawton, Mr, 19
Laycock, James, 49
Leeds, 15, 31, 47, 49, 50, 56, 58, 85, 86, 100, 133
—Choral Society, 31, 43, 46, 92, 98
—Festival, 46, 48, 51, 59, 69, 77, 78, 82, 84, 97, 100
—Festival Chorus, 47, 61, 97, 98
—Mercury, 16, 17, 22, 28, 30–33
—Parish Church, 44, 46, 123
—Philharmonic Society, 123
—Studios (TV), 136
—Town Hall, 43, 116, 136, 137
—Triennial Festival, 116
Leipzig, 85, 86
Leppard, Raymond, 134, 136
Lewis, Richard, 117, 120
Lincoln Cathedral, 6
Lind, Jenny, 43, 50
Linthwaite, 2
Liverpool, 40, 70, 91, 108, 125
—Philharmonic Hall, 108, 117
—Philharmonic Orchestra (See Royal Liverpool Philharmonic Orchestra)
—Post and Echo, 117
Lisbon, 122
Littlewood, William, 26
Liversidge, Luke, 27, 44, 54, 55
Lloyd, Edward, 60, 62, 63, 69, 72
Lockey, Charles, 40
Lockwood, 13, 39, 44
London
—Choral Society, 87
—Musical Festival, 105
—Orchestral Union, 42
—Philharmonic Choir, 93
—Philharmonic Orchestra, 115
—Symphony Orchestra, 83, 105, 115, 124, 142
Longfellow, 80

Longwood, 2
Loughran, James, 136
Luddite Riots, 8
Lunn, Clr J. E., 102
Lynn, Vera, 110

Maas, Joseph, 60, 62
Macann, Rodney, 136
Macfarren, George, 77
  WORKS: *Joseph*, 59
  St John the Baptist, 59, 76, 77
Mackerass, Charles, 136
Mackerness, E. D., 3, 7, 87
Magazine of Music, 1
Mahler, Gustav, 127, 130
Mainzer, 9
Manchester, 63, 74, 96, 108, 109, 119, 122, 136
—*Examiner*, 62
—Free Trade Hall, 101, 136
Manns, August, 82
Margaret, Princess, 129
Marina, Princess (Duchess of Kent), 123
Marshall, Charles, 58
Marshall, Charles (of Cullingworth), 63
Marshall, Joshua, 56, 58–60, 62, 63, 67, 68, 70, 75, 76, 90, 143
Masham, 4
Master of the Royal Music, 3, 40
McAlpine, William, 117
McGuckin, Bartin, 60
McNaught, W. G., 86
Mechanics Institute, 73
Mellor, Alfred, 53
Mellor, Joseph, 11, 12
Mellor, Richard, 2, 12, 74
Mendelssohn, Felix, 7, 40, 43, 55, 59, 77
  WORKS: *Elijah*, 43, 51, 62, 67, 68, 73, 75, 101, 107, 111, 117, 131, 142
  Hymn of Praise, 57, 91, 93, 97, 106
  A Midsummer Night's Dream, 57
  St Paul, 40, 41, 43, 46
  Walpurgis Night, 55
Midgley, Walter, 119
Miller, Glenn, 110
Milligan, James, 117, 118
Milnes, George, 11, 12, 16, 30, 31, 34, 35
Milnes, Miss, 16, 19, 20, 30
Milnsbridge, 12
Ministry of Information (Film), 107

Mirfield, 1
Mirror of Music (Scholes), 30, 71, 86, 103
Mitchell, Ena, 114
Mitchinson, John, 136
Montreal, 85
Morison, Elsie, 115, 117, 118
Morris, Wyn, 127–131, 133
Morrison, Herbert, 113
Moscow, 120
Mozart, W. A., 3, 20, 29, 30, 40, 102, 141
  WORKS: *Mass in C Minor*, 102, 104
  Requiem, 131
  Twelfth Mass, 47
Mullings, Frank, 89, 92, 101
Munich, 106, 122
—Philharmonic Orchestra, 122
Musical Herald, 72
Musical Pilgrimage in Yorkshire, A, (Sutcliffe-Smith), 30
Musical Reminiscences of Bradford (Cudworth), 1
Musical Times, 3, 21, 59, 69, 72, 77, 82
Musicians Benevolent Fund, 122
Musikverein Concert Hall (Vienna), 117

Nash, Heddle, 97, 105, 114, 115
National Anthem, The, 89, 101, 129
National Federation of Musical Societies, 130
Netherlands England Society, The, 95
Netherton, 12
Netherwood, Mr, 34, 35
Netherwood, Frank, 106, 109, 111, 112
Neu Österreich, 118
New English Glee and Madrigal Union, 42
New Inn, The, 22
New North Road Baptist Chapel, 75
New Philharmonia Orchestra, 133
New Zealand, 87
Nicholls, Agnes, 93
Noble, Dennis, 108, 115, 119
North, John, 67–70, 72–76, 104
Northern Philharmonic Orchestra, 106, 114
Northern Sinfonia Orchestra, 136
Novello's (Publishers), 9, 30, 71
Novello, Clara, 40
Novello, Ivor — *Rose of England*, 136

O'Neil, Doreen, 144
Oporto, 122

Organ, Huddersfield Town Hall, 63, 79, 94
Orpheus Society, 4, 61
Outlane, 12
Owen, Robert, 9, 26

Paddock, 2, 12
—School, 2
Pantheon, 7
Parish Church (old), Huddersfield, 9
    (of St Peter), Huddersfield, 3, 6, 8, 13, 16,
        18, 33, 44, 58, 68, 70, 74, 75, 126
Parratt, Henry, 3, 39, 63, 66
Parratt, Thomas, 3, 6, 16, 34, 41
Parratt, Walter, 3, 40, 63, 67
Parry, Hubert H., 75, 83, 86
    WORKS: *Blest Pair of Sirens*, 83, 92, 97,
        103, 113
    Judith, 83
    King Saul, 86
    Ode to St Cecilia, 75, 83
Parsons, William, 114
Patey, Janet, 62, 69
Patterson, Paul — *Stabat Mater*, 143
Peace, Dr A. L., 16
Peace, James, 16, 20, 30, 31
Peace, Mrs James, 16, 20, 30, 31
Peace, Lister, 16, 27, 31
Peace, Mrs Lister, 16, 31
Pears, Peter, 114
Phillips, Henry, 42
Philosophical Hall, The, 17–20, 23, 29, 30,
        34, 35, 41–44, 47, 50, 53, 54
Philosophical Society, 18
Piece Hall (Halifax), 7
Pizzey, George, 112
Plough Inn, The, 10, 11, 22, 23
Plug Riots, 9
Portugal, 122
Potter, Cipriani, 46
Priestman, Brian, 131
Prince of Wales, The, 69
Princess Royal, The, 112, 114, 115
Pritchard, John, 122, 123, 133–36
Proctor, Norma, 117, 119
Prokofiev — *Alexander Nevsky*, 131, 142
Promenade Concert (BBC), 125, 134, 135
Prout, Ebenezer, 71, 72, 76
    WORKS: *Hereward*, 70, 71, 77
    The Red Cross Knight, 71, 72, 75, 77

Puccini — *Turandot*, 142
Pyne, Louisa, 40

Quebec, 85
Queen Hotel, 37, 44
Queen's Hall, The (London), 62, 83, 86, 87,
        97, 102, 104
Queen St, 57, 73, 107, 115
—Court House, 2
—School Room, 54, 57
—Assembly Rooms, 54, 57
—Chapel, 33, 106
Rachmaninov — *The Bells*, 134, 137
Radford, Robert, 89
Railway, The, 55
Ramsden, Archibald (of Leeds), 70, 104
Ramsden, John L., 103, 105
Ramsden, Sir John William, 49, 50
Ramsden Street, 17, 43, 53–55
—Chapel, 2, 12, 74
Ramsden's Arms (and Glee Club), 4–6, 12
Rattle, Simon, 134
Raybould, Clarence, 108
Recordings, 94, 110, 111, 117, 130, 136
Reeves, Sims, 40, 50, 51
Reformation, The, 9
Reid, Charles, 99, 103, 105, 111, 125
Remedios, Alberto, 133
Reminiscences (Coward), 46, 69, 80, 81, 87
Rhodes, Keith, 128, 136, 144
Richter, Hans, 84
Riding School, The, 53
Ripley, Gladys, 105, 107, 112, 115, 117
Ripon Cathedral, 136
Rippon, Michael, 141, 142, 144
Robinson, Douglas, 133–35
Robinson, Clr Herbert, 129
Robinson, Stanford, 124
Romberg, Andreas, Jacob, 20, 28–30, 35
    WORKS: *Lay of the Bell*, 21
    Transient and Eternal, 20, 29, 35
Ronald, Sir Landon, 94
Rossini, 3, 40, 59, 62
    WORKS: *Messe Solenelle*, 125
    Stabat Mater, 59, 62, 75, 86, 91
Royal Academy of Music, 71
Royal Albert Hall, 70, 101, 105, 107, 112,
        115, 123, 125, 127, 134, 136
Royal Albert Hall Choral Society, 33
Royal Choral Society, 80, 105, 115, 116, 123,
        126, 127, 141

Royal College of Music, 75, 139
Royal Festival Hall, 115, 116, 122, 134, 143
Royal Liverpool Philharmonic Orchestra, 108, 111, 112, 117, 120, 122–24, 126, 128–31
Royal Liverpool Philharmonic Society, 117
Royal Northern College of Music, 142
Royal Philharmonic Orchestra, 134, 143
'Rule Britannia', 107
Rules and Regulations, 11, 13–15, 19, 23, 27, 36, 38, 81, 98, 113
Ruzdjak, Vladimir, 123

Sabata, Victor de, 114, 115
Sacred Harmonic Society, 6, 42
Saint-Saëns — Samson and Delilah, 93
San Francisco, 123
Santley, Charles, 62, 63
Sargent, Malcolm, 62, 94, 97, 99–107, 109–12, 114–30, 135, 138, 139
Sass, Sylvia, 142
Savoy Hotel, 122
Scarborough, 144
—Earl and Countess of, 114
Schmidt, Isserstedt, Hans, 124
Schnabel, Arthur, 112
Schofield, J. G., 1, 2
Scholes, Percy, 30, 71, 72, 86, 103
Schubert — Mass in E Flat, 137
Schwarzkopf, Elizabeth, 114, 115
Scougal, Dr, 74
Seaman, Christopher, 134, 136
Second World War, 58, 106, 108, 110, 111
Selby, 131
Senior, Whitfield, 106, 108
Settle, Luke, 5
Sewell, G. F., 4, 37, 40, 41, 46
Shakespeare Birthday Concert, 134
Sharp, Mrs Beth, 128
Sharp, William, 13
Shaw, John, 37, 84, 85
Sheffield, 38, 46, 51, 55, 80, 82, 85–87, 93, 96, 102
—Choral Society, 92, 96
—Musical Festival, 82
—Musical Union, 82, 85, 87
Shipton, Mother, 61
Silverwood, Irving, 103, 105
Simon, Elizabeth, 131
Sinfonia of Leeds, 135
Skipton Choral Society, 70

Smith, Samuel, 42
Social History of English Music (Mackerness), 3, 7
South Africa, 87
Spohr, Louis, 33, 34, 44
    WORKS: God Thou art Great, 77
    The Last Judgement, 33, 34, 44, 53, 62, 74, 86
Spring St Infants' School, 3, 11, 16, 17, 29, 137
St Anne's Church, Southowram, 5
St Bartholomew's Church, Armley, 100, 135
St Cecilia's Festival, 122
St David's Hall, Cardiff, 144
St George's Chapel, Windsor, 3
St George's Hall, Bradford, 40, 48, 137
St George's Hall, Liverpool, 16
St George's Square, 44, 70
St James's Hall, London, 63
St Patrick's R.C. Church, Huddersfield, 2, 58
St Paul's Cathedral, 30
St Paul's Church (— and Hall), 6, 13, 33, 39, 67, 85
Staincliffe, 75
Stanford — The Revenge, 77, 83
Stapleton, Robin, 134
Starkey, Abel, 19
Stead, George, 124
Stead, Reginald, 106
Steinitz, Richard, 144
Stevens, Horace, 93
Stiles-Allen, Lilian, 101
Stocks, Albert, 105
Stocks, Ben, 60, 73, 80, 86
Strauss, Richard, 130
Subscription, Annual, 23, 27, 28, 89, 98, 103, 114, 137
Suddaby, Elsie, 93
Sugden, Dan, 5, 6
Sullivan, Arthur, 91, 101
    WORKS: Golden Legend, 71, 76, 77, 91, 95
    In Memoriam, 89, 91
    Martyr of Antioch, 68, 86, 92
    O Gladsome Light, 87, 95, 96
Sun Inn, The, 22, 23
Sunderland, Henry, 6
Sunderland, Mrs, 5, 6, 12, 16, 17, 20, 29, 30–32, 34, 35, 38, 40–42, 44, 48, 49, 51, 53, 73, 84
    Musical Competition, 73–75
Sutcliffe-Smith, 30, 47
Sykes, D. F. E., 38

Sykes, James (Boro' Organist), 74
Sykes, James, 5
Sykes, John, 27
Sykes, Jos., 2
Sykes, Susan, 6, 16, 17, 19, 20
Swallow, Keith, 128
Sweden, 110
'Sweet and Low' (Barnby), 53
Switzerland, 102

Tanglewood, USA, 127
Tapp, S., 28
Tasmania, 87
Tattersall, William, 11, 12
Taylor, A. L., 118
Taylor, George, 108
Taylor Hill, 13
Tear, Robert, 126
Te Kanawa, Kiri, 131, 133
Tennyson (Ode), 51
Theatre Royal, Drury Lane, 133
Theatre Royal, Huddersfield, 17, 43, 53, 69
Thomas, Revd John, 54, 56, 57, 60, 67, 133
Thomas, Marjorie, 114, 117, 119, 120, 124, 126
Thudichum, Charlotte, 59
Ticket Prices, 27, 28, 117, 124
Times, The, 84, 87, 112, 115
Times, The Sunday, 110
Todmorden, 75
—Choral Society, 70, 75
Tomlinson, Miss, 57
Tonic Solfa, 43, 81, 82, 145
Toronto, 124
Toscanini, 105
Treacher, Graham, 135, 141
Tree, Charles, 83
Trinity College of Music, 122
Tubb, Carrie, 89
Turle, Mr, 30
Turnbridge, 12
Turner, Eva (Dame), 104, 109
Turner, James, 60
Typhus Fever, 17

Union Bank Yard, New St, 60
Unitarian Church, Fitzwilliam St, 56
USA, 87, 113, 123, 127
Usher Hall, Edinburgh, 112

Vaughan-Williams, Ralph, 93, 94, 102, 103, 105, 115
    WORKS: Dona Nobis Pacem, 103, 107, 108
    Five Tudor Portraits, 105
    In Windsor Forest, 134
    Sea Symphony, 93, 101, 102, 115, 131
    Serenade to Music, 134
Venn, Revd Henry, 9
Verdi, G.,
    WORKS: Aida, 93, 106
    Hymn of the Nations, 133
    Nabucco, 127, 128
    Requiem, 89, 101, 104, 109, 114, 129, 130, 134, 141, 142
    Te Deum, 123
Vert (London Agents), 72
Victoria (Princess), 18
—(Queen), 40, 43, 48, 49, 75, 84
Vienna, 86, 96, 117–19
Vienna Boys Choir, 118
Vienna Philharmonic Orchestra, 118
Vienna Symphony Orchestra, 117
Vivaldi — Kyrie, 135
Vulcan Inn, The, 22, 35
Vyvyan, Jennifer, 119

Wagner, 97, 102, 104
    WORKS: Mastersingers, The, 103
    Tannhäuser, 93
Wakefield, 43, 58, 136
Walker, Nina, 141, 142, 144
Walker, Norman, 109, 114
Wallace, Thomas, 13
Walton, William, 108, 110, 120, 129, 143
    WORKS: Belshazzar's Feast, 97, 100, 101, 103, 104, 108, 110, 112, 115, 117–19, 124, 130, 131, 134
    Gloria, 120, 122, 129, 143
    Te Deum, 123
War Relief Funds, 106
Water Street, 17
Watford, 133, 135
—Town Hall, 133
Watkin-Mills, 72
Watkinson, John, 71, 84, 85, 88, 90
Watts, Helen, 142
Webster, Dorothy, 91
Welt, Die, 119
Wesley, John, 9, 10
Wesley, Dr S. S., 46

West Berlin, 118
Westminster Abbey, 7, 30, 116
West Yorks. Rifles, Sixth, 53, 57
Wharncliffe, Lord, 30
Whitham, Miss, 29, 34, 35, 42, 43, 44, 48
Whittaker, Herbert, 138
Widdop, Walter, 104
Wilkinson, George, 11, 12, 30, 31, 43
Willcocks, David, 126
Williams, Anna, 74
Williams, Harold, 112
Wilmington, Miss, 28
Wilmshurst, Hilda, 100, 105
Wilmshurst, W. L., 2, 3, 9, 10, 26, 29, 30, 47,
    48, 58, 69, 76, 92, 95, 96, 103, 106, 120,
    145
Wilson, Hilda, 59
Wilton (Teesside), 124
Wood, Henry, 11, 12
Wood, Joseph, 55, 67, 69
Wood, Joe (of Kirkheaton), 57
Wood, Miss, 28
Wood, Mr and Mrs, 30
Wood, Sir Henry, 94, 104, 112
Wood and Marshall, 58, 67, 69, 72
Woodhead, Ernest, 104
Woodhead, Joseph (Ald.), 60, 62

Woolpack Inn, The, 4, 13, 16, 22
Workshop Weekends, 144
Wright, Brian, 137
Wrigley, Albert, 60
Wynne, Edith, 60

YMCA, 137
York, 55
—Festival, 114, 122, 124, 134
—Minster, 114, 115, 122–24, 131, 134,
    136
Yorkshire Choral (Vocal) Union, 48, 51
Yorkshire Musician, The, 68
Yorkshire Orchestral Union, 51
Yorkshire Post, The, 92, 113, 127, 136, 141,
    145
Yorkshire Queen of Song, The, 6, 41, 84
Yorkshire Symphony Orchestra, 114–16, 127
YTV, 136
Young, Alexander, 123

Zareska, Eugenia, 114
Zetland Hotel, The, 53